Patagonia-Sonoita Creek Sanctuary, Patagonia, Arizona.

G·R·E·A·T
BIRDING TRIPS
OF THE WEST

JOAN EASTON LENTZ

CAPRA PRESS
SANTA BARBARA

Acknowledgments

I wish to thank the following birders for their generous assistance: Kevin Aanerud, Larry Ballard, Allyn Bissell, Jane Church, Jon Dunn, Bill Gillespie, Sharon Goldwasser, Grace Gregg, Pat Kelly, Hugh Kingery, Mark Lewis, Helen Matelson, Jeri McMahon, Barbara Millett, Jean O'Kuye, Warner Reeser, Ron Ryder, Brad Schram, Nancy States and Dion Warren.

Karen Bridgers and Paul Lehman deserve extra thanks for their careful efforts in reading and criticizing the manuscript. I do, of course, accept full responsibility for the book's content.

My husband, Gib, was a constant source of companionship and encouragement, and my editor, Judith Young, guided me skillfully through the long process of making the book a reality.

The greatest help of all came from the many anonymous birders I met on my travels, who, seeing an out-of-town visitor, took the time to stop and freely give directions to the nearest good birding spot.

Cover design by Maureen Lauran.
Cover photograph by John Hendrickson.
Cartography by Ten-Ki Design.
Author's photograph by Lynn Rollins.
Editorial assistance, Judith Young.
Frontispiece photograph by Dave Bohn.
Design and typography by Jim Cook/Santa Barbara.

LIBRARY OF CONGRESS CATALOGING-IN-PUBLICATION DATA
Lentz, Joan Easton, 1943–
   Great birding trips of the West / Joan Easton Lentz.
     p. cm.
   Bibliography: p.
   ISBN 0-88496-296-2 : $10.95
   1. Bird watching—West (U.S.)—Guide-books.   I. Title.
QL683.W4L46   1989
598'.06'23476—dc 19   88-38832 CIP

Published by CAPRA PRESS
Post Office Box 2068
Santa Barbara, California 93120

Contents

Introduction

Every birder is a traveler at heart. The lure of unfamiliar birds in far away places turns even the most provincial backyard birdwatcher into a seasoned globetrotter. The quest for new bird species to observe and record, beyond the confines of everyday routine, leads the birder to explore all manner of regions. The thrill of a birding trip—the research, the planning, and the eventual journey—is unexcelled by any other bird-watching activity.

Birders are notorious for their wanderlust. Many carry only a backpack and binoculars, relying on the generosity of birding friends for a place to spend the night. Others spend thousands of dollars on airfare, lodgings and bird tours led by recognized experts. Some are on self-imposed deadlines to collect their "year lists," in which they attempt to count as many species as they can in a one-year period. Others roam the world on every continent, listing the thousands of birds they have seen during a lifetime.

Why do birders stand for hours on a rainy promontory in the San Juan Islands, surveying the gray seas for tiny specks? Or struggle out of bed at 4:00 A.M. to be in the midst of the Sonoran Desert at sunrise? Do they really *enjoy* waiting in the freezing snow of a Yosemite forest just to glimpse a certain species of owl?

Beneath all the intellectual knowledge we can absorb about birds, lies a feeling of deep wonder. From time to time, in our search for new birds and new birdwatching experiences, circumstances come together to create a truly magical moment.

At these rare opportunities, the self is left behind and all our concentration is transposed to the object before us. On a perfect day, observing the intricate movements of the tiniest flycatcher, or the plunging dive of a fishing osprey, or the slender outline of a perched falcon brings us a sense of extraordinary closeness with the natural world. Maybe the desire to reach this kinship with birds and their surroundings lies at the bottom of many a birder's quest.

As I went about my travels, eagerly sampling an abundance of bird species and journeying from one beautiful place to another, the importance of seeing birds as part of an ecological whole was brought home to me. If we diminish or destroy the fragile habitats in which most of our birds exist, we will lose them. It's that simple—they will disappear.

In the rush to add new species to our life lists or to "tick" off the key birds we have come so far for, we birders sometimes lose sight of the absolutely crucial need to preserve—not just the birds—but the habitats they need to survive. To this end, I urge all who read and enjoy this volume to support wholeheartedly the efforts of organizations whose costly battle to retain the West's lovely birding spots has just begun.

About This Book

In GREAT BIRDING TRIPS OF THE WEST I invite you to accompany me on my birding adventures. The book is designed as a series of selected birding trips to major habitat areas of the western United States, where we will observe the fascinating bird life that makes each of these destinations unique.

Even if you never leave your armchair, each trip should be "a good read" at home. On winter evenings by a cozy fire, with bird books and maps piled close at hand, many a birding venture has taken shape. And, when your trip becomes a reality, each chapter includes the specific directions necessary for finding birds in that part of the country.

In this book I have attempted a somewhat different approach from that of many regional bird finding guides. Each chapter emphasizes not only the birds to be found, but describes in detail the environment in which they live. The weather cycles, the plant life, the topography of the land—all contribute to the special conditions each bird species requires in order to thrive.

My choice of birding trips was a highly personal one, and, although the book includes many of the major habitats for birds in the West, it is just a beginning.

Also, I picked trips to places of intrinsic beauty, most of which will be pleasing to non-birders as well as birders. Each of the trips includes spectacular scenery with recreational facilities nearby; often birders are traveling with companions or family who are not as enthusiastic about birds as they are!

In order to share my birding experiences in the most useful way, each chapter of the book is divided into a number of sections. Following a short introduction, the bulk of the chapter is a description of the plant and bird life to be encountered on the trip. This is done by taking each habitat—for example, rocky shoreline or alpine tundra—and discussing it in detail. Where possible, one particularly interesting habitat—unique to that part of the country—will be featured in depth. At the end of the habitat description, a list of representative birding sites ties the discussion to specific birding spots.

Each chapter also contains short essays, a close-up of a typical bird of the area, and Notes from a Birder's Diary: all designed to give you a feeling for the place you are about to visit.

To avoid interrupting the main body of the text with detailed travel hints and mileage figures, the Traveler's Tips section at the end of the chapter provides all the details you need to prepare for your trip. Here, the birding sites have been grouped by geographic location rather than by habitat, with specific directions to guide you. Occasionally, potential birding sites were omitted because they were on private property, or special permission to enter was required. Be sure to ask local birders and call the Rare Bird Alert numbers listed.

Lastly, a local checklist of targeted birds—ones you can hope to find if you take that particular trip during the recommended time of year—has been included at the end of each chapter. The checklists are arranged in taxonomic order according to the American Birding Association Checklist (third edition, published in 1986). *They are not a substitute for an official checklist showing seasonality and abundance.* Use them as a general summary for your own information, and pick up a complete checklist (or send for one) before you visit.

Each chapter has at least one map. Those trips covering a relatively small territory have only the overview map at the beginning of the chapter. Trips of greater distances have an overview map as well as up to five area maps. The area maps, which are portions of the overview map in greater detail, have been placed at the back of the chapter near the birding sites they illustrate.

For valuable reading material prior to your journey, the Suggested Reading at the end of the book should provide lots of good references.

Bon voyage and good birding!

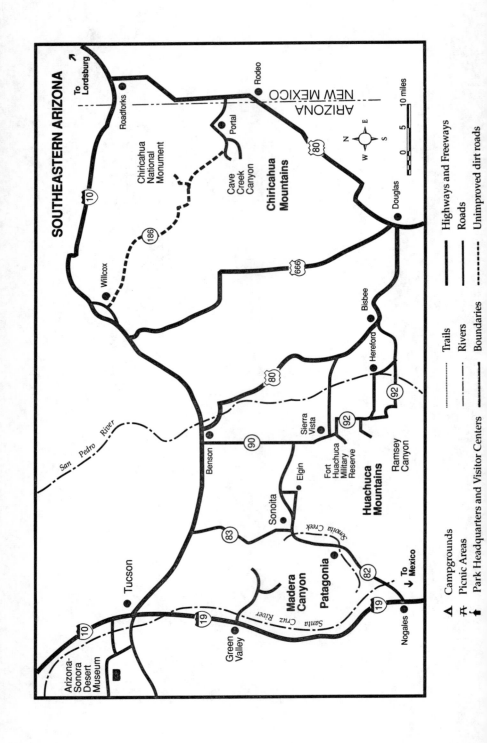

SOUTHEASTERN ARIZONA

Campgrounds
Picnic Areas
Park Headquarters and Visitor Centers

Trails
Rivers
Boundaries

Highways and Freeways
Roads
Unimproved dirt roads

$$\boxed{1}$$

SOUTHEASTERN ARIZONA:

Exotic birding north of the border

Birdwatchers are drawn to southeastern Arizona as golfers are to St. Andrew's in Scotland or baseball fans to the Cooperstown Hall of Fame: it's a pilgrimage. Almost from the onset of our birding careers, we've heard stories about the exotic species inhabiting the "Mexican mountains" of southeastern Arizona, and this trip is one of the tops for bird finding, not only in the West but in all of North America.

The birding is fantastic. Unique to Arizona alone are at least 25 species of North American birds, and several more are resident only in southern New Mexico and west Texas as well. The specialty birds you'll want to see are numerous. From owls to nightjars and from hummingbirds to warblers, tanagers and orioles, a southeastern Arizona checklist reads like a birder's dream.

Why is southeastern Arizona such a mecca for birders? The answer lies in its proximity to the Mexican border. Many of the rare birds, oblivious to international boundaries, are Mexican species that have colonized a few select mountain ranges in southern Arizona, mountains that form the northern end of the Sierra Madre Mountains of Mexico. Hence the term "Mexican mountains", and the presence in Arizona of many birds more commonly found farther south. Birdwatching buffs can check

13

off between 30 and 40 life birds on their first southeastern Arizona visit.

This chapter is designed to give you a taste of birding this famous region. We'll start off in Tucson, then drive south to Madera Canyon in the Santa Rita Mountains. From there, we go to the most famous Roadside Rest Stop in North America—for birders, that is—and later visit the Nature Conservancy preserve on Sonoita Creek in Patagonia. The Huachuca Mountains and Ramsey Canyon are the next attraction, and finally, the most unforgettable of all, Cave Creek Canyon in the Chiricahua Mountains.

In each of these places, the bounty of bird species and interesting new plants warrants a leisurely pace, a luxury, alas, most birders do not have. Even though we explore only a few of the many good birding spots in Arizona, pack your bags and binoculars and prepare yourself for a dazzling birding experience.

South and east of Tucson, Arizona, the land forms a rich complex of habitats for plants and animals. The bird life on this southeastern Arizona plateau includes bird species from Mexico, from the Rockies, and from the eastern United States.

The area marks the terminus of the Rocky Mountains in two mountain ranges to the north—the Catalinas and the Rincons—giving northerly life forms a stepping stone into the region. In patches to the east, a finger of the Chihuahuan Desert sends its thorny acacia bushes, sometimes side by side with remnants of the plains grasslands. To the west, the vast Sonoran Desert, characterized by saguaro and cholla cacti, impinges its arid conditions. And, from the south, marching in rugged splendor up from the Sierra Madre Mountains of Mexico, comes a series of isolated mountain ranges: the Baboquivaris, the Pajaritos, the Santa Ritas, the Patagonias, the Huachucas and the Chiricahuas.

For birders, these names have a mystical sound. Rising abruptly from the desert scrub and grasslands at their feet, these ranges harbor many special birds. The mammals and reptiles, as well as the birds, have attracted the attention of naturalists for years. The peaks and canyons of three of the ranges—the Santa Rita, Huachuca (Wah-chu-ka) and Chiricahua (Chi-ree-ka-wah) Mountains—stand out as the most attractive to birders.

These mountain ranges are sometimes dubbed "sky islands," appropriately describing their biological isolation from the surrounding desert and from each other. Each is its own archipelago, fostering a slightly different group of indigenous birds and plants. Their volcanic origin and steep topography contrast sharply with the mesas and plateaus of the northern part of the state.

For centuries the Apache Indians took shelter in these wild, remote mountains. In the late 1800's their tribes gained a war-like reputation, resisting attempts by the U. S. government to restrict them to reservations. Cochise and Geronimo, both chiefs of the Chiricahua band of the Apaches, led fierce raids against American and Mexican settlers and clashed with the U.S. Army.

Under the threat of intermittent Indian hostilities, early ornithological exploration was conducted by biologists stationed at such U. S. forts as Ft. Apache, Ft. Bowie, Ft. Defiance and Ft. Huachuca. Encouraged and guided by Professor Spencer F. Baird of the Smithsonian Institution, most of the early bird collectors were attached to the U. S. Army Medical Corps. By carefully, and often daringly, studying the unknown regions of the Southwest, they were able to discover many new bird species, some of which still carry their names. Charles E. Bendire (Bendire's Thrasher) and Elliot Coues (Coues' Flycatcher, now Greater Pewee), were two of the pioneers of bird study in southeastern Arizona.

Climate and Habitats of Southeastern Arizona

The weather in southeastern Arizona has a pattern of winter precipitation, spring drought, summer precipitation and fall drought. The winters are relatively mild, without snow except on the highest peaks. Summer temperatures in the lowlands can get very high. Fortunately, the majority of your birding will be in the oak woodland zone and above, where temperatures are considerably cooler.

Winter storms blow in from the north, and summer thunderstorms arrive from the southeast (Gulf of Mexico) and the southwest (Gulf of California). Summer moisture crosses the mountains, quickly rises, and forms huge rain clouds. Intense thunder and lightning storms follow, but blow over after an hour or so.

Birding in southeastern Arizona is similar to birding the Rocky Mountains or the Sierra Nevada—you ascend through a number of bird habitats with their characteristic plants as you climb each mountain range. (For a full discussion of life zones of the West, see Chapter Six.)

In southeastern Arizona, vegetation zones fall into the following general categories: desert scrub, desert grassland, deciduous riparian woodland, oak woodland, ponderosa pine forest and spruce-fir forest. To get the most out of your Arizona journey, stop at each of the bird habitats listed below as you climb the "sky islands."

Desert Scrub: Standing on the desert floor near Green Valley or Continental, you are surrounded by a portion of the Sonoran Desert, the hottest of our Southwestern deserts. The classic saguaro and cholla cacti regions of this habitat reach a peak of development just west of Tucson near the Arizona-Sonora Desert Museum. But at the base of the Santa Rita Mountains, before you begin the drive up to Madera Canyon, the dominant plants are creosote bush, paloverde and mesquite. Where more moisture collects, in the dry washes and arroyos, the catclaw, smoketree and desert willow afford shade and nesting for numerous birds.

Annual wildflowers (ephemerals) succeed particularly well in deserts, where the dry conditions aren't conducive to hold-over growth. A seed covered with earth has a better chance of survival than a perennial plant, because it can sprout and bloom quickly following a thunderstorm.

After good winter rains, spring annual wildflowers (February–April) in southern Arizona may be abundant, and the plants are largely Californian species of mustards, poppies, and sand-verbenas. However, flower displays during July–September, following good summer rains from the south, are largely "Mexican" species, such as amaranths and morning glories. As you travel across the Sonoran Desert from west to east, the cool winter precipitation of the California sections grades into the warmer summer rainfall of the Sierra Madrean sections.

Birds of the desert scrub seek food in the cool hours of the early morning and before dusk. The high temperatures of mid-day send them into hiding, resting in the shade of a convenient mesquite, or within the thick walls of the saguaro cactus.

Birders hoping to surprise these desert dwellers must be up before first light. Then, in the cool gray dawn, the desert comes alive.

Cactus Wrens and Curve-billed Thrashers grab the tops of shrubs and monopolize the best singing podiums. A Northern Cardinal flashes by—the first of several bright scarlet birds you'll see in Arizona. Somehow their color seems even more startling, when viewed against a backdrop of spiny shrubs and desert dust.

The Pyrrhuloxia, the cardinal's Arizona cousin, is more reclusive than the cardinal, but can often be spotted near washes in desert willows. Differentiating female cardinals from female Pyrrhuloxias is sometimes confusing. The bill color—yellowish in Pyrrhuloxia and reddish in the cardinal—should be a first clue. The thick, strongly curved bill of the Pyrrhuloxia contrasts with the more conical shape of the cardinal's. You can easily observe both birds at closer range by wandering through the open air exhibits of the Arizona-Sonora Desert Museum.

The Verdin, the Lucy's Warbler, and the Black-tailed Gnat-catcher are among the smallest inhabitants of the desert scrub. The Lucy's Warbler, looking somewhat like a gray and white Bushtit with a cocked tail, stakes out territory in mesquite trees or in cottonwoods near watercourses. The male's reddish crown patch and rump are difficult to glimpse, as the tiny bird flits from branch to branch. His loud warbler song, once recognized, will follow you everywhere in lowland habitats.

Lucy's Warbler was the first of three Arizona warblers—sometimes called "The Ladies" by birders—named after the female relatives of early ornithologists. The Lucy's Warbler was named for Professor Spencer Baird's daughter. To honor their loved ones back home, Elliot Coues commemorated his sister Grace with the Grace's Warbler and William Anderson, another

U.S. Army surgeon, remembered his wife with the Virginia's Warbler.

Representative birding sites:

Madera Canyon area: Florida Wash (and at lower elevations near Continental)

Tucson area: Arizona-Sonora Desert Museum.

Desert Grassland: The desert grassland reaches its lower limit at 3,500 feet elevation, and is best developed between 4,000–5,000 feet. Where soil is deep, perennial bunch-growth grasses such as black grama, blue grama, sideoats grama, slender grama and hairy grama may cover the landscape. More frequently, on the shallow-soiled, rocky slopes, the grasses mix with a variety of shrubs, trees, and cacti. Prickly pears, chollas, agaves, yuccas, ocotillos, catclaws and mesquite compete with the grasses. Over-grazing has encouraged these shrubs at the expense of former tracts of pure grassland.

The Santa Rita Experimental Range on the road up Madera Canyon is typical desert grassland habitat. Ash-throated Flycatchers perch on the yuccas, their crests blowing in the breezes, their tails balancing. A loud *prr-ipp* call, a flash of rufous, and they fly to the next post, this time an ocotillo.

Scaled Quail, their "cottontops" bobbing, hurry off into the roadside grass.

Near Florida Wash, you may glimpse a small, blackish-looking finch, which, in good light, transforms itself into a male Varied Bunting. A long look at his vivid, deep violet-and-maroon nuptial dress rewards the eager birdwatcher. The easiest way to find this uncommon Arizona specialty is to locate a singing male on territory as he pauses on top of a shrub; otherwise, they're hard to find in the dense mesquite thickets they prefer.

Brown Towhees and Rufous-crowned Sparrows can be found on the borders of the grassland: the Brown Towhee at the mouths of oak canyons and the Rufous-crowned Sparrow in rocky scrub. If you are a West Coast birder, notice how different the interior race of the Brown Towhee looks from those you see, for example, in coastal California. In southeastern Arizona, the Brown Towhee has a noticeable rufous cap, a brown necklace centered by a dot below the throat, and a completely different call. Ornithologists are considering splitting the Brown Towhee into two separate species, a painless way for birders to gain yet another life bird!

Representative birding sites:

Madera Canyon Area: Florida Wash
Patagonia-Sonoita Creek Sanctuary Area: Appleton-Whittell
  Research Ranch (and along Arizona 82 near Sonoita).

Deciduous Riparian Woodland: To explore this habitat, visit Sonoita Creek, where it flows just west of Patagonia at an elevation of 4,000 feet. Because the stream runs year-round, the lush stands of Fremont cottonwoods, sycamores and alders reach heights of 50 to 100 feet, and some of the cottonwood boles are 25 feet around. The cottonwoods, along with Arizona walnut, velvet ash, several willows, and Texas mulberry form a dense canopy above the narrow stream channel. All the trees are winter deciduous.

Immediately bordering the channel, a narrow floodplain valley supporting mesquite and acacia thickets reaches to the adjoining slopes of desert scrub. The edge situation formed by the presence of the running water alongside the dry hillsides attracts birds from both habitats, making for a mix of avifauna.

Once common along all major rivers in southern Arizona, riparian corridors have suffered from man's demand for farmlands and irrigation water. The Nature Conservancy saved this section of Sonoita Creek from a similar fate.

The Nature Conservancy's sanctuary along the stream and the Roadside Rest Stop south of the sanctuary are famous birding spots. Both migrant and resident birds congregate in the abundant leafy canopy above the stream, and several extremely rare birds nest here. Birders who fantasize about watching the Rose-throated Becard, Thick-billed Kingbird, and Gray Hawk at their nest sites, can see the reality along Sonoita Creek. These three rarities are next to impossible to find anywhere else in Arizona, much less the rest of the U.S.

The Rose-throated Becard behaves rather like a flycatcher,

but it is a member of the Cotinga family of the tropics. Once recorded in Arizona in 1888, it wasn't until 1947 that Allan Phillips, a renowned Arizona ornithologist, re-discovered the Rose-throated Becard nesting this far north. Since then, a breeding pair of becards has delighted birders most years by suspending their huge, foot-long nest from the tip of a sycamore branch hanging over Sonoita Creek.

Birders can find many other interesting birds breeding in the riparian woodland. Cavity nesters, such as the Acorn, Gila and Ladder-backed Woodpeckers, the Brown-crested Flycatcher, and the White-breasted Nuthatch use the dead cottonwood snags and hollow trunks for homes. Raptors build nests in the tops of the tallest cottonwoods; the lovely Gray Hawk is often spied circling high above its platform hidden in the sturdy branches.

Large and small members of the flycatcher family thrive at Sonoita. From the tiniest of all—the Northern Beardless Tyrannulet—to the big, noisy Thick-billed Kingbird, and including the Western Wood-Pewee, Dusky-capped Flycatcher, Brown-crested Flycatcher, and Cassin's Kingbird—the woods echo with the myriad calls of these insect-eating loud-mouths.

Several flycatchers here look very similar, and are best distinguished by their voice. For example, the Thick-billed Kingbird's harsh *kwa-reep?* heralds its arrival on the topmost branches of a sycamore, after a flycatching sortie. Nesting primarily across from the Roadside Rest Stop area near Sonoita Creek, the Thick-billeds tend to fly back and forth from the sycamores to the adjacent arid hillsides, where they can be discerned at a distance perched on yuccas. The Thick-billed Kingbirds, along with the Brown-crested Flycatchers and Cassin's Kingbirds, contribute to the raucous dawn chorus at Sonoita Creek.

The Northern Beardless-Tyrannulet, another of the Arizona specialty birds to be found here, is much less imposing than its long name suggests. Unless you know its call, this unassuming denizen of streamside shrubbery may be overlooked. Be alert for a loud *peer, peer, peer* series of notes. The tyrannulet flits about in the lower canopy of leaves, acting more like a warbler or vireo than a member of the flycatcher family to which it belongs. If you get your binoculars on the tyrannulet, you'll see a bird with a grayish-olive back and breast, a very tiny bill, and a ragged little crest.

The Vermilion Flycatcher's brilliant red and black form teeters on fencelines. In flying swoops, it partakes of the rich insect diet near the stream. The other scarlet flash in the thickets belongs to the male Summer Tanager. What other region in North America can boast so many birds with vivid red in their plumage?

Representative birding sites:
Patagonia-Sonoita Creek Sanctuary area: Roadside Rest Stop,
  Patagonia-Sonoita Creek Sanctuary
Huachuca Mountains area: San Pedro River.

Oak Woodland: In southeastern Arizona on hillsides between 4,000–6,500 feet, oak and pine-oak woodlands form a transition zone between the cooler coniferous forests above and the drier grasslands and deserts below. The dominant trees in the oak woodland are drought-resistant oaks, pines, and junipers— probably originating in Mexico.

In the oak woodland, rainfall is 12 to 18 inches per year, most of it falling during the summer rainy season. Compared to the oak woodland of California, which must sustain a long summer drought period, Arizona's woodland is more productive. More moisture is available during the summer growing season, encouraging a variety of wildlife.

Evergreen oaks prosper here, the most common being the Emory oak, a dark-barked tree with leathery, lustrous green leaves. The undersides of the leaves are pale. In addition, Arizona white oak and Mexican blue oak scatter over the hillsides and cloak the narrow canyons.

Alligator juniper, one-seed juniper and Mexican pinyon pine are mixed in with the oaks, giving this portion of the woodland a Sierra Madrean flavor. The understory consists of grass or shrubs and even some cacti. The term *encinal* is often used to describe this section of the evergreen oak woodland.

Between the *encinal* and the true ponderosa pine forest above, a unique pine-oak woodland exists. Here, the small Chihuahua pine and the long-needled Apache pine, both limited in their U. S. range to southeast Arizona and western New Mexico, blend with the evergreen oaks.

Both the oak *(encinal)* and pine-oak woodlands flourish in the foothills of the Santa Rita, Huachuca and Chiricahua Mountains. The shrubs include velvet-pod mimosa, woodland sumac, algerita, mountain yucca, golden-flowered agave and Parry agave. Buckbrush and locust reach down into the woodlands, too, as well as various kinds of penstemon, verbena, globemallow, lupine, mint, and calochortus. Blue grama is the common grass, coming up from the grasslands below.

Birding the oak and pine-oak associations of Arizona's woodlands means pure exhilaration for birders. Greedily, they feast on the sight of new bird after new bird. These woodlands support more Arizona specialty birds than any other local habitat.

The friendly Bridled Titmouse scolds, chickadee-like, the moment you get out of the car. Its gray and black crest and black throat make this titmouse the handsomest of its kind. Together with the Acorn Woodpeckers and Gray-breasted Jays, the Bridled Titmice gather acorns for sustenance and use the oaks for shelter. When these birds bury an acorn, they help propagate the oak trees. In turn, the oaks provide nesting cavities and a diet of nutritional acorns for the birds.

The Strickland's Woodpecker depends upon the oaks, too. Restricted largely to the evergreen oak belt, this bird's quiet habits and brown upperparts aid in camouflaging it against the brown-barked oaks. The Strickland's Woodpecker is a good deal more reclusive than the Acorn Woodpeckers you'll encounter everywhere, and can put birders through a trying search.

Bird life is most abundant along the narrow creeks that course down the arid canyons. Attracted to the Arizona cypress, Arizona sycamore, Arizona walnut and madrone growing beside the creeks, many species nest along the creekbeds and sing from nearby slopes.

This is trogon country! The gorgeous Elegant Trogon, an uncommon summer resident of a few canyons in these "sky islands," usually chooses a hole in one of the sycamores as a nest site (more about the trogon later). A trogon pair must vie with the aggressive Sulphur-bellied Flycatcher, which is apt to set up territory creekside, too. Listen for the rubber duck squeak of this big flycatcher, and you may see its long rufous tail protruding from a woodpecker-drilled cavity high above you, as it investigates a possible future home.

Where the pines and oaks mingle, search for the Painted Redstart. Both sexes display a stunning black and red outfit with white wing bars and tail feathers. Typically, this warbler prances and fans its tail as it explores through the trees. Rarely seen outside of a small fraction of the Southwest, the lovely Painted Redstart is easy to find in Arizona.

The mellow notes of the Hepatic Tanager's song may accompany your bird search. Frequenting the upper edges of the pine-oak woodland, male Hepatic Tanagers show themselves as a flicker of brick-red. Deliberately, they hunt amongst the blue-gray needles of the pines. Meanwhile, in late spring, their mustard-yellow mates quietly go about building a saucer-shaped nest high among the branches.

Nights in the woodlands are good for owling. In Madera Canyon, for example, an Elf Owl has occupied a hole in a telephone pole near the Santa Rita Lodge for several seasons. Recently, it was joined by a Whiskered Screech-Owl in a similar utility pole across the street. The Whiskered Screech's mate was often to be found nearby, a few yards up the hill dozing in a cypress. He resembled an old, but distinguished, whiskered gentleman, whiling away the daytime hours leaning against a tree trunk.

The only problem for birders occurred at dusk, when they had to decide which owl to watch as it awoke and flew off for the night.

Representative birding locations:

Madera Canyon area: Madera Picnic Grounds, Bog Springs Campground, Santa Rita Lodge, Nature Trail, Palisport Gift Shop

Huachuca Mountains area: Garden, Scheelite and Sawmill Canyons, Ramsey Canyon

Chiricahua Mountains area: Cave Creek Canyon.

Ponderosa Pine Forest: Between about 6,500–8,000 feet, the ponderosa pine forest takes over. At lower elevations, it is mixed with silverleaf oak, netleaf oak and madrone—the commonest broadleaf evergreen trees. Higher up, Gambel oak, big-tooth maple, aspen, alder and mulberry are the primary broadleaf deciduous trees. Towards the upper end of the zone, Douglas-fir and white pine occur on north-facing slopes. These are more cold-tolerant trees, commonly found in the spruce-fir forests of the Rocky Mountains.

Buckbrush is the main shrub on the forest floor. In the lower parts of the forest, chaparral-type shrubs are present such as buckthorn (*Rhamnus* species), deerbrush, manzanita and squawbush. Different kinds of lupine, peavine, cinquefoil, yarrow, goldenrod, paintbrush, penstemon, fleabane, deerweed, and groundsel bloom in spring and summer.

Many of the Mexican mountains in Arizona top out at this zone, because only the highest peaks of the Chiricahuas contain the spruce-fir forest. The mountains are so steep that few meadows or park-like landscapes soften the precipitous slopes.

The birds of the ponderosa pine belt feature further Arizona specialties, but not as many as those found lower down. The warblers, however, are exceptional here.

The Red-faced Warbler, another of those red-plumaged Arizona beauties, is one of the primary drawing-cards. From the pine-oak woodland up into the ponderosas, listen for the distinctive, loud song of the Red-faced. The bird is rather pugnacious, and will respond quickly to a Northern Pygmy-Owl imitation, either with your voice or on a tape.

In the pure stands of ponderosa pine, Olive and Grace's Warblers cavort. Way up in the very tops of the conifers, these two dainty warblers pick their way from branch to branch, often pausing to deliver their emphatic songs. The Grace's Warbler has a bright yellow throat and chest and a yellow eyebrow. It is white below with white wing bars and white tail spots.

The male Olive Warbler has a wonderful tawny orange head and upper breast. His song is a repetitive *weeta, weeta, weeta* or *peto, peto, peto* sounding rather like one of the titmouse calls.

Mexican Chickadees, Pygmy Nuthatches, Brown Creepers, Yellow-rumped (Audubon's) Warblers and Yellow-eyed Juncos roam the ponderosa forest, often in small flocks. Broad-tailed Hummingbirds are the common hummer here, feeding on the blooming iris and penstemon.

As if to make up for his dull plumage, the Greater Pewee whistles his lovely song, which sounds like *Jose Maria (Ho-say-mar-ee-ah)* from the branch of a pine. This large flycatcher, dressed in muted brownish-gray, shows an orange lower mandible and a slight crest. The Greater Pewee has a fondness for pines, sticking closely to them in southeast Arizona. Like many montane species here, it winters in the lowlands of Central America.

If you come across the tiny Western Flycatcher in this zone, listen carefully for its *whee-zeet* (accent on the last syllable) call. The bird sounds perceptibly different from the West Coast race's upslurred *zeeee-up? seet* call, and it may be a candidate for "splitting" into two species. A possible new life bird?

Representative birding sites:
Madera Canyon area: Mt. Wrightson Trail, Josephine Saddle Trail
Huachuca Mountains area: Miller Peak Trail
Chiricahua Mountains area: Rustler Park, Pinery Canyon.

Spruce-Fir Forest: Above 9,000 feet (Chiricahua Peak is 9,795 feet), small portions of the Chiricahuas support stands of Engelmann spruce and alpine fir. Aspen occurs in scattered clumps. Characteristic shrubs are species of currant, blueberry, Oregon-grape, black-fruited honeysuckle, red elderberry, dwarf juniper, and shrubby cinquefoil.

Sometimes you can find high elevation wildflowers such as primulas, gentians, violets, and columbines as well as skunk cabbage, baneberries, louseworts and many others.

The bird life here begins to resemble more that of the Rocky Mountains to the north, rather than Mexico to the south. Standard high mountain species such as Northern Goshawk, Red-breasted Nuthatch, Evening Grosbeak and Red Crossbill decorate the forest trees and call from the cool, north-facing slopes.

Golden-crowned and Ruby-crowned Kinglets reign in the firs, nesting and singing in the very treetops.

The Magnificent Hummingbird often wanders up to the firs, having nested at lower elevations. This large, sedate hummer sits erect on a branch, almost looking like a small sparrow. In good light, its metallic green throat and purple crown glisten.

Representative birding sites:

Chiricahua Mountains area: Rustler Park (along the Chiricahua Peak trail).

Attracting Birds with Taped Calls

Many birders carry taped recordings of the songs of the southeastern Arizona birds they wish to attract. While a definite advantage in some situations, playing tapes should be handled with great discretion. For example, when a pair of Buff-collared Nightjars set up territory in Florida Wash, one of the few accessible breeding locations in Arizona, birders were asked not to use tape recorders. Excessive tape playing may cause the birds to desert the area, as they fruitlessly respond to an imaginary rival—your taped call.

For this reason, Elegant Trogons are now protected by law from overzealous birders using taped calls. In the South Fork of Cave Creek Canyon, in the Trogon Management Area administered by the Coronado National Forest, the use of tape recorders to attract the trogons is strictly prohibited.

On the other hand, successful owling usually requires a tape recorder, which, if used in moderation, results in minimal disturbance to the owl. The playing of taped owl calls lures the owls closer, where they can be pinpointed for a moment in the beam of a strong flashlight (another essential tool of the owling trade).

Of course, some owl species are easy to call in, but difficult to locate even if directly overhead. Flammulated Owls, notorious for this behavior, can sit in a tree right above you, hooting away, and be impossible to see. By remaining motionless and perching very near the trunk, these owls can elude the most skilled owling expeditions.

As in birding other regions of pine-oak and ponderosa pine forests in the West, calls of the Northern Pygmy-Owl—by your own imitation or by tape recorder—agitate warblers and many other songbirds, sometimes bringing them closer to investigate you. In this way, you can call in a number of woodland species for closer viewing. Again, this tactic should be used in moderation, especially in heavily birded regions such as southeastern Arizona.

Watching Hummingbirds

No account of birding in this intriguing part of the Southwest would be complete without a mention of hummingbirds.

Hummingbirds, those tiny tyrants blessed with iridescent colors, will captivate your attention and provide endless hours of watching here. In Madera Canyon, Ramsey Canyon and Cave Creek Canyon, birders spend time glued to the hummingbird feeders. Not only is this the best way to study and photograph hummers, it's almost the only way the rare or accidental ones get discovered.

Identifying hummingbirds sounds easier than it is. The females and young males of some species look remarkably alike, and should be scrutinized carefully. For example, female Broad-billed Hummingbirds, common in southeast Arizona, can be confused with female White-eared Hummingbirds, an irregular but annual visitor.

However, by relaxing for awhile in front of a line-up of hummingbird feeders, you gradually begin to really recognize the common species. The males seldom pose a problem with their distinctive gorgets (patch of colored feathers on the throat), but even they can be tricky in poor light.

Their vocalizations can be another valuable clue in hummingbird identification. The Magnificent Hummingbird gives a loud chip like a Black Phoebe; the Blue-throated gives an equally strong *seep;* the Broad-billed Hummingbird stutters rather like a Ruby-crowned Kinglet; the Anna's Hummingbird makes a *click* sound resembling little castanets.

Some males produce trilling and whinnying sounds in flight with their wing and tail feathers, which are further aids in identification. The adult male Broad-tailed Hummingbird makes a buzzing trill, created by the wind rushing through two slots on his outer primaries. (The females lack these.)

Male Black-chinned Hummingbirds give a dry, whinnying sound with their wings as they rock back and forth in a shallow arc, displaying before the females. Using its spread tail feathers, the male Anna's Hummingbird makes a sharp popping sound at the bottom of its steep display dive.

The common hummingbirds present in Arizona May through August are: Black-chinned, Anna's, Broad-tailed, Magnificent, Blue-throated, and Broad-billed. In late July and August, many Rufous Hummingbirds migrate through on their way south.

The Elegant Trogon: A Birding Close-Up

"Almost at once the male approached, perching among the middle branches of the sycamore which hung idly over the canyon bed where I was standing. He showed little excitement but sat upright, parrot-style, on a small horizontal limb. Occasionally, he turned his gorgeous green head, and thus displayed the heavy yellow bill. Below the green hood is a pure white collar which seems to emphasize the striking crimson breast, while below the branch on which he sat hung his long copper-colored tail. The low morning sun made this elegant creature a veritable rainbow of color, as he sat in the tropical-like vegetation with the spectacular mountains forming a backdrop; here was a picture to be long remembered." (Herbert Brandt, *Arizona and Its Bird Life.*)

If Brandt's description strikes you as exaggerated, wait until you've seen your first Elegant Trogon.

The bird is truly elegant. It belongs to the Trogon family, a tropical group of birds of extreme beauty. The quetzal, another member of the same family, is considered by many to be the most beautiful bird in the Western Hemisphere, and was regarded as sacred by the Mayas and the Aztecs.

Trogons are adapted to life in the tropical forests, where they feed on fruit and large insects. Their large eyes are accustomed to focusing in the dim light. Their bill is short, wide at the base and has several teeth on the upper mandible. They have small legs and feet, with a strange toe arrangement—the first and second toes both turn to the rear.

The Elegant Trogon, formerly called the Coppery-tailed Trogon, lives in sycamore-shaded canyons, typically Madera, Ramsey, Scheelite, and Cave Creek Canyons in the Santa Rita, Huachuca and Chiricahua Mountains. Although their numbers fluctuate from year to year, the trogons usually make their trek north from Mexico by mid-May and depart by the end of September.

Long before the trogon becomes visible, you can hear its strange call in the distance. Carrying far, and bouncing off the canyon walls, the cry sounds like a cross between the *oink* of a pig and the gobble of a hen turkey. *Co-ah, co-ah, co-ah* repeated over and over in an unmusical croak. (In Mexico, the bird is called the Coa.)

Standing on the trail in the South Fork of Cave Creek Canyon in the Chiricahuas—with the call of the approaching trogon ringing in your ears—the impulse to chase after the bird is a natural one. But if you wait patiently, difficult to do if this is your first trogon, the bird will eventually fly very close. It may appear directly overhead, long tail fluttering. It may alight nearby, but further up the canyon's slope. Or, more often than not, the trogon will perch in a tree not ten feet away.

The birds are curiously tame, and once you've seen one, you can add your trogon story to those that circulate among the Arizona birding fraternity.

The male's bright red breast and glossy green chest, head and back are breathtaking! In good light, the coppery sheen to the upper tail feathers contrasts with the delicate white barring of the undertail spots. The female is brown above, dull rose on the belly, and has a teardrop white spot behind her eye.

Often, the bird calls while perched, tail hanging straight down, yellow bill held daintily skyward. If an insect should catch its eye, a quick sally into the air illustrates the function of the long tail. In smooth, graceful style, the trogon seizes its prey, returning at once to a favorite branch.

In selecting a nest site in one of the Arizona sycamores, usually along a creekbed, a trogon pair will pick a hole 12 to 40 feet up. The cavity is lined with hay, straw, moss, wool or down, and the female lays two to four eggs.

The rare status and exotic origins of the Elegant Trogon have endowed it with an aura of mystery for birders. If you spend some time in Cave Creek Canyon in the Chiricahuas, your diligence will be rewarded with a glimpse of this wonderful creature, the symbolic bird of southeastern Arizona's rugged canyons.

NOTES FROM A BIRDER'S DIARY

Southeastern Arizona

● June 9, 1977, 8:00 A.M., Roadside Rest Stop, Patagonia: This morning I rose early and drove here from Ramsey Canyon. A warm breeze rustles the cottonwood trees overhead, as I take notes in the car. The querulous cries of the Cassin's Kingbirds' ring out through the trees above me and bounce off the canyon walls.

Having just witnessed my first-ever Rose-throated Becard—a pair of them—building their strange nest, I want to record the experience while it is still fresh. . . .

Below the highway a narrow path, bordered by a fence paralleling a portion of Sonoita Creek, led me into a green amphitheater of huge cottonwoods and sycamores. Between the fence and the creek a level meadow area stretched to a chalky bluff.

Birds were everywhere. The cacophony of whistles and shrieks and scolds were deafening. Phainopeplas glided in and out; a Brown-crested Flycatcher squeezed into a nest hole in the sycamore; a Gila Woodpecker hitched up a tree trunk. All added to the general din.

Further on, the largest sycamore of all spread great boughs

overhead. There, about 30 feet up in the tree, at the end of a slender long, drooping branch, hung a large nest.

Suddenly, a medium-sized bird flew into the foliage above the nest and sat quite still. I got my binoculars on it: a gray silhouette with a marvelous deep rose color on the throat. The male Rose-throated Becard!

The nest was a large ball about 15 to 18 inches in diameter and just as long. It hung suspended in mid-air, inaccessible to all but the most daring predators. A disheveled mass of vegetation, the nest was still being built. The female soon landed on the structure, disappearing in a hole in the top with a long blade of grass. Squealing and sputtering, the male joined her. Hauling a twig twice his size, he entered the nest through a different hole at the bottom.

Spellbound, I watched as these two exceedingly rare birds went about their nest-building in such a natural manner, oblivious to my excitement at seeing this prized Arizona species at such close quarters.

• May 30, 1988, 9:00 P.M., Cave Creek Canyon, Chiricahua Mountains: Eleven years have elapsed since my first visit to southeastern Arizona. I have returned to do the loop once more, ending my trip in the Chiricahua Mountains.

As I approached Portal and saw the Chiricahua Mountains rising up purple—their feet firmly planted in the desert scrub, their cool forests hidden high above—I felt the magic of this place once more. At the entrance to the Chiricahuas, the red rock spires of Cave Creek Canyon thrust upward from the oak-and-pine-clad slopes. Gaping caves in the cliff faces formed dark, mysterious holes. No wonder the Apaches fled to this fortress of a canyon, so narrow and forbidding at its mouth, yielding its secrets only to those who follow it to its terminus at the base of Chiricahua Peak.

This morning very early I began the day at the head of the South Fork Trail. My goal: to locate the Elegant Trogon.

No sunshine peeped over the canyon walls, but the birding was good. I tracked down a singing Grace's Warbler, and followed a Painted Redstart; Hepatic Tanagers and Black-headed Grosbeaks serenaded from the trees. Bridled Titmice and Gray-breasted Jays harassed the Acorn Woodpeckers and the woodpeckers protested by ganging together and screeching in the upper branches of a sycamore.

Another group of birdwatchers came up behind me on the trail.

"Have you seen the trogon yet?" I queried.

"Nope. We hear it's supposed to be along this trail."

Wishing them well, I pushed on following the creek.

I stopped to listen. Very faintly from far, far down the canyon the *co-ah, co-ah, co-ah* call of the Elegant Trogon could be heard. Then, silence. Again, much closer, the gobbling sound reverberated from hillside to hillside.

Unable to stand still any longer, I took off up the slope in search of the bird, running with abandon through the poison ivy and boulders. Tripping and stumbling, binoculars swinging, I came to a breathless halt at last before an adult male trogon— the morning sun reflecting the copper highlights on his long tail. A bird to send the adrenalin surging each time one gazes upon it . . .

From the south fork of Cave Creek Canyon, the dirt road traced a dusty path up to Rustler Park. I followed the hairpin turns, intent upon reaching the coniferous forest and a chance to see the mountain warblers.

A Virginia's Warbler and an Olive Warbler—the Virginia's on the dry slopes in the shrubbery, the Olive in the ponderosas— were good finds. The Red-faced Warbler remained elusive until I got to Rustler Park, when, as I climbed up the trail behind the campground, I located one singing loudly, deep in a pine-oak thicket.

Returning to the Portal area, I spent the late afternoon hours at the Spoffords' Rancho Aguila. These generous bird-lovers have created a bird sanctuary in their backyard. Birders arrive and go straight to the rear of the house, where chairs and benches are arranged for viewing the great variety of birds. Feeders of all kinds—from hummingbird feeders to seed platforms to fruit and bread scraps—ring the yard.

I watched, entranced, as more than thirty different kinds of birds flew in to partake of the feast.

This is one of the best places in southeastern Arizona to watch hummingbirds. I have never seen so many, so tantalizingly close. Correctly identifying the females posed a challenge to all of us, but the males stole the show. As the evening light shone on their colorful crowns and throats, a sigh of admiration rose from the assembled group of birders.

Promptly at 6:00 P.M., Rhoda, the roadrunner, made her appearance. She ran, long legs flying, into the yard and hid behind a brushpile. Gradually, she eased her way up to the back porch. When Mr. Spofford opened the door to proffer a morsel of cat food, Rhoda waited for him to throw it in her direction. After dining on several tidbits, Rhoda left as she had come—on the run.

The wonderful, undeniable truth about southeastern Arizona the second time around: it is still terrific and the birds still abound, many of them to be found in the same locations they were eleven years ago. Yes, there are more birders. Yes, there are more bird tours and tour vans. Birdwatching's popularity has grown considerably all over North America in the last decade.

But the Rose-throated Becard still hangs its nest from the sycamore across from the Roadside Rest Stop near Patagonia; the Thick-billed Kingbirds continue to squeal from the treetops nearby; the Gray Hawk can still be found in the sanctuary at Sonoita; the Elegant Trogon flies up and down the South Fork Trail in Cave Creek Canyon. That is, these birds have continued to grace Arizona with their presence despite the pressure of enthusiastic birders and constantly shrinking habitat.

Arizona birding is alive and well in a spot to be treasured forever for its fantastic avifauna.

TRAVELERS' TIPS

Before You Visit: Most birding trips around southeastern Arizona begin and end in Tucson. In order to visit the many good birding spots in the area, birders typically travel in a loop. The loop often begins in Madera Canyon in the Santa Rita Mountains south of Tucson and culminates in a visit to the Chiricahua Mountains near the New Mexican border.

If you only have time for a very brief sample of birding southeastern Arizona, skip the full loop and try, for example, birding the Madera Canyon area only.

Whatever your route, you'll likely meet with birdwatchers along the way; Arizona's unique birds draw travelers from all over the world. At the lodgings, in the campgrounds, and along the trails, practically everyone you meet is a birder. And like you, they hope to see as many species as possible during their trip.

In birding the loop, it pays to exchange information with other birders. You will be surprised at their willingness to help. Frequently, nest locations change from year to year. Unexpected rarities show up even among the rare birds already there. By talking with other birders who have preceded you on the loop, or are going in the opposite direction, you augment your chances of up-to-the-minute information.

If you are visiting in late May or June, the hottest months, plan to be driving—preferably in an air-conditioned car—during the middle of the day. Save the early mornings and evenings for birding once you've arrived.

Southeastern Arizona has several overnight lodgings catering especially to birders. As such, the fun of your trip can be increased by staying at accommodations which welcome birders and provide well-stocked bird feeders! Since some of the birding locations are rather remote, you may save time and energy by staying in one of these lodgings situated near the good birding areas:

Madera Canyon: Santa Rita Lodge, Box 444, Amado, Az. 85645. Phone (602) 625-8746.

Patagonia/Sonoita: Stage Stop Inn, P. O. Box 777, Patagonia, Az. 85624. Phone (602) 394-2211.

Huachuca Mountains: The Mile Hi Cabins and Ramsey Canyon Preserve, RR 1 Box 84, Hereford, Az. 85615-9738. Phone (602) 378-2785.

Chiricahua Mountains: Cave Creek Ranch, Box F, Portal, Az. 85632. Phone (602) 558-2334. Also available: Cathedral Rock Lodge (602) 558-2254, Portal Store Bed & Breakfast (602) 558-2223, and Southwestern Research Station, Portal, Az. 85632, phone (602) 558-2396.

Inquiries should be made well in advance, in some cases many months ahead, due to the great popularity of these places with birders and bird tours.

Don't despair. If you find the above are already booked, there are motels in Green Valley (for the Madera Canyon area), Nogales, Sierra Vista, Douglas, and, of course, Tucson.

For details on camping in these areas and to obtain a map of the Coronado National Forest, write Supervisor, Coronado National Forest, Federal Building, Tucson, Az. 85701. Phone (602) 629-6483.

The best Arizona state map is available from Arizona Highways, 2039 West Lewis Ave., Phoenix, Az. 85009. Phone (602) 258-1000.

The Tucson Audubon Society, 30-A No. Tucson Blvd., Tucson, Az. 85716, phone (602) 323-9673, has books, checklists, and maps for sale. Many of the accommodations listed above have their own bird checklists, too.

The Tucson Audubon Society's statewide Rare Bird Alert number is (602) 798-1005.

When to Visit: For your first trip to southeastern Arizona, a visit between May 15 and August 15 should yield all of the species you seek. Before May 15 many of the birds migrating north from Mexico, such as the Elegant Trogon and Rose-throated Becard, may not have arrived yet, and after August 15, they may have departed or become scarce.

A trip during the last two weeks of May or the first week of June is suggested, because, though temperatures are warm, all the breeding Mexican species will be in, and the overall chances for owls are good. Late migrant warblers and other rarities frequently turn up at this season. However, Arizona's dry conditions in the past few years have created a serious forest fire threat this time of year. Call the Coronado National Forest Headquarters in Tucson at (602) 629-6483 for current information on possible forest closures.

Another rewarding time to visit is late July and August. The summer rains have cooled off the mountains, giving rise to a burst of singing and nesting activity among some species, particularly grassland sparrows. Although lowland temperatures soar at this season (Tucson will be scorching), the cooler oak woodland canyons remain quite pleasant. This is the best time to seek the rarer hummingbirds, such as the Violet-crowned and White-eared Hummingbirds, in addition to other unusual hummers and landbirds wandering north after breeding in Mexico.

Length of Visit: So many great birding locations and exotic birds keep turning up in southeastern Arizona, it really takes two or three trips to see all the sights. For a first bird finding tour of the area, spend at least a week, more if you can.

The trip outlined below takes six days and is somewhat of a whirlwind tour—whetting your appetite for a more leisurely stay the next time around. Everyone is bound to "miss" some of the Arizona specialties on the first trip, so have fun and see the most you can, knowing this famous birding area will be on your bird travel list for many years to come.

THE BIRDING SITES

Tucson area: A visit to the Arizona-Sonora Desert Museum before you begin your bird trip is highly recommended; whether you go before or after your trip, don't miss a stroll through this "live" museum.

ARIZONA-SONORA DESERT MUSEUM: Hardly a typical museum, this one contains living animals and plants of the Sonoran Desert region. The displays, tastefully landscaped, lure other wild birds, ones which you, as a birder, can "count." In addition, a walk in the aviary, surrounded by many of Arizona's native birds, allows you to study the wild birds close up, instead of straining through binoculars.

The Museum is located a half hour's drive west of Tucson. You can take two routes. The first follows Speedway Blvd. west over Gates Pass, and the second goes out Ajo Way (Arizona 86) and turns right (north) on Kinney Rd. The Gates Pass route is narrow and winding; motor homes and trailers should take Ajo Way.

Madera Canyon area: To reach the Madera Canyon Recreational Area, drive south from Tucson on I-19 for 24 mi.; use Exit 63, south of the town of Green Valley, and go east on Continental Rd. (1.2 mi.), then turn right (south) onto White House Canyon Rd., following the directional signs. Stay on this paved road to Madera Canyon (12 mi.).

FLORIDA WASH: Early in the morning the birding along the road to Madera Canyon is good. Watch carefully as you drive through the desert grassland with mesquite—the Santa Rita Experimental Range—and pull off for a chance to see lowland birds such as Gambel's Quail, Scaled Quail, White-winged Dove, Greater Roadrunner, Ladder-backed Woodpecker, Say's

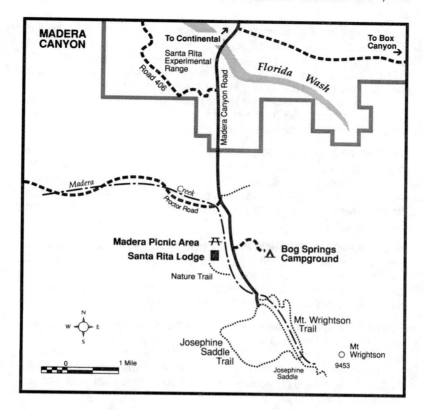

Phoebe, Ash-throated Flycatcher, Cactus Wren, Western Kingbird, Black-tailed Gnatcatcher, Phainopepla, Lucy's Warbler, Northern Cardinal, Pyrrhuloxia, Black-throated and Rufous-crowned Sparrows, and Eastern Meadowlark.

Approximately 7 mi. up the road to Madera Canyon, a dirt road goes off to the left to Box Canyon Rd. However, you proceed right on the paved road and shortly thereafter cross two narrow bridges. The second one crosses Florida (Flow-REE-dah) Wash, a well-known birding spot. Park and walk over the stile into the pasture to the left (northeast) of the road. From here, bird up and down the dry wash, where Bell's Vireo and Varied Bunting are found. If you're lucky, the elusive Crissal Thrasher may show itself, but the hardest bird to find here is the Rufous-winged Sparrow, also the most sought-after.

In the grasslands on either side of the road, Botteri's and Cassin's Sparrows breed after summer rains begin (July and August), when they perform their skylarking displays, making it easier to locate them. Road 406 is a good place to look.

Continuing past Florida Wash up the Madera Canyon Road, you will cross two cattle-guards. As you approach the second cattle-guard, watch on the right for a dirt place to pull off and park. A trail leads off to the left (east) across the road, following the fence to the edge of the ravine. The Buff-collared Nightjar has recently nested here—best heard, though seldom seen, at dusk. Please do not play tapes or harass these birds!

Proctor Road, at .1 mi. past the second cattle-guard, is a dirt road leading off to the right and down to the stream. Look along the first mile for other birds found in desert scrub and grasslands.

MADERA PICNIC GROUNDS: A mile past the Proctor Road turn off, on the main road, Madera Picnic Grounds on your right provides an oak and sycamore-shaded home for Acorn Woodpeckers, Black Phoebes, Cassin's Kingbirds, Dusky-capped Flycatchers, Sulphur-bellied Flycatchers, Western Wood-Pewees, Gray-breasted Jays, Bridled Titmice, Hepatic Tanagers, and Black-headed Grosbeaks.

BOG SPRINGS CAMPGROUND: Opposite the Madera Picnic Grounds, a road takes off to the east, with a sign pointing to Bog Springs Campground. In a half-mile, you'll come to the campground, worth searching for Strickland's Woodpecker, which has nested here recently. If the campers are putting out hummingbird feeders, ask to sit and watch!

SANTA RITA LODGE: Straight ahead on the main road, the Santa Rita Lodge has long been a landmark for birders along the Arizona loop. The main building burned to the ground in 1983, but the little cabins with kitchens are still very popular. One of the cabins serves as an excellent gift shop, selling books and bird checklists. The proprietors often have tips on the latest bird news in the area.

Hummingbird feeders hang everywhere in the lodge area. Relax in the shade and expect to see the following hummers: Anna's, Black-chinned, Blue-throated, Broad-billed, Broad-tailed and Magnificent. Ask for information about any vagrants that might have appeared, especially in July and August.

Santa Rita Lodge has always attracted owls! Check the telephone poles and ask at the office.

NATURE TRAIL: Continuing past the Lodge on the main road (.2 mi.), stop at the sign that says Nature Trail. Park and cross the creek on the bridge, following the cement pathway to your right around the little amphitheater and downstream. The path eventually ends up behind the cabins at the Lodge, and it's good birding all the way. Some Arizona specialties to look for, in addition to the ones mentioned for Madera Picnic Grounds, are: Strickland's Woodpecker, Montezuma Quail (rare), Greater Pewee, Brown-crested Flycatcher, Phainopepla, Hutton's Vireo, Black-throated Gray Warbler, Painted Redstart, Bronzed Cowbird, Hepatic and Western Tanagers, Rufous-crowned Sparrow, and Lesser Goldfinch.

At twilight, listen for Whip-poor-wills and Common Poorwills and Common and Lesser Nighthawks calling up and down the canyon.

PALISPORT GIFT SHOP: A quarter mile further up the road, the Palisport Gift Shop has more hummingbird feeders, and a picnic table out front to accommodate birders.

MT. WRIGHTSON TRAIL: The road ends at the topmost parking lot, from which two trails lead farther up into the Santa Rita Mountains. The first trail takes off to your left, at the lower end of the parking lot. If you're feeling full of energy, the seven-mile hike up to the summit of Mt. Wrightson provides a wonderful birding experience. The Elegant Trogon has nested in a sycamore about a mile up, and, if you get near the top, you can find all the high mountain Arizona birds such as Steller's Jay, Pygmy Nuthatch, Brown Creeper, Grace's, Olive, Red-faced and Yellow-rumped Warblers, Hepatic and Western Tanagers, Pine Siskin, Yellow-eyed Junco and Red Crossbill.

JOSEPHINE SADDLE TRAIL: The Josephine Saddle trail, which leaves the upper parking lot to your right, begins past the cable at the end of the lot and follows a dirt road. After a quarter mile, a trail turns sharply left, but you keep on the main trail up the canyon. At about .8 mi. up the trail, the Elegant Trogon has nested in the sycamores above the creek (ask at the Santa Rita Lodge office for current directions), and Northern Goshawks, Magnificent Hummingbirds, Sulphur-bellied Flycatchers and Painted Redstarts also breed in the area. A mile above the road, the trail leaves the stream bed and climbs into the oaks. Watch for such species as Wild Turkey, Montezuma Quail (rare), and Red-faced Warbler.

Note: The high mountain warblers—the Grace's, Olive, and Red-faced Warblers—and the Elegant Trogon are generally easier to see in the Chiricahuas. However, if you don't have time for a visit to the Chiricahuas, this is the next best spot.

Madera Canyon is great for owling too. You may hear Elf, Flammulated, Great Horned, and Spotted Owls (rare) plus Whiskered and Western Screech-Owls. Anywhere from the Lodge to the topmost parking lot at the end of the road, pull off and listen for owls or play a tape recorder.

Patagonia-Sonoita Creek Sanctuary area:
To reach the Patagonia area from Madera Canyon, go south on I-19 to Nogales, then take Arizona 82 north and east to Patagonia.

ROADSIDE REST STOP: Approximately 15 mi. north of Nogales (4 mi. south of the town of Patagonia), you'll come to the most famous roadside rest area in North America for birders. Both in the Rest Stop and across the highway on the west side, where Sonoita Creek flows close to the road, can be found a number of specialties.

In the trees at the Rest Stop and on the dry, brushy hillsides above it, look for White-winged Dove, Black-chinned and Broad-billed Hummingbirds, Cassin's Kingbird, Canyon Wren, Black-tailed Gnatcatcher, Phainopepla, Lucy's Warbler, Pyrrhuloxia, Varied Bunting, Rufous-crowned Sparrow and Lesser Goldfinch.

About 100 yds. north of the Rest Stop, cross to the west side of the highway and scramble down the bank to bird the sycamores and willows

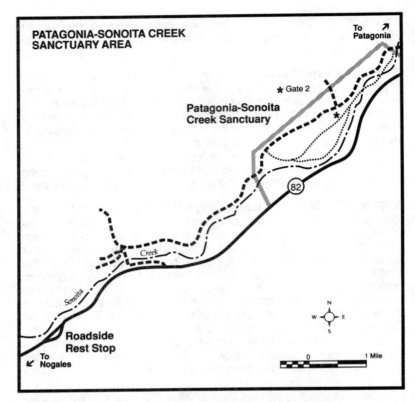

PATAGONIA-SONOITA CREEK
SANCTUARY AREA

To Patagonia

★ Gate 2

Patagonia-Sonoita
Creek Sanctuary

82

Creek

Sonoita

N W E S

**Roadside
Rest Stop**
To
Nogales

0   1 Mile

bordering Sonoita Creek. Although the property behind the fence is strictly private, belonging to the Circle Z Guest Ranch, all the good birds are visible from the path. The most notable, the Rose-throated Becards and the Thick-billed Kingbirds, are often in the trees above you. Other birds to look for in this incredible spot are Gray Hawk (flying over from its nesting spot in the Sanctuary), Brown-crested Flycatcher, Northern Beardless-Tyrannulet, Bell's Vireo, Summer Tanager, and Hooded and Northern Orioles.

PATAGONIA-SONOITA CREEK SANCTUARY: There are two approaches to the Sanctuary property, a stretch of riparian woodland along Sonoita Creek owned by the Nature Conservancy. The first is to go a mile north of the roadside rest area and turn left off the highway on a dirt road which doubles back, fording Sonoita Creek, and then continues to a fork in the road (.2 mi.). At the fork, you keep right, and you'll soon be driving along with the Sanctuary property on your right. Birding here is good, though you cannot enter the Sanctuary until you come to one of the four gates. Gate 2, the main entrance, has brochures and bird lists.

The second approach to the Sanctuary is to take Third Ave. west off Arizona 82 in the town of Patagonia. Go two blocks and turn left (south) on Pennsylvania Ave. and proceed .3 mi to the Sanctuary-posted property.

Walking in Gate 2, make your way to the right (south) on the network of trails through the lowland vegetation. Take your time, and be sure to get close to the creek in your tour. The tall cottonwoods and other lush growth attract many bird species including: Black Vulture (rare), Gambel's Quail, Band-tailed Pigeon, Common Ground-Dove, Greater Roadrunner, Western Screech-Owl, Broad-billed Hummingbird, Acorn, Gila and Ladder-backed Woodpeckers, Northern Beardless-Tyrannulet, Dusky-capped Flycatcher, Ash-throated Flycatcher, Brown-crested Flycatcher, Tropical Kingbird (rare), Cassin's and Western Kingbirds, Gray-breasted Jay, Bushtit, Bewick's Wren, Bell's Vireo, Yellow-breasted Chat, Summer Tanager, Black-headed and Blue Grosbeaks, Indigo (rare) and Varied Bunting, Bronzed Cowbird and Northern "Bullock's" Oriole.

While in the Patagonia area, you may wish to drive up Harshaw Canyon Rd., where a pair of Zone-tailed Hawks have nested. Get directions from local birders.

APPLETON-WHITTELL RESEARCH RANCH of the NATIONAL AUDUBON SOCIETY: The research ranch at Elgin, located east of Sonoita off Arizona 83 and 8.2 mi. south of Elgin, is a large tract of plains grassland, a former cattle ranch, now the property of the Audubon Society. Research projects are in progress, and prior arrangements should be made if you wish to visit: Box 44, Elgin, Az. 85611. Phone (602) 455-5522. Montezuma Quail are the prime attraction (look on north-facing slopes with scattered oaks), plus other grassland birds such as Botteri's and Cassin's Sparrows which nest there in summer.

Huachuca Mountains area: The town of Sierra Vista is a good place to headquarter for birding the Huachuca Mountains area, including Garden Canyon on the U. S. Army base at Ft. Huachuca, Ramsey Canyon, and the San Pedro River valley. To reach Sierra Vista, take Arizona 82 from Sonoita east for 19 mi., then turn right (south) onto Arizona 90 for 10 mi.

Note: If you're planning to visit the Chiricahua Mountains next, you might want to pick up many of your supplies in Sierra Vista, because groceries and other necessities are not plentiful in Portal.

GARDEN, SCHEELITE and SAWMILL CANYONS in FT. HUACHUCA: Upon entering the town of Sierra Vista, turn right (west) at the Ft. Huachuca entrance. The base is open to the public during daylight hours, unless special maneuvers are scheduled, when it closes. Stop at the information booth on your right as you drive in. Register for a permit and obtain a map to guide you to Garden Canyon.

The road to Garden Canyon leads you 6.7 mi. up into the foothills of Ft. Huachuca. Although the road is paved, it's not recommended for a long-wheelbase car due to many steep dips. You are traveling through grassland for the first 4 mi.; Botteri's and Cassin's Sparrows breed here in summer. For the next 3 mi. you'll pass three different picnic areas, the last and topmost one being the best for birding. Stop at the last picnic area, where the stream

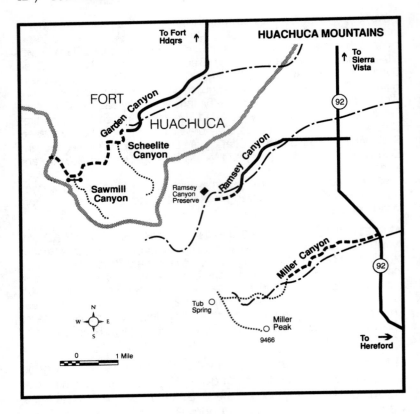

crosses the road, and poke around the picnic grounds (may be crowded on holidays and weekends) for Montezuma Quail (rare), Elegant Trogon, Acorn and Strickland's Woodpecker, Sulphur-bellied Flycatcher, Bushtit, Black-throated Gray Warbler, Lesser Goldfinch and many others.

After the last picnic area, the road, now gravel, continues to wind up .7 mi. to Scheelite Canyon on your left. Park and hike the steep trail along the dry stream bed about a half-mile to where a pair of Spotted Owls have nested and may be seen perched low in the conifers. Other possible species along the trail are Elegant Trogon, Strickland's Woodpecker and Virginia's Warbler.

From Scheelite Canyon, proceed up to Sawmill Canyon (2.1 mi.), and park beside the deserted log cabin. Walk behind the cabin and follow the rough road that leads from the cabled gate up into the Chihuahuan pine woodland. The best place in the U. S. to look for the Buff-breasted Flycatcher, Sawmill Canyon often has 6 to 8 pairs nesting in the area. Look for them as soon as you get out of your car, as well as further up the canyon.

As you walk the rough road beyond the cabin, you'll shortly come to six cement picnic tables, spaced among the pines on either side of the road. Evening Grosbeaks and Greater Pewees have nested here. Other interest-ing birds such as Northern Goshawk, Northern Pygmy-Owl, Steller's Jay,

Eastern Bluebird, Grace's Warbler, Hepatic Tanager and Yellow-eyed Junco should be looked for.

RAMSEY CANYON: To reach Ramsey Canyon, go south on Arizona 92 from Sierra Vista for 6 mi. to the signed road, which leads you west into the Huachuca Mountains up this narrow canyon. At the end of the road (4 mi.), the Nature Conservancy's Ramsey Canyon Preserve is renowned for its great variety of hummingbirds, which frequent the numerous feeders. Visiting birdwatchers can sit and watch from the benches provided. A well-stocked gift shop, nature trails, and six housekeeping cabins for rent, make Ramsey Canyon a popular place to stay.

If you are not an overnight guest, hours for the Preserve are 8 a.m. to 5 p.m. daily, the trails close at 4 p.m. and advance phone reservations are required for all visits on Saturdays, Sundays, and federal holidays. Phone: (602) 378-2785.

SAN PEDRO RIVER: Past Ramsey Canyon, drive 2.3 mi. and turn left (east) at the road to Hereford. Drive until you come to the bridge across the San Pedro River (about 6 mi.) and park off to the right. The area on either side of the bridge along the road is a good place to look for Gambel's Quail, Scaled Quail, Common Ground-Dove, Gila and Ladder-backed Woodpeckers, Say's Phoebe, Chihuahuan Raven, Verdin, Curve-billed and Crissal Thrashers, Phainopepla, Bell's Vireo, Cardinal, Pyrrhuloxia, Blue Grosbeak, Indigo Bunting, and Abert's Towhee.

Past the river .5 mi., the large ranch has a willow-lined pond often attractive to birds. Park and walk up on the railroad tracks to your left and scan for Crissal Thrasher and Scaled Quail.

MILLER PEAK TRAIL: The road up Miller Canyon to the best hiking spot in the Huachucas, Miller Peak Trail, lies .8 mi. beyond the Hereford Rd. turn-off on Arizona 92. After 2.7 mi. the road up the canyon ends in a parking lot. The trail starts up the hillside across from the parking lot, and, though steep in places, is a spectacular journey up through the oak forests into the ponderosa groves high above. About a mile and a half up the trail, start looking for Red-faced Warbler in the oaks. At about 2.5 mi., in the ponderosas, look for Wild Turkey, Band-tailed Pigeon, Northern Pygmy-Owl, Hairy Woodpecker, Western Flycatcher, Violet-green Swallow, Steller's Jay, Common Raven, Pygmy and Red-breasted Nuthatches, Brown Creeper, Ruby-crowned Kinglet, Olive, Yellow-rumped, Grace's and Red-faced Warblers, Western and Hepatic Tanagers, Evening Grosbeak, Pine Siskin, Red Crossbill, and Yellow-eyed Junco.

The hike to Miller Peak at 9,466 ft. is 4.7 mi., but you need only go as far as Tub Spring at 2.9 mi. to gain wonderful views of the San Pedro valley and most of the species mentioned above.

Chiricahua Mountains area: The Chiricahuas are located 54 mi. north of Douglas on U.S. 80. About 3 mi. north of Rodeo, N.M., take the road left (west) to Portal. After 7 mi., the hamlet of Portal offers a small store, post office, cafe (with take-out service), and gas. A stop at

the Portal store is mandatory for birders, not only to pick up a bird checklist or one of the T-shirts they sell, but to get directions to the Spoffords' ranch/sanctuary.

CAVE CREEK CANYON: A half-mile beyond the store, the road forks. Take the left (paved) fork and go 1.3 mi. to the display sign past the ranger station. The map here shows the roads and campgrounds in the Chiricahua Wild Area; it's a good way to get oriented.

Beautiful Cave Creek Canyon lies in the lee of Chiricahua Peak, and has two side roads which leave the main road to go to the South Fork area and to Herb Martyr Lake. The main road continues to the top of the ridge at Rustler Park.

The road to the South Fork (l.6 mi.) is the first one you come to. Turn left here and drive l.4 mi. to the end of the road, where a turn-around marks the South Fork Campground and the start of the South Fork Trail. All along the road, but particularly on the first half-mile of the trail, the birding is superb.

Look for Peregrine and Prairie Falcons nesting in the cliffs above the road, Band-tailed Pigeon, White-throated Swift, Acorn, Ladder-backed and Strickland's Woodpeckers, Elegant Trogon (best seen along the first half-mile of the South Fork Trail, but listen for it anywhere along the road), Cassin's, Sulphur-bellied, Brown-crested, and Dusky-capped Flycatchers, Greater

Pewee, Western Wood-Pewee, Western Flycatcher, Black Phoebe, Gray-breasted Jay, Bridled Titmouse, Bushtit, Bewick's, Canyon and Rock Wrens, Solitary and Hutton's Vireo, Grace's Warbler, Painted Redstart, Hepatic Tanager, Black-headed Grosbeak, Brown Towhee, and Hooded and Scott's Orioles.

At night, the following owls may be heard: Flammulated Owl, Whiskered Screech-Owl, Northern Pygmy-Owl and Spotted Owl up along the South Fork Trail, and down around the mouth of the canyon near Portal you might listen for Western Screech-Owl, Great Horned Owl and Elf Owl. An Elf Owl has nested in one of the sycamores behind the library in Portal. Both Whiskered Screech-Owl and Northern Pygmy-Owl have nested in trees at the start of the South Fork Trail.

After birding the South Fork of Cave Creek, return to the main road. You'll pass Sunny Flat Campground on your right, which is often good birding, but the route continues up the main road about 1.5 mi. to the Southwestern Research Station (property of the American Museum of Natural History). Here you turn left on Herb Martyr Road. If you wish to bird around the grounds of the Research Station, feel free to do so, but please don't disturb the students and naturalists. The Administration Office sells checklists and other literature on the region.

The road to Herb Martyr Campground takes you 2.2 mi. up into the headwaters of Cave Creek. From the road end, you may wish to hike the trail to the Little Dam (.25 mi.) or further. The Thick-billed Parrot, once a visitant from Mexico to Arizona's pine forests but unrecorded since the 1930's, has been re-introduced into the Chiricahuas and a small band of them often roams the trail up and down the creek. Ask local birders.

RUSTLER PARK: Return to the main road and start the climb up from the Southwest Research Station to Onion Saddle (7.3 mi.). The road is graded but unpaved, fairly narrow and winds up into the oak and conifer forests of the higher Chiricahuas. The marvelous views and the good birds to be seen in Rustler Park will spur you onwards. Look back towards the miles of western New Mexico in the distance. You can see forever.

At Onion Saddle, the main road continues over the ridge and down the other side to Pinery Canyon, but you'll turn left and proceed 2 mi. to a fork in the road. The left fork goes to Rustler Park, the right one to Barfoot Park.

Park your car here and bird the area. About 100 yds. north of the intersection, on the road to Barfoot Park, a signed trail leads up to Barfoot Lookout. Hike the trail for a half-mile or so. You should see Hairy Woodpecker, Western Flycatcher, Mexican Chickadee, White-breasted and Pygmy Nuthatches, Brown Creeper, American Robin, Hermit Thrush, Eastern Bluebird, Virginia's, Olive, Yellow-rumped, Grace's and Red-faced Warblers, Western Tanager, Black-headed Grosbeak and Yellow-eyed Junco.

When you're ready to leave, take the left-hand fork, and drive a mile to Rustler Park, pausing to listen and scan along the road. About a half-mile after you pass the cattle guard at the edge of the park, a spring on the left attracts many species of birds which drink there. Beyond the spring, the road forks again, the left one to the ranger station and the right fork to the campground.

Take the right fork, past the blue iris meadow (blooming in late May) up to the campground and picnic area. From here, a trail begins to climb the ridge. Take the right fork, the Barfoot Peak Trail, and prepare to scan the treetops for interesting warblers. The trail goes along just below the ridge, so you can look into the treetops. This is prime habitat for Yellow-rumped, Grace's and Olive Warblers, as well as the Red-faced Warbler. However, you may become a victim of "warbler neck" afterwards.

PINERY CANYON: If you still haven't seen the Red-faced Warbler and the Mexican Chickadee, Pinery Canyon is another good spot to try. Return to Onion Saddle and this time take the main road to your left (west). Stop along the road and listen for warbler song, for the Red-faced Warblers love the dense oaks here. In 2 mi. you'll come to the Pinery Canyon Campground. Continue past the upper section, on your right as you make the curve, and stop at the lower section. There's a place to pull off on your right, opposite a grassy clearing surrounded by pines to your left. The best birding is here. Flammulated Owls have nested in Pinery Canyon Campground.

To reach I-10, proceed down the ridge from Pinery Canyon Campground and turn right in 10 mi. at Arizona 181. When Arizona 181 meets Arizona 186, go northwest to Willcox (31 mi.).

PORTAL AREA: Our tour continues by exploring some of the lowland habitats back in Portal. Along the road to Paradise (take the right fork a half-mile west of the Portal Store) look for Scrub Jays and Plain Titmice on the juniper-covered hillsides. The old cemetery (4.2 mi.) on the Paradise road may harbor Montezuma Quail at dawn and dusk.

When you're leaving Portal traveling east, just after you cross the cattle-guard that signifies your entry back into New Mexico (about 5 mi.), you'll come to a straight gravel road that heads south (Stateline Rd.). Turn right and bird along it for any lowland species you might have missed, such as Scaled Quail. To return to I-10, take U.S. 80 28 mi. north to Roadforks, N. M., and then head west to Tucson (about a 3 hour trip).

Willcox Municipal Golf course: On your way back to Tucson, whether via Roadforks, N. M., or by way of Chiricahua National Monument and Arizona 186, stop to look for shorebirds and waterfowl at Willcox Lake and several ponds on the golf course.

To reach the golf course, which is on the south edge of town, exit I-10 at the sign for Arizona 186 south and follow Arizona 186 south about half a mile out of town. Cross the railroad tracks and proceed a short distance until you come to a faded sign on your right saying Municipal Golf Course. Turn right on the paved road to the golf course, and drive to Willcox Lake, surrounded by a dike on which you can drive. Some smaller ponds are located at the edge of the golf course. Many interesting waterbirds have been discovered here.

SOUTHEASTERN ARIZONA:
Exotic birding north of the border
Checklist of Common Birds by Habitat

DESERT SCRUB:
Swainson's Hawk
Gambel's Quail
White-winged Dove
Mourning Dove
Greater Roadrunner
Elf Owl
Lesser Nighthawk
Gila Woodpecker
Ladder-backed Woodpecker
Western Kingbird
Verdin
Cactus Wren
Black-tailed Gnatcatcher
Northern Mockingbird
Curve-billed Thrasher
Phainopepla
Lucy's Warbler
Northern Cardinal
Pyrrhuloxia
Rufous-crowned Sparrow
Black-throated Sparrow

DESERT GRASSLAND:
Turkey Vulture
Montezuma Quail (rare)
Scaled Quail
Common Nighthawk
Common Poorwill
Ash-throated Flycatcher
Horned Lark
Chihuahuan Raven
Crissal Thrasher (in washes,
    mesquite)
Varied Bunting
Rufous-winged Sparrow
Lark Sparrow
Grasshopper Sparrow
Eastern Meadowlark
Scott's Oriole

**DECIDUOUS RIPARIAN
WOODLAND:**
Turkey Vulture
Gray Hawk
Cooper's Hawk
Common Ground-Dove
Western Screech-Owl
Great Horned Owl
Broad-billed Hummingbird
Gila Woodpecker
Ladder-backed Woodpecker
Northern Beardless-Tyrranulet
Vermilion Flycatcher
Dusky-capped Flycatcher
Ash-throated Flycatcher
Brown-crested Flycatcher
Tropical Kingbird
Cassin's Kingbird
Thick-billed Kingbird (local)
Rose-throated Becard (local)
White-breasted Nuthatch
Bewick's Wren
Bell's Vireo
Yellow-breasted Chat
Summer Tanager
Blue Grosbeak
Indigo Bunting (uncommon)
Bronzed Cowbird

**OAK AND PINE-OAK
WOODLAND:**
Zone-tailed Hawk (uncommon)
Band-tailed Pigeon
Spotted Owl
Flammulated Owl
Whiskered Screech-Owl
Northern Pygmy-Owl
Elf Owl
Broad-billed Hummingbird
Blue-throated Hummingbird
Magnificent Hummingbird

Black-chinned Hummingbird
Elegant Trogon
Acorn Woodpecker
Strickland's Woodpecker
Greater Pewee
Cassin's Kingbird
Western Wood-Pewee
Western Flycatcher
Buff-breasted Flycatcher (local)
Black Phoebe
Dusky-capped Flycatcher
Sulphur-bellied Flycatcher
Gray-breasted Jay
Bridled Titmouse
Hermit Thrush
Solitary Vireo
Hutton's Vireo
Warbling Vireo
Black-throated Gray Warbler
Painted Redstart
Hepatic Tanager
Western Tanager
Black-headed Grosbeak
Brown Towhee
Yellow-eyed Junco
Hooded Oriole
Northern Oriole (Bullock's)
Lesser Goldfinch

PONDEROSA PINE FOREST:
Wild Turkey
Flammulated Owl
Northern Pygmy-Owl
Broad-tailed Hummingbird
Greater Pewee
Violet-green Swallow
Steller's Jay
Mexican Chickadee
Pygmy Nuthatch
Brown Creeper
Eastern Bluebird
Virginia's Warbler
Yellow-rumped Warbler
    (Audubon's)
Grace's Warbler
Red-faced Warbler
Olive Warbler
Hepatic Tanager
Yellow-eyed Junco

SPRUCE-FIR FOREST
Northern Goshawk
Whip-poor-will
Hairy Woodpecker
Steller's Jay
Mexican Chickadee
Red-breasted Nuthatch
Golden-crowned Kinglet
Ruby-crowned Kinglet
Hermit Thrush
Western Tanager
Red Crossbill
Pine Siskin
Evening Grosbeak

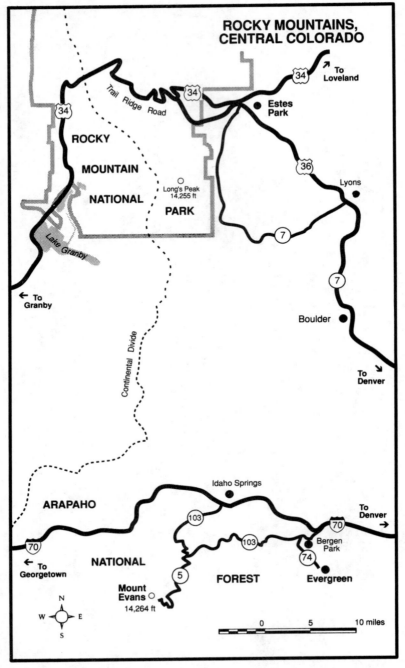

ROCKY MOUNTAINS,
CENTRAL COLORADO

To Loveland

Estes Park

Lyons

ROCKY

MOUNTAIN

NATIONAL

PARK

Long's Peak
14,255 ft

Trail Ridge Road

Lake Granby

To Granby

Continental Divide

Boulder

To Denver

ARAPAHO

Idaho Springs

To Denver

NATIONAL

FOREST

Bergen Park

Evergreen

To Georgetown

Mount Evans
14,264 ft

N
W   E
S

0   5   10 miles

▲ Campgrounds   Trails   Highways and Freeways

🛆 Picnic Areas   Rivers   Roads

🛉 Park Hq and Visitor Centers   Boundaries   Unimproved dirt roads

COLORADO'S ALPINE TUNDRA:

Tracking the White-tailed Ptarmigan

High in Western mountains above the timberline lies a region known as the alpine tundra. It is a land of incredibly harsh weather with frequent wind and heavy snowfall; it is a land of no trees, and flowers so tiny you almost need a magnifying glass to see them. It is a land where the clear atmosphere and intense sunlight make far-off mountain ranges appear within walking distance. And, for birders, it is the land of the White-tailed Ptarmigan and the Rosy Finch.

These two avian pioneers are among the few birds that brave the stringent environment of North America's alpine tundra. Living on the barren tundra slopes, surrounded by a mosaic of wildflowers in summer and sheltered by huge snowdrifts in winter, the chicken-like White-tailed Ptarmigan is unique—the only species of ptarmigan to be found south of Canada. The Rosy Finch, a plump brown-and-raspberry colored finch, is well-suited for survival under Arctic conditions, nesting in the crags and precipices of the highest mountains. Here in the Rocky Mountains, birders have a good chance of observing the Brown-capped race of the bird.

At elevations above 11,000 feet, the spectacular Colorado terrain boasts an unusual ecosystem, one similar to that of the

Arctic tundra to the north in Canada and Alaska. During the summer months, the mountain summits burst into a many-hued carpet of tiny wildflowers. As you trek across the wind-swept ridges in search of the White-tailed Ptarmigan or scan the edges of a glacial lake for Rosy Finches, take a moment to enjoy the stunning views out over the Rockies.

Although you may be able to hike to many areas of alpine tundra in the western United States, only a few can be reached by automobile. Among those tundra regions accessible by car, two of the most well-known to birders lie in the Rocky Mountains of Colorado: Trail Ridge Road in Rocky Mountain National Park and the summit of Mount Evans.

This bird finding trip centers around a visit to Rocky Mountain National Park, an excellent place to begin your search for the tundra-dwelling species. En route to the tundra, plan to stop at several other birding locations in the verdant forests of the Park, prime habitat for a variety of birds of the Western mountains.

An alternate trip—a drive to the summit of 14,260 foot Mount Evans—has the advantage of being located within 60 miles of Denver, should time and convenience preclude a stay in Rocky Mountain National Park. The road to the top of Mount Evans, said to be the highest paved road in the United States, winds up through the spruce-fir stands of Arapaho National Forest, offering good birding along the way and stupendous views of the Rockies.

Join me as we travel through the mountains of Colorado, ascending through the forests to the highest habitat for birds in the United States—the alpine tundra.

As early as the 1870's, the land destined to become Rocky Mountain National Park was a scenic landmark in the West. The Estes Valley, at first occupied by farmers and ranchers, eventually attracted wealthy vacationers and game hunters with its beautiful landscape. Luxurious hotels and resorts, such as the famous Stanley Hotel built in 1909, became the nucleus of the town, now known as Estes Park. To accommodate his guests, Mr. Stanley ran a fleet of automobiles—Stanley Steamers—between his hotel and the main depot in what is now the town of Lyons. The Stanley Hotel still stands on a hill overlooking Estes Park and is well worth a visit.

In 1915, Enos A. Mills, the famous naturalist and writer, and his friends had the satisfaction of realizing their vision when Rocky Mountain National Park was formed from the purchase of extensive hunting and homestead lands by the federal government.

In 1932, Trail Ridge Road was constructed, crossing the park as a main artery from east to west, winding through the tundra country and following in part the old Ute Indian trail. This is U.S. Highway 34, a miraculous engineering feat of its day, now enabling nearly three million tourists per year to share in the gorgeous alpine scenery.

The gateway to Rocky Mountain National Park, the town of Estes Park, gets its name from the fact that people in Colorado use the term "park" as a synonym for a large or small mountain valley. The beautiful Estes Valley is one of these mountain valleys, and the town of Estes Park nestles within it.

Rocky Mountain National Park, spanning 266,000 acres and lying across the Continental Divide, contains more than 68 peaks above 12,000 feet. The Park's highest mountain is Long's Peak, 14,265 feet, a favorite of climbers and hikers.

Rocky Mountain National Park shows the geologic effects of Ice Age activity on Colorado's mountains during the past two million years. The grandeur of the snow-capped vistas was formed by glaciers scouring U-shaped valleys and steep precipices. The creation of tundra, the presence of alpine plants, and the still-remaining glaciers in the Park are all evidence of the most recent brief cold period, "The Little Ice Age," which lasted until 1300 years ago.

During that time, the valleys were filled by glaciers hundreds of feet deep. The glaciers carved huge bowls called cirques at the heads of the valleys. They scooped out alpine lakes and pushed great masses of rocks and boulders into ridges called moraines. These rocky ridges are the remains of the debris carried by the glaciers. They are terminal moraines if they were dumped at the end or "toe" of the glacier's path, and lateral moraines if they were deposited at the glacier's sides. The road to Moraine Park, just past the Beaver Meadows Entrance, climbs over a lateral moraine. The topography of Rocky Mountain National Park, with its gorges and waterfalls, wide valleys and meandering streams, makes geology come alive as a part of your trip.

Climate and Habitats of the Southern Rockies

The Southern Rockies, so-called to distinguish them from the Rockies farther north, are the highest part of the Rocky Mountain chain in the United States. The Continental Divide winds through them from north to south, separating areas draining to the west into the Gulf of California and areas to the east with rivers flowing into the Gulf of Mexico.

Colorado's climate is marked by extreme variations in temperature and rainfall, due to the influence of the mountains and the lack of a large body of water to moderate the weather conditions. Wide temperature variations can occur relatively close together, because elevations change abruptly within short distances. The differences in average annual temperature between the summit of Pike's Peak and Las Animas, 115 miles to the southeast, is about 35 degrees F., comparable to the difference between south Florida and Iceland. You will experience something akin to this if you drive from Denver to the top of Mount Evans.

In general, air temperature decreases with gain in altitude at the rate of 3 degrees F. with each 1000 feet of elevation. By the time you crest Colorado's highest peaks, the temperature of the air becomes very low, and the air grows very thin. The thinner air, which lets more ultraviolet light penetrate the atmosphere, means greater sunburn to skiers, hikers and birders enjoying the crystal clear weather.

Most days are sunny and dry, particularly in the summer months, but be ready for rain showers or even snow flurries—though they may clear off quickly—at almost any time of year.

Like all mountainous regions in the West, the Rockies show a vertical succession of plant associations as you journey upwards from the foothills to the alpine tundra, each inhabited by its own unique bird species. (For a full discussion of Western life zones, see Chapter Six).

Ponderosa Pine Forest: The forests are magnificent here. At lower elevations, between 5500–7800 feet, tall cinnamon-barked ponderosa pines space themselves evenly throughout the sagebrush that covers the slopes of the valleys. The ponderosas form savanna-like parklands, with patches of meadow containing bunch grasses and wildflowers making a ground cover between the trees. This dry, warm forest gets the least moisture from winter storms, and the trees need wide spacing to accommodate their roots.

On moister north-facing slopes, Douglas-firs drape their feathery green boughs in the cool shade.

Growing at somewhat higher elevations, lodgepole pine and quaking aspen invade sites from which other trees have been removed, due to logging or forest fires. Both are pioneer species, especially in disturbed places where the natural plant succession has been interrupted. The lodgepoles and aspen thrive on the sunlight available to them in deforested tracts, and in five to ten years invasion is complete. Between 25 and 50 years later, the young seedlings of spruce and fir will replace the lodgepoles and aspen, as they grow to maturity in the shade provided by the "pioneers."

Streamside vegetation here—consisting of the lovely Colorado blue spruce (the state tree), narrowleaf cottonwood, alder, various willows and river birch—attracts great numbers of breeding birds, some of which nest in the adjacent forests. The streams course through the ponderosa forests creating a sunny, open habitat filled with bird activity in late spring and summer.

Williamson's Sapsuckers hitch their way up the trunks of ponderosas. Male and female Williamson's Sapsuckers look so unlike they were at first thought to be separate species. The male's striking white vertical wing-patch and black upperparts make it a real contrast to the female's subdued plumage. She looks like a small, brown woodpecker with a ladder-backed pattern. In the summer months, when lots of juvenile sapsuckers follow their parents through the trees, it is helpful to remember that they will look like a duller version of each of their parents.

Red-naped Sapsuckers are especially fond of aspen groves, where rows of tiny holes encircling the white aspen bark leave evidence of this plentiful species. The sapsuckers attend the holes to drink the sap, and devour the insects which collect in each little cavity.

MacGillivray's and Wilson's Warblers breed near the rushing streams, never far from moist underbrush or lakeside shrubbery. On the dark, slippery rocks beside the Fall River, the Big Thompson River, and other swift streams, look for the gray form of the American Dipper doing its deep knee-bends as the water churns and splashes around it.

Cassin's Finches, the most common finch at this elevation, give their dry *kee-up* call and loud, warbling song from the highest branches of the conifers. The forest hillsides echo their friendly, jubilant tones all summer long.

Mountain Chickadees, Pygmy Nuthatches, and Dark-eyed Juncos, often joined by interesting migrant warblers in late summer, move in roving bands through the trees. Virginia's Warblers may tag along at lower elevations where the ponderosas mix with sagebrush.

Representative birding sites:

Rocky Mountain National Park: Moraine Park, Upper Beaver Meadows Trailhead, Little Horseshoe Park, Horseshoe Park, Endovalley Picnic Area.

Engelmann Spruce-Subalpine Fir Forest: Somewhere above

8,000 feet, the lodgepole-aspen forest relinquishes the majority of Colorado's mountain slopes to the great green tracts of Engelmann spruce and subalpine fir. This is a dense, dark forest of narrow-crowned Christmas trees, nudging each other in quiet ranks. Heavily snowed upon in winter and never warm in summer, the subalpine forest reaches up to timberline, often trapping the snow blown down from the tundra region above.

Subalpine firs have upright, erect cones near the top of their very regular spire-like crowns. They have soft, flat needles rounded at the tip. The Engelmann spruces, with cones hanging downwards, have rigid, square needles with pointed tips, and rather ragged crowns.

The forest floor, frequently wet from the winter snowpack into early August, displays exquisite wildflowers of all kinds. If you should visit the Rockies in mid-summer, Colorado blue columbine, the state flower, may still be blooming at this elevation. Its delicate blue flower with a yellow center can be glimpsed in nooks and crannies of boulders near timberline.

This cool, moist forest has fewer birds than forests of lower elevations, but several species are highly sought-after. Less visible in the close stands of trees, the birds of the subalpine forest hide high in the conifers' branches or cling quietly to the trunks.

If you take a picnic with you on a hike here, a silent cluster of watchful Gray Jays may suddenly materialize, waiting for a handout.

The bolder Clark's Nutcrackers can be found at many turnouts on mountain highways at this elevation, taking peanuts from the hands of friendly tourists and competing with the Steller's Jays, chipmunks and ground squirrels for free morsels.

Yellow-rumped Warblers abound. Their black and yellow nuptial plumage stands out against the dark forest trees.

Scan the skies above for a Northern Goshawk, or a Cooper's or Sharp-shinned Hawk in late summer. You may flush a family of Blue Grouse near the trail, or come upon a Pine Grosbeak pair feeding in a willow patch. The Three-toed Woodpecker, scarce even in its preferred habitat, would be a lucky find; its insistent loud tapping is a good clue to the bird's whereabouts.

Representative birding sites:

Rocky Mountain National Park: Old Fall River Road, Chapin Creek Trail.

Mount Evans area: Echo Lake.

Alpine Tundra: The word tundra derives from the Lapp word *tundar* meaning marshy plain or the Russian *tundra,* a land of no trees. It describes a region and a type of vegetation which, in the United States, lies above the tree limit and below the line of perpetual snow in our highest mountains.

The term "alpine" tundra distinguishes this mountain habitat from the arctic tundra which, though similar in appearance, exists far to the north near the Arctic Circle. In part, you can find the same plant species on the tundra in Lappland, in the Alps, in Alaska or in Colorado, tundra plants being more uniform throughout the world than any other major plant community.

The presence of numerous Arctic plants and animals in the Rocky Mountains is explained by the uninterrupted series of north/south ranges down which they migrated thousands of years ago from more northerly climates. Many characteristically Arctic plants reach the southernmost tip of their ranges in the Southern Rockies.

The tundra habitat begins at around 11,000 feet or near timberline. Here, the Engelmann spruce and subalpine fir give up their battle against the constant pruning action of the wind and snow. The trees that do survive have a twisted, deformed shape. They are called *krummholz* or "crooked wood." Buffeted by winter winds and pummeled by blizzards, these dwarfed and bent trees are the last outposts of the forest, giving way at last to the tundra above.

As you begin to explore the tundra in the summer months, picture the landscape in the dead of winter. Although you cannot see it, the ground beneath is still very much in the grip of winter. Underneath the surface, the soil is permanently frozen, as it has been for thousands of years. This is permafrost, created by permanent moisture that never completely thaws during the brief summer season.

Above ground, notice the rocky areas called "fellfields." The continual freezing and thawing of the bare rock surfaces breaks the rock apart, creating new fragments. Over time, boulders break down into smaller rocks, talus, and the talus becomes gravel. The gravel decomposes to sand, making new soil for the alpine plants to root in.

Enveloping everything, the power of the constant wind on the tundra distributes the snow, which is the most important factor in controlling the growth of plants in the alpine region. Under the snow, plants are protected from the wind; above it, their growth is severely stunted.

Alpine tundra, like Arctic tundra, is dominated by herbs because the climate is too harsh to support tree life. Of the 300 alpine species of plants, all are perennials and none are annuals. A fresh start every year would waste too much of the plant's valuable energy.

When tundra plants bloom, they produce oversized flowers in proportion to their short stems and few leaves. The large relative size of their flowers, plus the tendency to flower early in the growing season, insures a good crop of seeds. Seeds need prolonged warmth to mature, so the earlier in the season the plant comes to bloom, the more quickly the seeds can form. Then, the seeds will take advantage of the remaining summer days to ripen fully.

Plants on the tundra grow incredibly slowly. Some may take four years to go from seed to bud to flower. This is due to the short growing season and their habit of hugging the ground. They grow small instead of tall, thus protecting themselves from buffeting winds, while exposing their maximum leaf surface for photosynthesis.

The cushion and mat plants exemplify the dwarfing process. The little pink moss campion, found in tundra areas worldwide, grows in a dense, rounded cushion on the ground. Mat plants, like the dwarf clover, have more of a spreading habit. The dwarf clover, sprawled across the corner of a huge boulder or wedged into the cracks of a rock pile, has astonishingly large purple flowers compared to its miniaturized leaves and stems.

Alpine plants have other tricks for survival too numerous to mention here. Among them, succulence (a protection against high altitude dryness), hairs (to reflect the sun), and reproduction underground via bulbs, rhizomes and runners.

You are sure to become a wildflower enthusiast after your first tundra visit. The tiny plants cover the otherwise barren mountainsides with masses of blue, yellow, white and orange blooms. No wonder birders take time to stoop down and study the beautiful blossoms, surprising themselves at how quickly alpine wildflowers can be recognized and identified.

Some tundra species, such as alpine avens and American bistort, are found in many types of tundra plant communities, but most are limited by specific environmental requirements to certain locations on the tundra. These requirements are often correlated with the length of time snow covers the ground. Thus each alpine plant community is unique—as it clings to a rock crevice or springs up in a moist meadow or covers a fellfield—reflecting the diversity of ecological niches throughout the expanse of tundra.

Below are a few of the more common flowering plants:

Alpine sunflower or Rydbergia have vibrant yellow daisy-like blooms which always face towards the east. By far the largest bloom on the tundra (two to four inches across), they are also called "Old Man of the Mountain," commemorating Per Axel Rydberg, an early Rocky Mountain botanist.

American bistort and alpine avens are the most numerous wildflowers on the tundra during July and August. Alpine avens sports a clear yellow buttercup blossom and bright green leaves. It crowds the hillsides in company with the American bistort, which looks like a little white bottlebrush on a slender stem.

Both marsh marigold and greenleaf mertensia or chiming bells are early bloomers on the tundra. On the fringes of the snowpack, these two—the white-flowered marigold and the midnight blue chiming bells—greet the tundra summer.

The harebell, with its bell-shaped, light lavender flower, grows everywhere in Colorado's high country, particularly along roadsides and in disturbed areas.

Alpine tundra is a very fragile ecosystem. After disturbance, whether it be from soil movement, small animals or human trampling, rejuvenation is very slow because of the short growing season and the harsh climate. Recovery may take years. For example, one candy wrapper carelessly tossed aside can kill the plants it covers in three or four weeks, plants which may take 20 years to return to normal size.

The birds inhabiting the tundra equal the plants in their ability to withstand the rigors of life at this altitude. Although bird species here are few, two in particular lure intrepid birders to these heights, glad to search out the White-tailed Ptarmigan and the Brown-capped race of the Rosy Finch. Aside from these two, only the Water Pipit, the Horned Lark and the White-crowned Sparrow breed in the tundra zone.

The quiet, rather non-descript Water Pipit nests on the ground in tundra meadows, and is at home amongst the grasses and boulders of this high altitude prairie. Its habit of bobbing its tail up and down, and walking, rather than hopping, along the ground make the pipit easy to spot.

The Horned Lark frequents the alpine zone, too, though not abundantly. Both the Water Pipit and the Horned Lark employ similar mating displays. They fly sharply upward and then spiral down in fluttering flight, singing their gurgling songs.

The White-crowned Sparrow wanders up onto the tundra, having nested at treeline in the *krummholz* and willow thickets. White-crowneds are seen hopping about the snowbanks, sometimes using the Rosy Finch's method of taking frozen insects from the melting snow.

Of all the tundra-dwellers, it is the Rosy Finch which favors the steepest crags and crevices of the mountain peaks, feeding on seeds near melting snowdrifts or catching insects that lie frozen on the surface of the snowfields.

The Rosy Finch was formerly recognized as being made up of three distinct species: the Gray-crowned, the Brown-capped, and the Black Rosy Finch. Now, all the Rosy Finches have been lumped into one species, due to interbreeding where the ranges of the various subspecies overlap. Birders, however, are still interested in observing each of the races of the Rosy Finch, their plumage differences being frequently discernible in the field.

In this southern portion of the Rockies, from southern Wyoming to northern New Mexico, the Brown-capped race of the Rosy Finch is the one you will see in summer. The Brown-capped Rosy Finch has an all-brown head, lacking the gray crown found in Rosy Finches of the mountains of Washington, Oregon, and California. Both males and females have brown bodies with pink on the rump, at the bend of the wing, and on the belly and upper breast. The pink coloration is duller in the females, so that they look almost entirely brown against the snowpack.

Rosy Finches nest in cracks in the cliffs, from which they make long flights to the meadows and snowfields to feed. In winter, they descend to lower elevations, where flocks gather in open areas, such as farmlands or roadsides, and even at bird feeders.

Rosy Finches fit perfectly into an alpine environment. They

are very strong fliers, enabling them to fly far to obtain the insects and seeds they need to nurture their nestlings. They also have a protective snow mask of feathers over their nostrils.

W.L. Dawson in *The Birds of California* delightfully describes the eating habits of the Rosy Finch: "What, now does [the Rosy Finch] eat? To all intents and purposes, *snow*. Watch a company of them deploy over a snowfield, hopping sedately from crest to crest of the tiny ridges, or else escalading into the pits which the sun has made. They are pecking industriously at the surface as they go, and accumulating—well, not snowflakes, nor yet snowballs, but *frozen insects,* instead. It is marvelous what a varied diet is offered to these patient gleaners of the glaciers. The warm winds wafted up from the great valley bear moths and beetles, bugs and winged ants—they know not whither; and these, succumbing to the sudden cold of the heights, fall in a beneficent shower over the [Rosy Finch's] table."

During the breeding season, the Rosy Finch develops a pair of pockets in the floor of its mouth, which enables it to store large quantities of food while on the way to the nesting area. Males and females develop the pouches only when they are feeding young, making a distinct bulge in the bird's throat.

Another characteristic of the Rosy Finch, its concept of territoriality, protects the pair bond against outside challengers. Instead of defending a particular nesting territory, the male finch defends the female. Male Rosy Finches outnumber females by about six to one, so it's necessary for them to defend their mates against a number of bachelor males. During nest building and courtship, furious fights between rival males result in aerial twisting and turning and feathers flying.

When birding the tundra in search of Rosy Finches, watch for the stocky finch-like shape of these birds, as they hop about the fellfields and melting snow patches. They also frequent alpine lakes above timberline. At a distance, the finches are easily distinguished from the two other common birds found at this elevation—the White-crowned Sparrow and the Water Pipit. The White-crowned's silhouette appears much longer-tailed than that of a Rosy Finch, and the Water Pipit walks along the ground bobbing its tail, never hopping about in the way of the Rosy Finch.

Patience is a virtue when searching for Rosy Finches. They can suddenly appear out of nowhere, their strong undulating flight carrying them across the tundra. Then, just when you think they'll stay put for a good look, off they go, uttering a musical *turttl-ew* as they fly.

Of the tundra birds you hope to find, the White-tailed Ptarmigan probably tops the list. Ptarmigans are members of the Grouse family, distinguished by their heavily feathered legs and toes, which help shield them during the harsh Rocky Mountain winters. (The Latin name for the genus is *Lappus,* meaning "rabbit-foot.") About the size of a common pigeon, the White-tailed Ptarmigan is practiced at blending into its background. In summer, its plumage of mottled black, brown and tan blends with the bird's tundra surroundings, and in winter, its all-white feathering renders it nearly invisible amongst the snowdrifts.

During their spring and fall molts, the birds stay on the periphery of the snowbanks. The brown and white patches of their plumage are often the size, shape and color of old willow leaves. Unless flushed, the ptarmigans are invisible even from a few feet away.

Ptarmigans are monogamous during the breeding period and pairs usually mate for life. Breeding begins in early May, when the male ptarmigans establish territories on the tundra and the females soon join them. Once mating has been completed, the males show no further interest until the following year; the females are left to raise the chicks alone, while the males retire to the higher ridges.

During late June and July, female ptarmigans are sitting on eggs, their nests made in a depression on open ground, well-hidden among tundra plants. By August, the broods have hatched. For ptarmigan chicks, bad weather is the greatest cause of mortality, although Prairie Falcons and Common Ravens patrol the area, taking their share.

As the brief alpine summer comes to a close, all ptarmigans—young birds of the year and adult males and females—change into their pure white garb in preparation for the snowy months ahead. They will winter in separate flocks—the females in thickets below timberline, and the males on the tundra itself.

Representative birding sites:

Trail Ridge Road area: Sundance Mountain Basin, Forest Canyon, Rock Cut Overlook, Medicine Bow Curve

Mount Evans area: between Summit Lake and the top of Mount Evans.

Tracking the Ptarmigan

Skillful as the ptarmigans are at camouflaging themselves in their surroundings, they can still be located fairly easily during the summer breeding season in June, July and August. Ptarmigans are rather tame, foraging about the landscape oblivious to human observers. The key is to detect their movement, for if they freeze in fear, you can walk within ten feet of them and never know their whereabouts. Incidentally, do not count on noticing the white tail from which the bird gets its name, for it lies concealed by the upper tail coverts, unless the bird is in flight.

Birders occasionally attempt to use taped calls to attract the male White-tailed Ptarmigan. While tape recorders should always be used with great discretion, it is possible to lure the male closer by playing his call. By the time the roads are open in the high country—in late May or June—the ptarmigans are finished mating, and the hens, already on their nests, will not respond to the male's call. If you visit the tundra this early in the season, your chances of attracting the male birds with a tape are reasonably good, and you may avoid considerable damage to the tundra plants by not climbing all around.

However, should you visit in July or August, a taped call will be useless, since the males have already dispersed to the high rocky ridges, inaccessible to birders. But a birding trip to the tundra at this time of year may produce ptarmigans without the need of a tape at all. By mid-July, the broods have hatched, and the chicks and hens move about cautiously on the tundra, often preferring moist spots near willows. The trick is to spot the foraging broods; absorbed in searching for food in the early morning and watching over the chicks, the hens can be quite approachable.

Trail Ridge Road in Rocky Mountain National Park is by far the best place to start your ptarmigan search. (For some reason, the birds are much more difficult to locate in the Mount Evans area.) Birding Trail Ridge Road for the ptarmigan requires a very early start, not only because the birds are most active in the early morning, but to avoid the crowds. Dress warmly and plan to spend a couple of hours seeking this tundra treasure!

The Three-toed Woodpecker: A Birding Close-Up

The Three-toed Woodpecker (formerly named the Northern Three-toed Woodpecker) inhabits the great circumboreal forests of Eurasia and North America. This hardy woodpecker remains year-round in the cold, snow-laden spruce forests, content to sustain itself by searching for the wood-boring insects hiding beneath the bark of the trees.

Where the northern forests dip south into the United States, as they do in the Southern Rockies, small populations of Three-toed Woodpeckers may be found scattered locally at 9-11,000 feet, quietly going about the business of making a living, and often successfully eluding would-be observers.

Like other members of the woodpecker family, the Three-toed drums and hammers vigorously at the bark of trees, excavating a steady supply of beetle larvae. The bird's nostrils are covered with bristle-like feathers, protecting it from the wood-dust raised by the sharp bill as it drills into the tree. The woodpecker's skull is encased in a thick-walled membrane, which cushions the brain from the constant shock of pounding.

Ornithologists believe woodpeckers such as the Three-toed depend upon their hearing to detect insects gnawing within the bark of trees, or hibernating in the wood. With an extraordinarily long, barbed tongue, which the bird protrudes when feeding, its prey is uncovered and neatly snared. A pair of long muscles called hyoids are capable of extending and retracting the bird's powerful tongue.

Equipped with such a feeding mechanism, no wonder Three-toed Woodpeckers readily move into forests that have undergone forest fires, wind storms or insect infestations. Sometimes, the dead or rotting wood the bird prefers for nesting holes and foraging lure it down to lower elevations, away from the spruce-fir forest. For example, in the Horseshoe Park and Little Horseshoe Park areas of Rocky Mountain National Park, below the woodpecker's habitual range, the Three-toed has followed the mountain pine beetle infestation. The beetle lays eggs between the bark and the wood of trees in late summer, which hatch into larvae and feed upon the trees during the winter. The Three-toed has joined other woodpeckers to reap the harvest of beetle larvae here, well-fed enough to disregard even the coldest winter months.

Although the Three-toed Woodpecker should not be confused with the Black-backed Woodpecker, a bird of more southern distribution in North America's forests, the two share a common trait: both have three toes, not the standard four of other woodpeckers. Instead of two toes pointing forward and two backward, these woodpeckers are missing one of the backward pointing toes, the hallux.

Apparently, being without the hallux enables the Three-toed and the Black-backed to deliver a more powerful blow without impairing their climbing ability. Because the woodpeckers develop most of their blow's momentum from the body, not with the head and neck, the bird can increase its force by rotating its heels outward before delivering the blow, then rotating them inward as the blow is struck. The absence of one of the backward toes facilitates this rocking motion.

The Colorado race of the Three-toed Woodpecker somewhat resembles a Hairy Woodpecker, except that the Three-toed has some barring toward the bottom of the white back patch, whereas the Hairy does not. A foolproof way to tell the Three-toed from the Hairy is to look for the blackish-gray bars on the sides and flanks of the Three-toed. This is particularly helpful when identifying female Three-toeds, as the males will have a nice yellow crown patch, making their recognition much easier. (The Black-backed Woodpecker is not found in Colorado, which eliminates that species as a source of confusion; in any case, the Black-backed always has a solidly black back.)

Usually silent except for an occasional squeak note, Three-toed Woodpeckers may still leave clues to their presence. Watch for chips of bark and excavations at lower levels on the tree trunks, often only four or five feet off the ground. Listen for the whacking and thumping of the bird as it extracts the wood-boring beetles with its strong bill. Expect to track down many a Hairy Woodpecker in your search for the Three-toed, but, when at last you locate the bird, it may belie its shy reputation. Alternately hammering and preening, positioning itself in a single spot for several minutes, the Three-toed Woodpecker rewards the waiting birder with a good, close-up view.

NOTES FROM A BIRDER'S DIARY
Rocky Mountain National Park

● August 5, 1986, 6:00 A.M.: I've been up since 4:30 A.M. and now that the car is rounding Rainbow Curve on Trail Ridge Road, the sun is just beginning to tinge the magnificent, snowy peaks of the park with shades of rose and purple.

Nobody is on the road at this hour, and we sail up around the curves, climbing higher and higher. Soon we pass through the spruce-fir forest, and tundra meadows unfold on either side. The little alpine plants—the orange daisies, the blue chiming bells, the purple asters and the yellow paintbrushes—flank the road in swatches of color.

This is the domain of the White-tailed Ptarmigan, and my morning's quest is the product of much research and several phone calls to local bird authorities. One phrase keeps running through my head as a warning, "Remember, this time of year the ptarmigan looks more like a rock than a rock." In the gray, weathered rocks that clutter the hillside interspersed with dwarf willows, how will I ever spot the perfectly camouflaged ptarmigan?

We crest the top and finally come to Medicine Bow Curve, a

marked pull-out off the road. From here we must walk out onto the tundra. I get out of the car, amazed at the chill of the summer morning. The view of the high, remote mountains beyond the headwaters of the Cache la Poudre River spreads before me.

I slip and slide on the icy ground. The little grasses and mat plants glisten with dampness. I try to walk gently on this precious alpine carpet. The air is so thin at this altitude I am out of breath after a few steps.

As time passes, I begin to lose hope, plodding around with my boots getting wetter and my feet colder. We've wandered a good distance from the parked car, and have examined every inch of the surrounding area through binoculars.

Thinking I hear a noise, I stop and listen. Nothing. A slight breeze rustles a lone willow bush. Dejectedly, I look down the steep slope at the sheer immensity of the landscape.

As I scan the ground once more, the sun's rays catch an unfamiliar profile. It looks like part of the landscape—a rock or a plant—but it sticks up in an odd way.

"I've got it!" I whisper. There she is! A female White-tailed Ptarmigan stands watchfully on a little hummock of green with a background of yellow alpine flowers. Her pretty, soft brown-and-black-and-beige feathering merges completely into the gray boulders and brown earth patches of the summer tundra.

She's moving about this morning attending her brood of young. I count five chicks—their brownish-gray little forms hunkered down as they explore widely in an area surveyed by the hen ptarmigan. The chicks like this boggy swale, where the new shoots are tastiest. Occasionally, the mother bird keeps in touch with her chicks by making a clucking noise, and the chicks respond with a *peep* as they hunt about for food.

On the quiet tundra slope, it is hard to imagine a more auspicious beginning to my ptarmigan search!

● Same day, 10:00 A.M.: On our way back down the mountain, we decide to pull off and hike Toll Memorial Nature Trail, a short pathway leading from the Rock Cut viewpoint. I am still reeling from the thrill of seeing my first ptarmigan. The whole morning assumes a radiant glow.

I lug myself up the nature trail, draped with spotting scope, binoculars, and camera. Although this was another spot recommended for the ptarmigan, I cannot imagine any birds feeling at home here. Too many people! Crowds of tourists are beginning to make their assault on the higher parts of the Park. Large families fill the station wagons and vans which pull up and disgorge their passengers to enjoy the alpine scenery.

Just then, a friendly-looking woman with short, dark hair and a smiling face came towards me down the trail.

"You must be a birder!" she said, eyeing my scope and binoculars. We chatted for a minute. She told me she was from Ohio and was here with her family on vacation. I feigned interest but I was anxious to move on up the trail.

"By the way, I assume you saw the ptarmigan as you came up the path . . ." she mentioned.

"WHAT PTARMIGAN?" I exclaimed incredulously. This was totally unexpected—a ptarmigan up here with all these people walking around?

Pointing out into the rocks near the trail, the lady showed us a plump female ptarmigan, calmly watching over her brood as she foraged, partially hidden by the succulent tundra grasses. Soon after, the whole ptarmigan family managed to scurry across the paved pathway, one by one, and disappear into the meadows that camouflaged them so well.

I laughed, and thanked this helpful stranger for sharing her discovery with us. I was embarrassed to admit I'd flown halfway across the country and spent countless hours preparing for my ptarmigan search. Without binoculars, lengthy phone calls or explorations through the icy tundra, this lady had succeeded in tracking the ptarmigan much more easily than I had, proving once again what Colorado birders had told me from the start, "As for ptarmigans, you just have to take them where you find them!"

TRAVELERS' TIPS

Before You Visit: Whether you plan to seek lodging facilities in Estes Park or to camp within Rocky Mountain National Park, it's necessary to make reservations well in advance. To obtain a map, a checklist of birds, information on camping, and other publications, write Superintendent, Rocky Mountain National

Park, Estes Park, CO. 80517. For accommodations in Estes Park, write the Chamber of Commerce in Estes Park, CO. 80517, or National Park Village South, 900 Moraine Av., Estes Park, CO. 80517. (Staying in accommodations in the National Park Village South area along Moraine Ave. can be convenient for birders; many establishments back up to National Park lands and afford good birding.)

There are two entrances to Rocky Mountain National Park on its eastern border, the south entrance, where U.S. 36 enters the Park, and the north entrance, where U.S. 34 enters. The north entrance, known as the Fall River Entrance, is not as heavily used as the southern one, the Beaver Meadows Entrance. If this is your first visit, use the Beaver Meadows Entrance—the adjacent Visitor Center and Park Headquarters are a good place to find books, maps, trail advice and campground information.

For general information about travel in Colorado and the location of state parks and outdoor recreation areas, write the Division of Commerce and Development, State Office of Tourism, 1313 Sherman St., Denver, CO. 80203.

For a Forest Service map of the Mount Evans area, in Arapaho National Forest, write to Clear Creek Ranger District Visitor Center, P. O. Box 730, Idaho Springs, CO. 80452. There are numerous towns with accommodations that have access to the Mount Evans Wilderness, including Idaho Springs, El Rancho and Evergreen, plus the Denver metropolitan area.

The Denver Museum of Natural History should be one of your first destinations on a Colorado visit. A great place to get a sense of Colorado's flora and fauna, the Museum offers excellent dioramas of Colorado wildlife and a comprehensive collection of birds. The displays of Colorado's life zones help to interpret the ecosystems you will soon observe in the field. Many natural history publications are available at the bookstore within the Museum, and a list may be obtained by writing Denver Museum of Natural History, Denver, CO. 80205, phone (303) 370-6363. The Museum is located in City Park, not far from Stapleton Airport; from Quebec St., take Montview Blvd. until it deadends into City Park.

The Statewide Rare Bird Alert for Colorado is (303) 423-5582.

When to Visit: A visit to alpine habitats is usually restricted to the summer months, due to road closure until the end of May, and the threat of early snowfall in autumn. Trail Ridge Road in Rocky Mountain National Park and Colorado 5 to the summit of Mount Evans are both closed from the first snowfall (usually mid-September) to Memorial Day, and occasionally to mid-June.

Come to see the tundra and its bird life from mid-June, through mid-August. During these months, you can enjoy the wildflowers in full bloom, and birds will be abundant in the mountain forests as well as on the alpine tundra.

Even in the warmest months, the temperature at the tops of the highest peaks is unpredictable. Do not expect to guess the weather atop Mount Evans from what it's like in Denver! Besides the temperature difference in the high country, summer thunderstorms regularly drench the mountains for an hour or more during mid-afternoon. Come prepared with warm clothing in layers, a rain jacket, sunscreen and a hat.

A last word about birding the tundra regions in Colorado: if you are flying in from sea level to Denver, known as the mile-high city, be aware of the slight effects altitude may have on your body. If you plan to drive to the higher mountains, give yourself a day to acclimatize if possible. Even so, the air on the highest peaks is very thin and you will need to walk slowly to avoid shortness of breath. Frequent snacks help, and so do lots of glasses of water.

Length of Visit: To fully explore Rocky Mountain National Park, birding the forests at lower elevations and the tundra habitats as well, allow three or four days. Of course, if you go straight to Trail Ridge Road and only wish to bird that section of the Park, your stay can be considerably shorter.

A trip to the summit of Mount Evans can be made in a half-day from Denver. Before noon you can reach the top of the mountain, and be back in Denver late that afternoon. If you spend the night closer to the Mount Evans area, at one of the smaller communities nearby, you will have more time for a leisurely drive up Mount Evans, with plenty of birding along the way.

THE BIRDING SITES

Rocky Mountain National Park: The route described below begins at the Beaver Meadows Entrance Station to the Park, and finishes high in the tundra habitat on Trail Ridge Road. All locations are best birded in early morning to avoid the crowds on the main roads.

Rocky Mountain National Park can be reached via several routes, depending upon your travel plans. If you are coming from the the Pawnee Grasslands, take U.S. 34 from Greeley. From Denver via Boulder, take U.S. 36 on a lovely route along the base of the Front Range, thence to Lyons and Estes Park. The back way, Colorado 7, is an alternative route from Lyons.

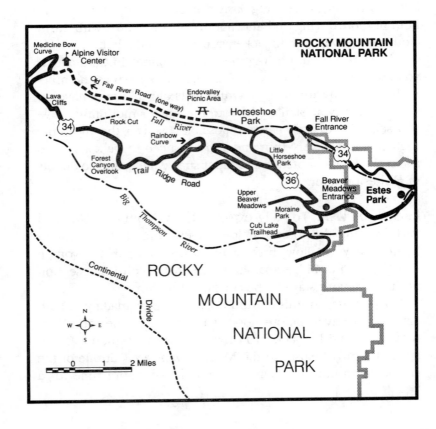

MORAINE PARK: Drive east through the Beaver Meadows Entrance Station and go .2 mi. to the sign that says Moraine Park, then turn left until you come to Moraine Park Campground (1.3 mi.). Turn right, then left, onto the road leading to the Cub Lake/Fern Lake Trailheads. Anywhere along here is good birding for species found in the ponderosa pine zone such as Broad-tailed Hummingbird, Rufous Hummingbird (late summer), Red-naped Sapsucker, Williamson's Sapsucker, Western Wood-Pewee, Tree Swallow, Violet-green Swallow, Steller's Jay, Mountain Bluebird, Western Tanager, Chipping Sparrow and Pine Siskin. At dawn and dusk, scan the sky above for possible Black Swifts as they come down Forest Canyon.

UPPER BEAVER MEADOWS TRAILHEAD: Return to U. S. 36 and turn left, proceeding further west into the Park. Take the next left turn at a sign that says Beaver Meadows. Follow the road until it dead-ends at the second picnic stop. Look for more species typical of the ponderosa pine forest such as Mountain Chickadee, Townsend's Solitaire, Western Tanager and Cassin's Finch.

LITTLE HORSESHOE PARK: This stop is suggested for the Three-toed Woodpecker, which has nested here in recent years. Proceed along U.S. 36, reaching Deer Ridge Junction where U.S. 34 intersects. Be sure to notice square-topped Long's Peak (14,255 ft.) to your left (south) as you climb to the junction. Turn right down the hill towards Horseshoe Park and Fall River Rd. Halfway down the hill (about .9 mi.) a dirt road with a gate across it takes off to your right (east). It has a sign saying Little Horseshoe, but it faces the other direction. (If you come to an overlook on your right, you've gone too far).

Park by the highway; walk past the gate onto the dirt road. Bird quietly up and down the road. You're in the midst of a beetle-infested stand of pines here, so it's not pretty, but the woodpeckers love it. At the end of the road is a dilapidated wooden building, a reminder from the 1920s and '30s when hunting parties used to stay there to shoot elk. Respect private property, please.

HORSESHOE PARK: Return to U.S. 34 and head down the hill (north) to the intersection of Fall River Road (about .9 mi.). Turn left at Fall River Road, driving past where the bridge crosses the main slide area. The slide occurred in 1982, when a dam broke at Lawn Lake; the resultant surge of mud and boulders killed four people. The gorge of the Roaring River has been greatly enlarged here.

After passing the main slide area and the Alluvial Fan Trailhead parking lot on your right, you'll come to a pull-out on your left with two picnic tables. Park here; bird the road on either side. The stands of aspen and dead ponderosa here and further on are excellent for woodpeckers, namely, Red-naped and Williamson's Sapsuckers, Hairy Woodpecker, and Three-toed Woodpecker (rare). If you feel like hiking, go back to the Lawn Lake/Ypsilon Lake Trailhead and start up the moderate slope for nice views out over Horseshoe Park.

ENDOVALLEY PICNIC AREA: After birding along Fall River Road, drive to the end of the road to the Endovalley Picnic Area, a shady campground for picnicking and a good place for observing montane species preferring a streamside habitat. Among species to look for are Western Flycatcher, Warbling Vireo, Yellow, Yellow-rumped, MacGillivray's and Wilson's Warblers, Black-headed Grosbeak and Lincoln's Sparrow.

A pair of American Dippers, resident on the stream—the Fall River—can be found by walking upstream from the west end of the picnic grounds. Keep an eye out overhead for possible Black Swifts cruising down Fall River Canyon, which rises steeply above you. Also, notice Colorado's state tree, the lovely blue spruce, growing around the picnic grounds.

OLD FALL RIVER ROAD: From Endovalley Picnic Area the road becomes Old Fall River Road, a one-way rather dusty and narrow road that winds up through beautiful scenery to the topmost ridges of the Park. It is 9.4 mi. long, and you'll eventually arrive at the Alpine Visitor's Center and hook up with Trail Ridge Road high on the tundra. (Not suggested as a quick way to reach the tundra areas; use U.S. 34 instead.)

Old Fall River Road is interesting from a scenic and historic viewpoint. Be sure to purchase the pamphlet available at the roadside before you start up. Although you may find good birds anywhere along the road—the turn-outs are haunted by Clark's Nutcrackers begging from tourists—it's sometimes difficult to get beyond the roadway to observe the birds. Try the Chapin Creek Trail, which winds through the moist spruce forest, bordered by wildflowers.

Trail Ridge Road Area: The following locations on Trail Ridge Road in Rocky Mountain National Park are your best chances for finding Rosy Finch and White-tailed Ptarmigan. Directions start from the east end of Trail Ridge Road.

SUNDANCE MOUNTAIN BASIN: About .5 mi. past Rainbow Curve, pull off to the left. (A sign identifies the Ute Trail here.) Park there. Cross the road to your right and climb over a little ridge into what looks like a basin—about .25 mi. from the road to the basin. Scan here for ptarmigan.

FOREST CANYON: Continue up to the Forest Canyon Overlook. Past the overlook is a parking spot on your left for two cars. Park here and cross the road. Walk up the hill and scan for ptarmigan (you are on the back side of Sundance Mountain Basin).

ROCK CUT OVERLOOK—TOLL MEMORIAL NATURE TRAIL: Proceed on up Trail Ridge Road until you come to this signed parking area. Park and walk up the nature trail. You may have people pointing out the ptarmigan to you as I did!

LAVA CLIFFS: This is the best place in Rocky Mountain National Park to try for Rosy Finches. Proceed 2.1 mi. up the road from the Rock Cut Overlook to the Lava Cliffs viewpoint. Scan the reddish volcanic cliffs, which rise sharply above the perpetual snowfields. Be sure to bring a scope, because you're pretty far from the birds.

ALPINE VISITOR CENTER: Go 2.1 mi. from Lava Cliffs, and stop at the Alpine Visitor Center to see exhibits about the tundra (also, a store and restaurant). Rosy Finches have nested around the buildings here, so scan the area.

MEDICINE BOW CURVE: About a mile west of the Alpine Visitor Center on Trail Ridge Road, you'll come to this turn-out. Park and walk east and slightly uphill from the parking area. Good for ptarmigan!

Mount Evans area: To begin your trip up Mount Evans, take I-70 west from Denver to the El Rancho Exit (Exit 252). Take Colorado 74 toward Bergen Park and Evergreen. After 2.5 mi., turn right (east) onto Colorado 103, which leads upwards toward Echo Lake and the summit of Mount Evans.

Through the great expanse of green conifer forest, the road winds up over Squaw Pass and Chief Mountain. Don't hesitate to stop at the many pull-outs and picnic areas, where you may come upon the following: Gray Jay (bring a picnic to lure these out), Clark's Nutcracker, Mountain Chickadee, White-breasted and Red-breasted Nuthatches, Ruby- and Golden-crowned Kinglets, Townsend's Solitaire and Evening Grosbeak, among others.

ECHO LAKE: At the juncture of Colorado 103 and Colorado 5, stop at Echo Lake; this spot is heavily used on summer weekends. Go round to the parking lot at the northwest end of the lake. From here, follow the path around the edge of the lake, where Wilson's Warblers, Lincoln's Sparrows and White-crowned Sparrows breed. In the spruce forest surrounding Echo Lake, look for: Yellow-rumped Warbler, Gray Jay, Clark's Nutcracker, and Dark-eyed Junco.

SUMMIT LAKE: From Echo Lake (10,700 ft.) to the summit of Mount Evans, you are on the highest highway in the United States! When this road is open (Memorial Day through Labor Day), the views and the birds are terrific.

On the way to Summit Lake, the road winds past a stand of gnarled bristlecone pines at timberline. If you've never visited the tundra before, stop at the Mt. Goliath Nature Trail. Otherwise, proceed to Summit Lake (9 mi. from Echo Lake).

At Summit Lake, birders are seldom disappointed in their search for the Brown-capped Rosy Finch. From the parking lot, scan the whole area for Rosy Finches. Walk around to the north end of the lake, where the finches nest on the cliffs overlooking the Chicago Basin. The Rosy Finches often hop around on the rocks at the lake's margin.

TOP OF MOUNT EVANS: Another 6 mi. from Summit Lake, the road finally ends at the cold, windy summit of Mount Evans. On the way up, look for

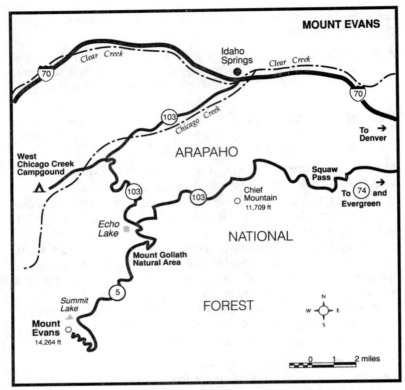

White-tailed Ptarmigan (particularly at a spot .25 mi up the road from Summit Lake on the hill to your right). However, this is not an easy place to find the bird.

At the top of the mountain, put on a jacket and grab your camera to record your visit to this desolate, high peak. The walk up the last 65 feet to the very top is worth it, if you're in good physical condition. The views are out of this world!

To make a spectacular loop trip, retrace your route down Colorado 5 and go north on Colorado 103 to the little town of Idaho Springs, which brings you back to I-70 at Exit 239. As you descend Mount Evans on Colorado 103, further opportunities to bird the montane forest present themselves at any of the view points and picnic areas. When you get to Idaho Springs, a Colorado mountain town with real western flavor, drive the residential streets looking for bird feeders. A number of houses have feeders, which attract everything from Broad-tailed Hummingbirds to Evening Grosbeaks and Cassin's Finches. (Also, Idaho Springs is a quaint place to spend the night, should you wish to do this loop up Mount Evans in reverse.)

COLORADO'S ALPINE TUNDRA:
Tracking the White-tailed Ptarmigan
Checklist of Common Birds by Habitat

PONDEROSA PINE FOREST
Turkey Vulture
Northern Harrier
Red-tailed Hawk
Golden Eagle
American Kestrel
Band-tailed Pigeon
Red-naped Sapsucker
Williamson's Sapsucker
Downy Woodpecker
Hairy Woodpecker
Three-toed Woodpecker (rare)
Common Nighthawk
Common Poorwill
Black Swift
White-throated Swift
Broad-tailed Hummingbird
Western Wood-Pewee
Hammond's Flycatcher
    (uncommon)
Willow Flycatcher
Western Flycatcher
Violet-green Swallow
Tree Swallow
Steller's Jay
Black-capped Chickadee
Mountain Chickadee
Pygmy Nuthatch
White-breasted Nuthatch
House Wren
American Dipper
Western Bluebird
Mountain Bluebird
American Robin
Solitary Vireo
Warbling Vireo
Yellow Warbler
MacGillivray's Warbler
Wilson's Warbler
Western Tanager
Black-headed Grosbeak
Dark-eyed Junco (Gray-headed)

Chipping Sparrow
Cassin's Finch
Evening Grosbeak

**ENGELMANN SPRUCE-
SUBALPINE FIR FOREST**
Northern Goshawk
Sharp-shinned Hawk
Blue Grouse
Three-toed Woodpecker (rare)
Olive-sided Flycatcher
Hammond's Flycatcher
Gray Jay
Clark's Nutcracker
Red-breasted Nuthatch
Brown Creeper
Golden-crowned Kinglet
Ruby-crowned Kinglet
Swainson's Thrush
Hermit Thrush
Townsend's Solitaire
Yellow-rumped Warbler
    (Audubon's)
MacGillivray's Warbler
Wilson's Warbler
Lincoln's Sparrow
White-crowned Sparrow
Dark-eyed Junco (Gray-headed)
Pine Grosbeak
Red Crossbill
Cassin's Finch
Pine Siskin

ALPINE TUNDRA
Prairie Falcon
White-tailed Ptarmigan
Common Raven
Horned Lark
Water Pipit
White-crowned Sparrow
Rosy Finch (Brown-capped)

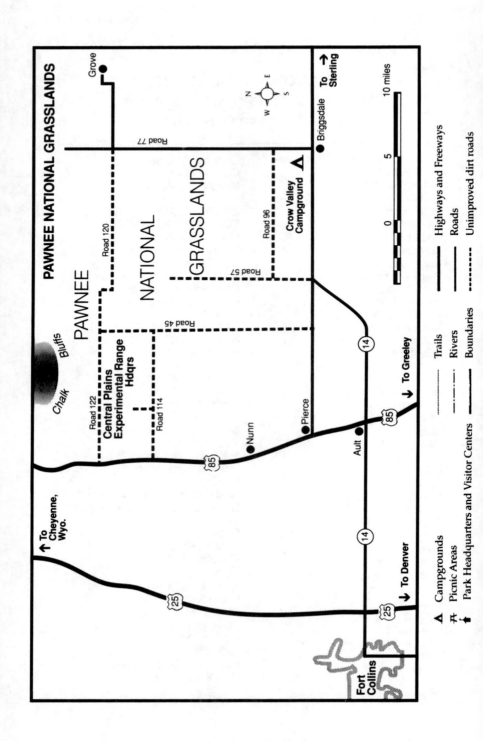

PAWNEE NATIONAL GRASSLANDS

Grove

Road 77

To Sterling

Briggsdale

Road 120

PAWNEE

Chalk Bluffs

Road 122

Central Plains Experimental Range Hdqrs

Road 45

Road 114

NATIONAL

Road 57

GRASSLANDS

Crow Valley Campground

Road 96

Nunn

Pierce

Ault

To Greeley

To Cheyenne, Wyo.

Fort Collins

To Denver

N
W   E
S

0   5   10 miles

△ Campgrounds
⌗ Picnic Areas
† Park Headquarters and Visitor Centers

.... Trails
— · — · Rivers
▬▬▬ Boundaries

━━━ Highways and Freeways
——— Roads
- - - - Unimproved dirt roads

3

COLORADO'S SHORT-GRASS PRAIRIE:
Birding Where the Buffalo Roamed

To see the bird life in what was once a vast grassland stretching across the Great Plains, a trip to the Pawnee National Grasslands in eastern Colorado promises an unusual birding experience. A healthy remnant of North America's famous short-grass prairie survives in the gentle hills and flat pasturelands of the Pawnee. This habitat, now greatly diminished in the United States and Canada due to overgrazing, agriculture and development, supports a very specialized group of birds, several of them difficult to find elsewhere.

The Lark Bunting, the Chestnut-collared Longspur, and the McCown's Longspur are prime examples of species breeding in the grasslands. The possibility of seeing nesting Mountain Plovers and Long-billed Curlews adds to the excitement of a visit to the bunch grasses and wildflowers of the Pawnee in late spring.

This corner of the Great Plains reaches into eastern Colorado, north to eastern Wyoming, and south into eastern New Mexico—a region of arid lowland prairie traversed by an occasional river or stream. The vegetation along these streamside corridors lures a variety of bird species desirable to birders because they are at the eastern or western limits of their ranges.

Historically a barrier to east-west travel, the Rockies have deterred Eastern bird species from westward expansion, and most Western birds do not venture eastward from these rugged mountains. Because of this, birding at the base of the Front Range and out along the watercourses on the western edge of the Great Plains produces an interesting mix of Western and Eastern birds.

The possibility of finding these borderline species tempts birders to scour the watercourses and ponds en route to the grasslands. Western birders, intrigued at the prospect of glimpsing such Eastern birds as the Red-headed Woodpecker, Blue Jay or Brown Thrasher, search the deciduous thickets along the streams. Likewise, Eastern birders can hope to spot Western Wood-Pewees, Western Kingbirds and Say's Phoebes on this trip.

The route commences with a night's stay in Ft. Collins, Colorado, ideally situated as a stop-over on the way to either the Pawnee National Grasslands or Rocky Mountain National Park. After exploring Ft. Collins, with its fine examples of streamside habitat and foothill woodlands, the trip leads east to the wide open spaces of the Pawnee, a land of longspurs, prairie dogs and pronghorns.

Here, on the prairies of eastern Colorado, spend a morning where the fresh smell of the prairie grasses waving in the breeze and the immense sky spanning the horizon make a serene setting for birding where the buffalo once roamed.

For miles and miles these grassy flatlands stretch north into Wyoming and through eastern Colorado towards Kansas and Nebraska. Before the earliest white settlers arrived, this was Indian and buffalo country. You can picture scenes of Pawnee Indian braves as they gathered for the annual buffalo-hunting season, their tepees pitched, ready for the huge herds of bison that roamed the Great Plains. Pronghorn antelope thrived here too, preyed on by gray wolves.

The land was rich in native grasses which held the soil against the erosion of the fierce prairie winds and rainstorms. These grasses formed compact mats mixed with bunches of taller grasses. Even though the buffalo herds grazed heavily in their own path, there were no fences to restrict them and they moved on, permitting the grasslands to resprout naturally.

With westward expansion, homesteaders and farmers began

to till the soil for cultivated crops. The deep roots of the heavy sod made plowing with the original iron plows difficult. When steel plows came into use, the soil yielded plentiful crops, but without sophisticated agricultural methods, the land was stripped of its natural vegetation.

Economic deprivation during the 1930's led to widespread bankruptcy and many families abandoned their farms. Severe drought and destructive winds ruined the already barren land. The Dust Bowl, as it was called, affected parts of Colorado, Wyoming, Nebraska, Kansas, Oklahoma, Texas and the Dakotas. The soil began to drift in great clouds of dust, which carried as far as the Atlantic Coast.

Pawnee National Grasslands is one of the few places you can see what the early short-grass prairies of the western Great Plains must have looked like. Since the Dust Bowl years of the 1930's, the federal government has purchased many of these marginal lands with poorer soils and set up experimental tracts.

The Pawnee National Grasslands now encompasses 775,000 acres of prairie. The Soil Conservation Service has created demonstration areas, interspersed with privately-owned farms and livestock ranches, where native grasses are being re-planted in an effort to restore the land to its original productivity.

Climate and Habitats of Eastern Colorado

All of Colorado's weather is influenced by the great Rocky Mountains. A feature of late spring and summer days are the convective storms, born high above the Continental Divide in late morning. These intense thunderstorms, a result of the earth's warm air rising rapidly and causing moisture to condense, drift eastward as the day progresses. Once over the plains, they can become quite violent. Pelting rain and hail, accompanied by a 20 degree drop in temperature, is not unusual. Within half an hour, however, the storm's fury abates and the sun shines brightly once again. Ft. Collins residents take such weather in stride, for this part of northern Colorado and southern Wyoming are known as a hail belt.

Ft. Collins, situated along the banks of the Cache la Poudre River at the base of the Front Range, provides several examples of streamside habitat. Out on the open plains of the Pawnee, the streamside vegetation bordering the rivers and ponds abuts that of the grasslands, increasing the diversity of bird species in the two ecosystems.

Lowland Streamside (Riparian): Early explorers on the plains gravitated to the watercourses, the only places on the rolling grasslands where deciduous trees grew. In the shade of the magnificent plains cottonwoods, early forts were established and settlers built their farmhouses.

The broad domes of plains cottonwoods, visible from far away on the grasslands, signify an oasis for bird and animal life. Their fissured trunks support huge crowns of heart-shaped leaves, which quiver and sigh in the wind.

Along the major rivers such as the South Platte, box-elder, American elm, green ash and Russian-olive have been introduced, joining the native cottonwoods and the peach-leaved willow, another tall tree of the prairies.

These riparian ecosystems are constantly in flux, responding to changes in the river channels. Dry oxbows leave sandy soil, which is soon invaded by willows. Eventually cottonwoods take over from the willows. Both trees lure numbers of nesting and migrant birds.

The Red-headed Woodpecker and the Blue Jay, both Eastern bird species, have successfully expanded their ranges west from their origins in Eastern deciduous forests, making use of the lush vegetation along plains' watercourses. Orchard Orioles fly through the cottonwoods, and Brown Thrashers sing from the hawthorns, a welcoming sight to Western birders unfamiliar with these Eastern species.

In the same way, Western birds venture east, following the streams issuing from the Rocky Mountains' snow melt out onto the Great Plains. Eastern Kingbirds can be seen flycatching in the same woods as Western Kingbirds and Western Wood-Pewees. The Yellow-billed Cuckoo, a Western species, may skulk in a streamside thicket in the vicinity of its Eastern relative the Black-billed Cuckoo. The Say's Phoebe and the Brewer's Sparrow, both Westerners, may be found here, too.

The further east you explore on the Colorado plains, the

greater the preponderance of Eastern species in streamside habitats.

Representative birding sites:

Ft. Collins area: Martinez Park, Northern Colorado Nature Center, Spring Canyon and south end of Horsetooth Reservoir
Pawnee Grasslands area: Crow Valley Park and Campground
Areas east of Sterling: Red Lion Wildlife Area, Duck Creek, Julesberg Reservoir.

Grassland: Short-grass prairie, differentiated from the tall-grass prairie of wetter sites to the east, predominates on the Pawnee Grasslands. Most of the perennial grasses on the Pawnee are blue grama or buffalo-grass—low grasses no more than five inches tall with curly leaves.

Short-grasses are accustomed to the semi-arid conditions of this section of the plains. Most major storms, carrying precipitation in the form of rain or snow, have already dumped the bulk of their moisture over the Rocky Mountains, resulting in dry conditions over the western prairies. Fortified with deep root systems, the short-grasses can withstand the limited rainfall and frequent wind.

Buffalo-grass develops a wide network of fine roots just below the surface, as well as deeper roots. The surface network quickly drinks up large quantities of water from the brief spring and summer thundershowers.

Blue grama, a native bunch grass, also has an extensive root system which helps it to survive the irregular rainfall. To propagate, blue grama forms a series of side branches or clumps from the base of the plant, known as tillers. The tillers result in a bunch effect, crowding out other plants and contributing to a ground cover of dense sod.

Western wheat-grass and buffalo-grass both reproduce by means of stolons—thin stems that scoot along the surface of the ground. With good rainfall, the stolons grow buds at intervals, creating new plants and assuring the spread of the grasses.

Grasses multiply by seeding themselves as well as by vegetative growth, increasing the competition amongst each other for survival.

Taller grasses of moister sites on the Pawnee, and farther east on the tall-grass section of the prairie, grow nearly three feet high. Needle and thread, sand dropseed, side-oats grama, western wheat-grass, June-grass and red three awn are among these.

Flowering plants join the struggle to exist on the prairie, too. Some flowering plants produce seeds earlier in the spring, before they are overwhelmed by the grasses. Other flowers manage to extend their stems high above the level of the grasses to facilitate pollination.

Flowering plants produce a marvelous color display May through July. Brilliant yellow and purple cactus blooms add an exotic dimension to the landscape. Look for amaranth, Rocky Mountain bee plant, mountain bladderpod, pincushion cactus, prairie evening primrose, white stemless evening primrose, Kansas gayfeather, milk vetch, prairie clover, prickly pear cactus, pasture sage, common sunflower and yucca.

Cacti, tumbleweeds, yuccas and sagebrush are unwanted trespassers, thriving during dry periods and all too soon elbowing out the grasses in their immediate vicinity.

This great sweep of sky and golden expanse of tufted grasses is home to many birds. Although you will see few trees, except along the occasional streams and near the farmhouses, the grass itself is where much of the bird activity lies. Look closely in the pastures and fields for Mountain Plover, Long-billed Curlew, Burrowing Owl, Horned Lark, Loggerhead Shrike, Brewer's, Vesper, Lark and Grasshopper Sparrows, Lark Bunting, McCown's Longspur and Chestnut-collared Longspur, all of which breed here.

Say's Phoebes and Eastern and Western Kingbirds live near the farmhouses and under bridges.

Search the sky above and scan the utility poles for the raptors that hunt on the plains and nest high on the distant buttes and escarpments. Northern Harrier, Swainson's Hawk, Red-tailed Hawk, Ferruginous Hawk, Golden Eagle, American Kestrel, and Prairie Falcon are among those to expect in spring and summer. (The Greater and Lesser Prairie Chicken and the

Sharp-tailed Grouse, once common on the prairies, are restricted to a few remaining strutting grounds, none on the Pawnee.)

Birds of the grassland sort themselves out in remarkable ways. The height and density of the grasses and low shrubs hold the key to a variety of techniques for gaining food.

Within any selected patch of grassland, you will notice that some species feed on or near the ground, while others forage higher up in the tops of the grasses and low shrubs, each consuming different types of insects and seeds. The Western Meadowlark uses its long, sharp bill to probe in the ground searching for insects and grubs. The longspur uses its short, thick bill for cracking seeds and grains it finds in stubble and low grasses.

Some birds move rapidly through the grass as they search for food, stopping sporadically. Others move more slowly, methodically searching for insects and seeds in every clump. Apparently, the main competition among birds on the prairies is not for food, but for high perches from which to sing!

Most grassland birds have rather short tails, enabling them to slip through the dense vegetation easily and crouch low to the ground to avoid predators. For example, longspurs will squat behind a dirt clod or clump of weeds, perfectly matched to their background, and remain there until flushed; after a short flight, they will run a few feet and squat, motionless, again.

The Burrowing Owl has carved out an important niche on the prairie. So dependent is this little owl on open grassland, its very existence is threatened because of disappearing habitat in much of the West. Seen perched on fenceposts or standing guard at the low mound before its burrow, this sandy-brown colored owl with no ear tufts has a peculiar erect, long-legged stance. On the ground in front of its burrow, it watches for enemies, while swiveling its head back and forth constantly. When the owl sees anything of a suspicious nature, it reacts with a queer bobbing motion from side to side.

Burrowing Owls are quite gregarious, and formerly nested in colonies, using the abandoned burrows of the black-tailed prairie dog in which to raise their broods. Increased agricultural activity has caused a reduction in the size of Burrowing Owl communities, but the birds still reside in loose groups of four or five families, employing the tunnels of the prairie dog as nest sites whenever possible.

Both adult and juvenile Burrowing Owls possess a highly effective vocal defense mechanism. Any intruder attempting to enter, reach into or dig up an owl burrow will be greeted by a strange buzzing sound, exactly mimicking the rattle of the western rattlesnake. Often the rattling will be accompanied by a snake-like hissing—enough to put a stop to the most determined predator.

Contrary to popular belief, Burrowing Owls and western rattlesnakes do not use the same burrows, and have no close relationship aside from their similar-sounding rattle. The rattlesnakes do usurp vacant prairie dog burrows, however, and they can be found throughout the grasslands. Tread carefully in Pawnee country!

In the swales and dips of dry, short-grass prairie, the Mountain Plover occasionally shows itself. Although a member of a shorebird family—the Plovers—this bird breeds mostly on the high plains. Here on the Pawnee, the Mountain Plover's pale brown back and breast camouflage it, nesting as it does on the bare, open ground. Scan the fields painstakingly to spot this cleverly concealed bird. If you should flush a Mountain Plover, and the bird has a nest, it will play the "broken wing" game to lure you away, just as the Killdeer does.

Watching Longspurs

This is the land of longspurs. These finch-like birds, which dwell on the ground seeking food skillfully and often secretively among the bunch grasses, are the goal of many a birder on the Pawnee. To fully appreciate the sight of longspurs on their nesting grounds, you must study the pastures and fields for a look at the beautiful males in their nuptial dress. In typical longspur fashion, once on the ground, these birds can hide simply by posing without moving in front of a clump of grass or a furrow. The brown, beige, and rust tones of their plumage completely assimilate them into the patterns of dark earth and lighter grasses of the prairie.

McCown's Longspurs are locally common on the short, buffalo-grass sections of the Pawnee, and in the drier stubble fields. They are more abundant here in dry years than in wet years. Males and females stick close together, walking through the grazed-over tussocks of grass. During the breeding season in May and June, the male McCown's is more likely to sing in skylarking fashion (as does the Lark Bunting and Horned Lark) than the male Chestnut-collared, making the McCown's easier to locate. Named for the European Skylark, skylarking refers to the elaborate display flight engaged in by many prairie-nesters, in which the male ascends high in the sky and flutters— singing melodiously—to the ground.

Male McCown's Longspurs have a black cap, a white throat and a black breastband. Unlike other longspurs in breeding plumage, they have a gray—not chestnut—nape. Both males and females show a rufous shoulder patch, although it's some-times not as apparent on the female.

A visit to the Pawnee even into early August is sure to produce the Chestnut-collared Longspur as well as the McCown's, though the former may be more difficult to find. The Chestnut-collared Longspur, perhaps more common to the east of the Pawnee Grasslands, prefers the lusher grasses. The buffy throat, solid black underparts, and bright chestnut collar of the distinctive male Chestnut-collared Longspur are easily recognizable.

In looking for longspurs on the grasslands, watch for the distinctive tail patterns in flight. If you see a bird fly over with large white patches in the tail be on the alert for a longspur. Male and female McCown's show a black inverted "T" patch on a white tail. Male and female Chestnut-collareds have a dark triangle on a white tail.

Scan carefully through the mixed flocks of Horned Larks, Vesper Sparrows, Lark Sparrows, Lark Buntings and Western Meadowlarks for the longspurs. Seeing the dark tails of the Horned Larks and the white outer tail feathers of the Vesper and Lark Sparrows can help you to eliminate these species in your search.

In flight, Chestnut-collared Longspurs give a finch-like *kittle* or *kittle-kittle*. McCown's Longspurs utter a soft, dry rattle, interspersed with *pink* notes. The point is, you need to be able to pick out these calls from the *tsee-ee* of the Horned Larks with which they mingle.

In the late spring and summer, begin your tour of the Pawnee Grasslands early in the day, since bird activity markedly subsides during the mid-day warmth. Although not absolutely necessary, a spotting scope in the grasslands is often an advantage. By scoping large flocks of birds at a distance, you can examine individuals, before flushing them with your approach.

Representative birding sites:
Pawnee National Grasslands.

The Lark Bunting: A Birding Close-Up

The Lark Bunting speaks to us of the wide open spaces and its home on the prairie grasses with the endless sky above. In friendly flocks, the Lark Bunting ushers in spring on the Great Plains with its arrival from the south. In early March, hundreds of buntings pass through Kansas on their way north to Colorado and southern Canada, " . . . the ones at the rear of the flock fluttering continually to the fore, the whole appearing like some enormous wheel rolling over the greening prairies . . ." (John K. Terres, *The Audubon Encyclopedia of North American Birds.*).

Here on the Pawnee, the Lark Bunting, Colorado's state bird, is found everywhere in the fields and on fences, giving its low, sweet *hoo-ee* call. In spring, the jet-black males with their large white wing patches sing from the tops of grasses or fencelines or, more frequently, on the wing. The skylarking display flight of the male bunting begins with a steep ascent as high as 30 feet or more above the ground. Then, with set wings, the bird floats downward, circling ever closer to the grasses below, all the while giving forth a song of clear piping whistles and trills, mingled with some harsher notes.

Meanwhile, the female Lark Bunting, befitting her rather sober, streaky plumage, sits silently waiting on the ground or on a fence wire, while the male completes his dazzling flight.

Male buntings are sociable creatures and will tolerate each other close by. Since territories are not strongly developed, pairs often nest 100 feet apart in the low prairie grasses. The birds construct a nest of weed stems and rootlets lined with plant down, concealed near a tussock of grass or in a depression. Four or five light-green eggs are laid during the nesting season, which is from May through July.

The male Lark Bunting's black plumage punctuated by a large white wing patch renders him almost unmistakable. In fall and winter, after the breeding season, the males molt their black and white feathers, making them resemble the females and immatures. In this plumage the buntings look like large, streaky brown sparrows with thick silver-blue bills and a buffy-white wing patch; the tail has white at the outer corners.

The Lark Bunting loves the windy prairie and the bird seems to deliberately soar into the stiffest gale, revelling in its freedom to fly over the grasslands whatever the weather. No wonder the male bunting does not require the tall trees and tight little territories of other backyard birds, for its home is the sweeping plains and its territory is bounded only by the arching sky.

Birders who have never traveled to this part of the country will be surprised at the abundance of the Lark Bunting, a bird seldom encountered on either coast. Leaving the grasslands, you will take with you a lasting impression of the myriad gatherings of buntings, lifting off in unison from the fencerows and circling back to land again after your car has passed on.

NOTES FROM A BIRDER'S DIARY
Pawnee National Grasslands

● August 3, 1986, 8:30 A.M.: I love tromping about in this open country. There are little cacti and tufts of grasses of several kinds and scattered sagebrush and wildflowers—all mixed together. From a distance, the fields have a greenish-gray cast, sometimes golden, depending upon the make-up of the grasses and shrubs. Up close, I watch carefully to avoid the spines of the prickly pincushion cacti, which nestle amongst the buffalo-grass. The purple cleome and the white evening primrose are still in bloom. In the next pasture, cattle crop the nourishing grasses, creating ideal habitat for the Mountain Plover and McCown's Longspur.

Walking up a little rise, I put the scope down and settle it firmly on the ground. Peering through it—far, far away, almost obscured by the heat haze—I can make out a herd of prongh-orn antelope. A feeling of nostalgia and wonder creeps over me. How fitting and wild for them to be here in the early morning, a symbol of the prairies and a memory of the old West. When I look again, a puff of dust in the scope is all that's left, as the pronghorns vanish swiftly out of sight.

A long-winged Swainson's Hawk flies up from the ground and alights on a telephone pole. Its cowl-like plumage shows a white throat. A Red-tailed Hawk soars lazily overhead in a sky that seems to go on forever.

Driving and stopping, we progress eastward along the gra-velly road. A Burrowing Owl, its spindly legs silhouetted against the morning sunlight, sits atop a fencepost. As the car approaches, the owl flies off scolding.

A pair of Prairie Falcons are skimming along, flying fast and low with sandy wings. When one banks I check to make sure of the black patches under its wings. The falcons probably nest on the buttes to the north, and hunt these grasslands for prey.

We turn north and come to some plowed fields interspersed with pastures of yellow stubble. Huge flocks of Lark Buntings and Horned Larks fly up from the roadside, then circle back to land in another golden field. Driving slowly, our heads leaning out the window, we begin to scan anxiously for McCown's Longspurs.

Right here looks like a good patch of short-grass prairie. Cattle have grazed heavily, and the hills and gentle swales are shorn of all but the shortest tussocks. It's time to examine carefully every bird that flies over.

I spot a finch-like bird with a lot of white in the tail flying beside the car. It plummets across the road and lands in a field not far off, then simply disappears!

"Stop!" I cry excitedly. We back the car up to the spot where I could have sworn the bird landed. It must be rummaging around in the clumps of stubble not 20 yards from the car.

A couple of lazy-looking red-faced cows amble towards us, and I fear for the bird's safety under their clumsy hooves. Cautiously, we get out of the car in slow motion and use the scope to scan the area. Meanwhile, one of the cows is still coming on strong. No sign of the longspur. What has happened to our bird?

At last the longspur shows itself—an exquisite adult male McCown's! It has been foraging in a shallow depression and now comes out into view. Its black and white head pattern, rufous shoulder patch, and characteristic thick bill stand out in the scope. Perfect. There must have been a female there, too, for when it finally flushes, two birds fly off, giving a dry rattling call as they depart. Relief and joy flood over me. It's the beginning of a memorable birding day on the Pawnee!

TRAVELERS' TIPS

Before You Visit: Before you visit Pawnee National Grasslands, send for a map (fee) at the following address: Pawnee National Grasslands, 2009 Ninth St., Greeley, Colorado 80631. Phone: (303) 353-5004. Three other publications are available: a field checklist of birds of the Pawnee Grasslands showing seasonality and abundance, "Birding Auto Tour" and "Auto Winter Birding Tours."

While visiting the Pawnee Grasslands, your best bet is to stay in Ft. Collins or Greeley or camp at Crow Valley Campground, .5 mi. north of Briggsdale on Road 77. There is no park headquarters at the Grasslands and no food or lodging facilities nearby.

If you should arrive without a map, they are available at the following locations on the Grasslands: Pawnee Grasslands Work Center, .25 mi. north of Crow Valley Campground on Road 77, and at the Briggsdale Cafe and the Briggsdale Market in Briggsdale. (Since the hamlet of Briggsdale might not be active if you arrive early in the morning, it is better to come prepared with a map. Also, should you wish to explore the area on your own, a map is indispensable.)

The Grasslands is laid out on a grid-work of roads. Even-numbered roads run east and west, and odd-numbered roads run north and south, with a mile between each of the two numbers. Some of the land here is privately owned, while other tracts are used as demonstration plots by the U. S. Department of Agriculture. As long as you walk carefully, the farmers don't mind birders in their pastures. You'll see experimental vegetation studies in progress. Please don't disturb them.

Caution: many of the roads on the Grasslands are impassable after heavy rains. Take care not to get stuck! Also, start with a full tank of gas.

When to Visit: The best time to visit the Pawnee Grasslands is late spring. From mid-May through early July, the wildflowers are blooming and the breeding birds are in full territorial display, highly visible as they perform their flights above the nesting grounds.

If you wish to combine a visit to the Grasslands with one to the alpine regions of Rocky Mountain National Park (see Chapter Two), it is advisable to wait until early July to visit the Pawnee. By this time, all the mountain roads should be open and accessible in the Park, and you will be able to observe the grassland birds and the tundra birds on the same trip.

Late July and early August are a little late in the season for the plains' species—the males may not be singing and display-ing—but the birds are definitely still present. Summer rains can keep the wildflowers blooming into August, too.

Length of Visit: If you get to the Grasslands very early, and spend a morning birding, you will probably see most of the targeted species for this area. Of course, the Pawnee Grasslands covers an enormous stretch of prairie, and you may wish to explore further, especially in the country east of Briggsdale out to Sterling, which will take a full day at least, and perhaps two.

THE BIRDING SITES

Ft. Collins area: Listed below are directions to some birding spots in and around Ft. Collins. To reach Ft. Collins from Denver, take I-25 north 60 mi. to Colorado 14. Exit Colorado 14 west for 4 mi. to Ft. Collins.

MARTINEZ PARK: From the corner of Laurel and Shields streets in downtown Ft. Collins, drive north on Shields 1.3 mi. to Cherry St. Turn right 1.2 mi. and then left .3 mi. on Sherwood. This park on the Cache la Poudre River has large trees and riparian thickets. The following are among the birds breeding here: Red-headed Woodpecker, Bank, Cliff and Barn Swallows, Belted Kingfisher, Black-billed Magpie, Blue Jay, Common Yellowthroat, and American Goldfinch.

NORTHERN COLORADO NATURE CENTER: Starting at the intersection of Laurel and College Ave., go south on College 1.7 mi. and turn left at Drake for 1 mi. to Lemay. Continue on Drake 2 mi. and bear right over the bridge and turn left on Road 9 for .1 mi. to Northern Colorado Nature Center. This network of riparian nature trails, owned by Colorado State University, is another good spot on the Cache la Poudre River for woodland birding. Among the birds found here are: Black-crowned Night-Heron, Great Horned Owl, Western Screech-Owl, Yellow-billed Cuckoo, Common Flicker, Red-headed, Downy and Hairy Woodpeckers, Eastern and Western Kingbirds, Western Wood-Pewee, Black-billed Magpie, Brown Thrasher, Northern "Bullock's" Oriole, and perhaps Blue Grosbeak. During migration, expect any warbler, but most frequently you'll find Orange-crowned, Yellow-rumped, MacGillivray's and Wilson's Warblers and Northern Waterthrush, plus Western Tanager, Black-headed Grosbeak, Lazuli Bunting and Green-tailed Towhee.

SPRING CANYON AND SOUTH END OF HORSETOOTH RESERVOIR: Starting at the intersection of Laurel and Shields, go south .2 mi. and turn right on Elizabeth and left after 2 mi. onto Overland Trail. After 1.2 mi. turn right at Road 42C and go up the hill until you reach Horsetooth Reservoir where a left turn on Road 23 will take you to Spring Canyon Dam. Park at the top and walk, or drive down and park at the gate. A partial list of birds you might see in these habitats includes Scrub and Steller's Jays, Canyon and Rock Wrens (cliffs directly below the ponderosa pines), Dusky and Western Flycatchers, Bushtit, Yellow-breasted Chat, Virginia's Warbler (in oak brush), Veery, Western Tanager, Indigo and Lazuli Buntings, Rufous-sided and Green-tailed Towhees, Lincoln's, and Brewer's Sparrows, plus most western warblers and sometimes uncommon transients.

Return to the Y of Road 23 and Road 38E and continue around the south end of Horsetooth Reservoir. On the road to Masonville, there are several places to observe the following breeding species: White-throated Swift,

Broad-tailed Hummingbird, Three-toed Woodpecker (rare), Western Tanager and Indigo and Lazuli Buntings.

Pawnee National Grasslands area: From Ft. Collins, travel 18 mi. east on Colorado 14, crossing I-25 and arriving at the little agricultural town of Ault. Here, turn left (north) onto U.S. 85 and pass through the towns of Pierce and Nunn. Seven miles north of Nunn, you will see a large sign that says "Central Plains Experimental Range," with a dirt road leading off to the right (east). This is Road 114, a good way to begin your tour of the Pawnee Grasslands.

As you follow the route below, remember to park your car and get out often. Leisurely scan the many pastures and fields, for only by taking your time can you expect to find the many species of birds foraging in the stubble.

PAWNEE NATIONAL GRASSLANDS: Immediately upon turning into the Experimental Range, park your car and get out. Scan the field at the southeast corner of the intersection of Highway 85 and Road 114. In this mixture of grasses you should see both McCown's and Chestnut-collared Longspurs. Don't be afraid to walk out into the field itself.

Proceed along Road 114, stopping whenever you want to observe the birds. At about 2.5 mi. from Highway 85 you should come to some experimental pastures on the north side of the road. These are short-grass pastures that may contain Mccown's Longspur and Mountain Plover. Remember to look at skylarking birds, they may be either species of longspur. Mountain Plovers are difficult to see when they sit down motionless on the prairie. Scan the ground.

Proceed along Road 114 until it dead-ends at Road 45. Go left (north) on Road 45 for 2.5 to 3.5 mi. and watch the road on both sides for Mountain Plover and McCown's Longspur. (There's a good pasture just before the intersection with Road 122.)

When you come to Road 122, turn right (east). Look for raptors as you go along. Prairie Falcons and Ferruginous and Swainson's Hawks like the phone poles here. You can see the Chalk Bluffs to the north in the distance, where they nest.

Go along Road 122 for 5 mi. until you come to Road 55, where you'll turn right (south) and then left (east) onto Road 120, which will take you 11 mi. all the way to Road 77. Along the fences you could see Vesper, Lark, Brewer's and even Grasshopper Sparrows.

Turn right on Road 77, which leads you back south towards Briggsdale. To try another area of the grasslands, follow Road 77 for 12 mi. and then turn right (west) onto Road 96 (unmarked dirt road and a cattle guard). This is another good spot for McCown's Longspurs and Mountain Plovers. After about 3 mi. on this road, the grass gets longer, the preferred habitat of Chestnut-collared Longspur.

To return to Road 77, the main road back to Briggsdale, retrace your route on Road 96 back to Road 77. From here turn right (south) and go 2.8 mi.

towards Briggsdale, when you'll come to Crow Valley Park and Campground. This riparian oasis in the grasslands is a nice place to end your visit. To return to I-25, go west on Colorado 14 for 39 mi. from Briggsdale.

CROW VALLEY PARK AND CAMPGROUND: Once you have explored the open prairies and located the typical grassland species, you may wish to visit a riparian area on the Pawnee. Crow Valley Park and Campground near Briggsdale is a nice place for a picnic, and a good chance to see some Eastern bird species. Look through the willows and cottonwoods near the creek for Great Horned Owl, Yellow-billed Cuckoo, Red-headed Woodpecker, Northern Flicker, Blue Jay, Western Wood-Pewee, Eastern and Western Kingbirds, Barn Swallow, Black-billed Magpie, Northern Mockingbird, Northern "Bullock's" Oriole, Orchard Oriole, and House Finch.

Areas east of Sterling: If you are a Western birder, and want more of a look at Eastern bird species, continue east on Colorado 14 past Briggsdale to Sterling. The riparian streambeds and other bodies of water, such as the Julesberg Reservoir, are excellent birding.

RED LION WILDLIFE AREA, DUCK CREEK AREA NORTH OF CROOK: To explore further east, take Colorado 14 to Sterling and go north on U.S. 138 (or I-76) to Crook along the South Platte River. About 14 mi. east and west of the Crook road, between I-76 and U.S. 138 along the river, are two sites where the Colorado Division of Wildlife has established ponds for waterfowl breeding. The Red Lion Wildlife area (north of U.S. 138 about 8 mi. east of Crook), including Jumbo Reservoir, and the Duck Creek area (north of Crook) are both worth exploring.

COLORADO'S SHORT-GRASS PRAIRIE:
Birding where the buffalo roamed
Checklist of Common Birds by Habitat

LOWLAND STREAMSIDE
Great Blue Heron
Snowy Egret
Black-crowned Night-Heron
Canada Goose
Mallard
Northern Bobwhite
Ring-necked Pheasant
Spotted Sandpiper
Yellow-billed Cuckoo
Black-billed Cuckoo (rare)
Great Horned Owl
Belted Kingfisher
Red-headed Woodpecker
Northern Flicker
Western Wood-Pewee
Western Kingbird
Eastern Kingbird
Barn Swallow
Cliff Swallow
Northern Rough-winged Swallow
Blue Jay
Black-billed Magpie
Black-capped Chickadee
House Wren
American Robin
Northern Mockingbird
Brown Thrasher
Yellow Warbler
Common Yellowthroat
Red-winged Blackbird
Yellow-headed Blackbird
Orchard Oriole
Northern Oriole (Bullock's)

GRASSLANDS
Northern Harrier
Swainson's Hawk
Red-tailed Hawk
Ferruginous Hawk
Golden Eagle
American Kestrel
Prairie Falcon
Killdeer
Mountain Plover
Long-billed Curlew
Mourning Dove
Burrowing Owl
Common Nighthawk
Say's Phoebe
Horned Lark
Loggerhead Shrike
Chipping Sparrow
Brewer's Sparrow
Vesper Sparrow
Lark Sparrow
Lark Bunting
Grasshopper Sparrow
McCown's Longspur
Chestnut-collared Longspur
Western Meadowlark
Brewer's Blackbird
Common Grackle
Brown-headed Cowbird

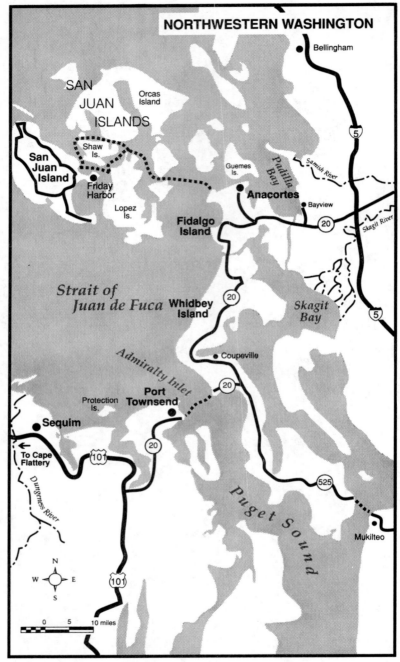

NORTHWESTERN WASHINGTON

San Juan Islands

Orcas Island

San Juan Island

Shaw Is.

Friday Harbor

Lopez Is.

Bellingham

5

Guemes Is.

Padilla Bay

Samish River

Anacortes

Bayview

20

Skagit River

Fidalgo Island

Strait of Juan de Fuca

Whidbey Island

20

Skagit Bay

5

Coupeville

20

Admiralty Inlet

Protection Is.

Port Townsend

Sequim

101

To Cape Flattery

Dungeness River

20

525

Puget Sound

Mukilteo

101

N
W   E
S

0   5   10 miles

▲   Campgrounds

🛆   Picnic Areas

👤   Park Hq and Visitor Centers

·········   Trails

—·—·—   Rivers

———   Boundaries

━━━   Highways and Freeways

———   Roads

- - - - -   Unimproved dirt roads

4

WASHINGTON'S ISLAND WORLD:

Masses of seabirds and waterfowl in the Pacific Northwest

Adventurous bird finding on Washington state's splendid protected waterways is one of the best-kept secrets of the birding world. Many birders have yet to discover the innumerable seabirds, waterfowl and shorebirds to be seen from Washington's "inland coasts." The shallow bays and narrow inlets afford shelter for quantities of waterbirds, and the rocky shorelines lure several desirable species of shorebirds. From September to May, a trip to the islands and rocky promontories north of Puget Sound should yield a plethora of bird species which thrive in the food-rich waters of the cool Pacific Northwest.

This birding tour commences with a visit to Whidbey Island north of Seattle. Here, in the deep coves, the flotillas of scoters, goldeneyes and other sea ducks come so close to shore you can see every detail of their exquisite plumage.

Continuing north, the route follows the coastlines of Whidbey and Fidalgo Islands, where all manner of waterbirds—particularly loons, grebes and cormorants—can be seen swimming offshore.

In the vicinity of Anacortes, visits to Fidalgo Bay, March Point and Padilla Bay offer migrating shorebirds in season and large flocks of wintering waterfowl, including over twenty species of ducks and one of the largest congregations of wintering Brant on the west coast.

Next, the scenic ferry ride through the San Juan Islands ushers you into an island world, where Bald Eagles perch grandly above the rocky coastlines, while oystercatchers and turnstones deftly pick their way along the shore. Everywhere, the views out over the straits produce sightings of loons, grebes, cormorants and many other birds, including alcids.

Watching for alcids—the murres, auklets and puffins—is a highlight of any birding visit to the Northwest. The next destination, Port Townsend, offers good views from shore of these fascinating seabirds as they swim and dive in the tidal rips of the Strait of Juan de Fuca.

The trip concludes at Dungeness, near Sequim, on the northern edge of the Olympic Peninsula. The bay at Dungeness offers further opportunities to look at huge flocks of migrating Brant, plus wintering ducks and geese. A spot near the Dungeness River estuary is one of Washington's foremost shorebird stop-offs.

Emphasis during this bird finding tour is on the waterbirds and waterfowl of western Washington, and the shorebirds found on its rocky shores. Although there are many good places to observe landbirds along the route, it is left up to you, the individual birder, to uncover them. For our purposes in this chapter, it is the birds inhabiting the waters of the Pacific Northwest that lure the first-time visitor.

Join me on a bird quest in Washington. The pristine shores and peaceful birding conditions, added to the hundreds of waterbirds you are sure to see, make this trip to the Northwest an outstanding one.

Washington's history has always been intimately tied to the sea. In April 1792, after English captain George Vancouver met American captain Robert Gray at the entrance to the Strait of Juan de Fuca, Vancouver proceeded through the strait to Puget Sound, while Gray went south to discover the mouth of the Columbia River. Gray's forays gave the U. S. a claim to the Oregon country, reinforced in 1805 with the Lewis and Clark expedition. The journals of William Clark (Clark's Nutcracker) and Meriwether Lewis (Lewis' Woodpecker) stirred early interest in the natural history of the Pacific Northwest.

Meanwhile to the north, Vancouver was searching for the Northwest Passage, a route which might link British commercial ventures on the Atlantic to a closer route to China. As he explored, Captain Vancouver named many familiar Northwest landmarks after his crew members. For example, Whidbey Island was named after Captain John Whidbey and Puget Sound after Peter Puget, Vancouver's lieutenant.

Until 1846, when the boundary was settled at the 49th parallel, Britain and the U.S. occupied the Pacific Northwest jointly. However, the treaty was vague about the ownership of the San Juan Islands, and in June, 1859, on San Juan Island, when a British pig raided an American potato patch and the farmer shot it, tempers flared on both sides. In fact, the two countries nearly went to war over the pig.

For 12 years afterwards, the Americans and Britishers maintained separate military camps on San Juan Island (both of which are excellent birding spots today). Eventually, the U.S./Canadian line was drawn through Haro Strait, and the San Juans officially became American territory.

The topography of western Washington, dominated by the giant marine estuary Puget Sound to the south and an assortment of islands and channels to the north, was created by glaciation thousands of years ago. Puget Sound is a typical glacial trough, lined with glacial deposits forming hundreds of miles of bays and coves. The San Juan Islands are examples of the exposed dome outcroppings left behind when the glacier retreated. Unlike the harder rock formations of the San Juan Islands, Puget Sound's softer materials weathered more easily, creating spectacular bluffs and cliffs along a shoreline of 1750 miles.

Two great mountain ranges embrace western Washington's waterways: the Olympic Mountains, crowding the Olympic Peninsula, and the Cascade Range, separating this part of the state from eastern Washington. The Cascades, looming icebound for much of the year, include Mount Baker at 10,788 feet, and Mount Rainier, 14,410 feet. Unsurpassed vistas of both the Olympic and Cascade ranges towering in the distance enhance the beautiful birding locations to be found in this region of Washington.

Climate and Habitats of Western Washington

Western Washington has a marine climate of comparatively mild, dry summers and cool, wet winters, with most of the precipitation falling between October and March. During this season, prevailing winds circle in from the southwest bearing storms from the Pacific Ocean. As they strike the western slopes of the Olympic Mountains, the air rises and cools, drenching the Olympic rainforests with the accumulated moisture.

But northeast of the Olympic range—in an area from Sequim and Port Townsend to Whidbey Island and the San Juan Islands—the climate is much drier, falling in the rain shadow of the Olympics. For example, the San Juan Islands average between 20-30 inches of rainfall annually, considerably less than that of the western Olympic Peninsula, and less than Seattle. Sometimes referred to as Washington's "banana belt," this section includes most of the birding spots covered in the chapter.

The wet winters and overcast summers encourage coastal forests of Douglas-fir, western hemlock, western redcedar and grand fir which cloak the islands and headlands. Bigleaf maples lend their broad green leaves to the associations of forest trees on moister sites, while Pacific madrone occurs as an understory tree in drier areas. Red alders and black cottonwoods line the streams.

Although space precludes detailed mention of the landbirds of western Washington, part of the delight of birding here comes from the juxtaposition of the forest birds—creepers, siskins and warblers—with the gulls and seabirds. A typical morning's walk leads you from the birds of the dense coniferous forests out onto the beaches and saltwater lagoons of the shore. The calls of the warblers echoing in the woods behind you are soon supplanted by the cries of the seabirds and the sounds of the ocean, a wonderful medley characteristic of birding in the Pacific Northwest.

Rocky Shoreline: Habitats for birds in a marine environment blend together much more so than those on land. Birds' great mobility allows them to wander from rocky coast to open ocean to inshore waters and back again. However, for convenience in this discussion, the bird species inhabiting the rocky shoreline are grouped in one section, those found swimming just off-shore in another, those nesting in seabird colonies in a third, and those frequenting the tidal mudflats in a fourth.

Walking along Washington's rocky shorelines, the vegetation catching your eye is apt to be some form of seaweed. Seaweeds are a kind of algae. Despite their large size, they are closely related to the microscopic planktonic plants that float freely throughout all ocean waters.

Seaweeds grow mostly in rocky intertidal or continental shelf areas. They need no roots, stems or leaves, because they gain nourishment from the ocean around them, just as the micros-copic algae do.

Seaweed communities or kelp beds are extremely productive: they serve as perches for seabirds, harbor abundant fishes and invertebrates on which seabirds and mammals feed, and, when washed ashore, are fed upon by sand fleas and kelp flies, tasty prey for shorebirds.

Along the rocky strand, one of the characteristic large seaweeds is the bull kelp or bull whip kelp. These plants can grow to 100 feet long in a single season, after which they are often destroyed by winter storms. You will probably notice the visible portion of the seaweed, an inflated, ball-like float four to six inches in diameter. The float supports a number of strap-like blades that trail in the water. The long, hollow "stem" of the seaweed is anchored to the rocks by a holdfast.

The rocky shoreline habitat attracts several species of shore-birds, to be sought here in the tide-washed crevices and barnacle-encrusted rocks of the San Juan Islands, Penn Cove on Whidbey Island, and other suitable locations.

The American Black Oystercatcher (not to be confused with the American Oystercatcher of the East and Gulf coasts) reigns as the resident specialist of the Pacific's rocky shores. Few other birds are as well-equipped to forage up and down the slippery rocks. Little structures on the oystercatcher's feet allow it to cling to wet surfaces. Its bright red bill and pink feet may be the only visible parts of the bird as it picks its way with dark brown body camouflaged against the dark, wet rocks.

Unlike other shorebirds which use their bills for mudflat probing, the oystercatcher's bill is strong and laterally compressed. Wielding it like an oyster knife, the oystercatcher uses its bill as a tool to deal with the hard-shelled mollusks and barnacles that cling tightly to the rocks. Prizing mollusks and chitons from their berths, the oystercatcher then inserts its bill into the animal, severing the muscle holding the shell together, and giving the oystercatcher a chance for a nourishing meal.

Of the shorebirds inhabiting Washington's rocky coasts, the American Black Oystercatcher is the only one to breed here. In spring, the harsh cries of oystercatcher pairs proclaim territorial squabbles, as they set up nesting sites on offshore islets or deserted reefs above the high tide line. Often, a mound of mollusk shells nearby is evidence of the oystercatchers' nesting area.

Besides oystercatchers, look for the "rockpipers"—Black Turnstones (and occasionally Ruddy Turnstones), Wandering Tattlers, Surfbirds, and Rock Sandpipers—all of which spend time on the rocky shores searching for prey at low tide, and rest on sheltered promontories at high tide. Although nesting far to the north, these species migrate through western Washington in spring and fall and some individuals stay throughout the winter.

One species of sea duck, the lovely Harlequin Duck, forages along the rocky coast at low tide, not by land but by sea. The Harlequin Duck feeds by swimming in the eddies and tidal rips that wash around the exposed rocks. Ignoring the sharp rocks and dangerous currents, the Harlequin dexterously nibbles at the tiny creatures stirred up by the swirling waters. The steel-blue and maroon nuptial plumage of the adult male shows up boldly in good light, looking as though he were decorated with white paper cut-outs. From a great distance, these white dots and crescents on the head and neck make identification easy. Even in dark eclipse plumage, the dainty silhouette and unique feeding behavior of this duck are diagnostic.

Harlequin Ducks nest far inland along swift streams in the

Cascades and northern Rockies, coming to the coast only to spend the winter, except for a few individuals which may linger over the summer.

Representative birding sites:
Whidbey Island: Penn Cove, Ft. Ebey State Park, Swantown.
San Juan Island: Cattle Point.
Port Townsend area: North Beach Park.

Inshore Waters: As you watch the huge flocks of seabirds and gulls that make their living along the Pacific coast, ponder the incredible productivity of the ocean waters that support them. Burgeoning with tiny marine plants, the ocean's rich vegetation enables numerous birds, fish and mammals to survive.

The microscopic algae, tremendously important as one of the primary food sources for life on earth, represent the first stage in the marine food chain. They are consumed by millions of equally tiny planktonic creatures, which in turn are fed upon by all sorts of invertebrates. The fishes feed upon the invertebrates, and the birds and mammals upon the fishes, so perpetuating the fine interdependence of all sea life.

Ninety-five percent of the sea's vegetation, therefore, is invisible, because it's mostly comprised of microscopic algae. Known as phytoplankton, these one-celled little plants conduct their own photosynthesis, utilizing water, carbon dioxide and sunlight as they float along. They are eaten directly or indirectly by everything that feeds in the sea. When nutrient-rich waters provide the right conditions, clouds of these minute algae burst into frantic fertility, resulting in a meal for the small, filter-feeding fishes, which in turn attract numbers of hungry seabirds.

Besides the algae, there's another group of marine plants—the submerged seagrasses, eelgrass, and surfgrasses—which occur along the edges of estuaries and shallow bays. Eelgrass is particularly vital as food for migrating waterfowl.

In shallow bays and estuaries of the more protected marine environments, such as Fidalgo and Padilla Bays in Washington, eelgrass, a seed-producing marine plant, grows in thick stands. Eelgrass occupies the lower parts of the flats, those that are covered by water most of the time. Its roots and stems serve to bind and stabilize the mud, and the blades are home to diatoms and small invertebrates.

In spring and summer, the long, greenish eelgrass grows fast, but by early fall the plants have flowered and the blades die back and decompose, providing nutrients for many other microorganisms to flourish. The microorganisms, a by-product of the dying eelgrass, are devoured by little fishes and bivalves.

Whether they graze on the eelgrass of shallow bays or sip the tiniest phytoplankton from the ocean, birds find the inshore waters of Washington bountiful. Bird species of the inshore waters can be divided into two groups—those that winter here or stop to rest and feed as they migrate through, and those that nest nearby in the seabird colonies (more about them later). The loons, grebes, most ducks and geese, most gulls, and some shorebirds exemplify the first group. Many of these birds have nested far inland on freshwater lakes and marshes, or to the north in Canada and Alaska, but they will spend their winters on the coast in sheltered bodies of saltwater.

In fall, as the birds move to the Pacific coast to follow the southward flow of migration, population numbers are greater than in spring—their ranks swelled by the juveniles accompanying them. Lured by the mild climate and plentiful food supplies in the shallow bays and lagoons, many species remain for the winter months. These huge wintering flocks attract unusual raptors—falcons and even owls—preying upon the odd, unwary waterbird that may have become separated from its companions.

In migration, many of the ducks, geese, shorebirds, gulls, and terns count on the eelgrass communities to fuel their southward flights, and often sustain them throughout the winter. The Brant, a small sea goose, is particularly dependent upon eelgrass, seeming to eat most parts of the plant. While the Brant flocks float on shallow bays, they feed on the eelgrass by snipping portions of the grass in a sideways movement, not unlike grazing.

Other ducks, such as Northern Pintails, feed on the seeds of the eelgrass, and still others munch on the tiny crustaceans clinging to the eelgrass stems. Shorebirds probe in the nearby mudflats to uncover tiny clams sheltering in the eelgrass beds.

Other birds make their livelihood on a variety of prey. Surf and White-winged Scoters dive to the bottom of bays like Penn Cove in search of mussels, clams, and small scallops. With their powerful bills, they swallow the whole animal, shell and all, utilizing what must be a truly enviable digestive system. Common and Barrow's Goldeneyes feed on mussels, plus clams and marine worms. Buffleheads dive for shrimp, and small fish in Fidalgo Bay. Other species of ducks, and of course the Brant, rely on the aquatic vegetation and algae found in Padilla Bay.

In spring, the wintering flocks in Washington are joined by other individuals of their species which may have spent the winter further south along the Pacific coast. Huge flocks of loons, grebes, sea ducks and waterfowl congregate in the shallow bays and lagoons. The spots where these birds gather to prepare for their northbound journeys are known as staging grounds. The staging grounds offer prime birding opportunities for observers from shore. Dressed in high breeding plumage, and calling to each other in a series of groans, grunts and whistles, the flocks tank up for the final leg of their journey to northern breeding destinations.

Representative birding sites:

Whidbey Island: Penn Cove, Ft. Ebey State Park, West Beach in Deception Pass State Park.

Anacortes and vicinity (Fidalgo Island): Rosario Beach, March Point, Washington Park.

Padilla/Samish Flats area: Bayview State Park.

San Juan Island: Ferry ride to Friday Harbor, Cattle Point, False Bay.

Dungeness area near Sequim: Dungeness Bay shoreline, Dungeness River estuary, Dungeness Recreation Area.

Seabird Colonies: Most seabirds remaining in Washington's inshore waters from May through August nest on the nearby islands and isolated rock stacks offshore. Double-crested and Pelagic Cormorants, Glaucous-winged Gulls, Pigeon Guillemots, Rhinoceros Auklets and Tufted Puffins nest there, often in huge colonies. These traditional nesting sites, protected by their remoteness from predators such as foxes and rats, are occupied year after year. However, human disturbance poses a constant threat, and only by observing seabird colonies from a boat can you leave the birds undisturbed on the ragged cliffs and grassy burrows where they nest.

Protection Island, a two mile long islet in the Strait of Juan de Fuca near Port Townsend, is famous as the nesting habitat for most of the alcids in the area. More than 60,000 birds call this island home, including 17,000 pairs of Rhinoceros Auklets—half the breeding population of the Rhinos in the contiguous forty-eight states. The Rhinos are joined by Pigeon Guillemots, Pelagic Cormorants, Tufted Puffins and Glaucous-winged Gulls, all of whom share the windswept island.

The tubby Rhinoceros Auklets, seen from shore in bullet-straight flight, webbed feet sticking out behind and wings going a mile a minute, are typical members of the alcid or auk family. Alcids are the Northern Hemisphere's counterpart to the penguin, sharing the same chunky body build, erect posture on land, and the method of "flying under water" by beating their wings rapidly while swimming beneath the surface. Penguins and alcids have short, fat wings, great for underwater swimming, but rather useless on land. Ornithologists speculate that some of the alcids are evolving towards flightlessness, like the penguins.

Seabirds that pursue fish underwater, like the alcids, have a unique plumage pattern—dark above and white below. The white is confined to the part of the bird below the waterline, and acts as a camouflage against marauding aquatic predators from below.

In the breeding season, both male and female alcids develop colorful plumes and bright bills. The Rhinoceros Auklet acquires a pale yellow horn at the base of the bill, together with two white plumes on either side of the head. The Tufted Puffin's bill, a bulbous red and yellow affair, can be spotted from great distances. A pair of pale yellow head plumes droop down its back, too.

Rhinoceros Auklets and Tufted Puffins lay their eggs in burrows tunneled deep into the grassy hillsides of offshore islands. During the day, and often into the night, the adults fly back and forth from their nesting islands to the feeding grounds, where they fish for sandlance and herring. The birds capture the fish with stiff tongues, pinning them to the roof of their mouth, so four or five fish can be delivered to the chicks in one foraging trip.

The three species of cormorants—the Double-crested, the Brandt's and the Pelagic—are well-represented in seabird colonies. The Brandt's prefers to nest close to the open ocean on the outer coast of Washington, but both the Double-crested and the Pelagic breed on islets off the San Juan Islands and on Protection Island. To alleviate competition for nesting sites, Double-crested Cormorants build their stick nests in cylindrical stacks on the flatter portions of the nesting islets, while Pelagic Cormorants pile a few pieces of seaweed on a ledge of one of the steeper cliff faces and call it home.

Cormorants swim and dive up to 100 feet to catch their prey, their dense bones and strong feet aiding their efforts. In *Birds of the Pacific Northwest,* Ira Gabrielson and Stanley Jewett describe watching a cormorant fishing: " From the float at the landing where he was sitting, little schools of a small anchovy type of fish appeared to be moving through the water much as swarms of gnats travel in the air. Locating one of these schools of fish by the broken surface of the water, the bird dove some distance away and came up through the swarm of fish, driving them to the surface. The fish in panicky confusion bolted to the surface making the water fairly boil with their struggles. The dark fisherman, darting up from below almost invariably succeeded in catching two or three fish before they scattered and regained the depths. The successful catcher crushed its prey in its bill, swallowed the fish head first, and then, locating another swarm repeated the performance. This was repeated until the bird could not eat another fish, when he hauled out on the rocks and spread himself out in the sunshine for his feathers to dry. During the performance, the wings were not used at all under the water, the motive power being supplied solely by the huge feet and legs."

Cormorants, unlike other seabirds, do not have feathers that are completely waterproof, and they hold their wings outstretched when resting on offshore rocks or buoys. Ornithologists used to explain spread-wing postures in cormorants as a deficiency in their preening glands, due to insufficient oil production. Recently, experiments have shown that cormorants and other members of their family hold their wings outstretched to re-arrange their feathers. Evidently, the extremely intricate construction of their feathers renders them almost waterproof, but they require a certain amount of "drying time" in between diving underwater for prey.

Fortunately for birders, most nesting cormorants, alcids and gulls can be seen from shore as they fly by, or discerned through a spotting scope as they swim and dive in the straits. To get closer views of the seabird colonies you will have to charter a boat or join a wildlife cruise (see Before You Visit).

Representative birding sites:
Whidbey Island: Ft. Casey State Park, Ft. Ebey State Park.
Port Townsend area: Ferry from Keystone to Port Townsend, Point Hudson, Fort Worden State Park, North Beach Park.

Tidal Mudflats: Thousands of migrant shorebirds use Washington's mudflats as resting and refueling stops in spring and fall. The principal mudflats in the region are created by river estuaries and by very shallow bays uncovered at low tide. Since a detailed description of the tidal mudflat habitats along the Pacific coast can be found in Chapter Eight, suffice it to say that shorebirding here will add numerous species to your list.

Representative birding sites:
Whidbey Island: Crockett's Lake.
Anacortes and vicinity: March Point.
Padilla Bay/Samish Flats area: Bayview State Park.
Dungeness area near Sequim: Dungeness River estuary.

Watching Seabirds

In birding Washington for seabirds, an awareness of two phenomena will make your search more productive: the importance of the tides and the significance of feeding frenzy behavior.

Since the greatest tidal ranges occur in areas where narrow straits have a funneling effect, the upper reaches of Puget Sound undergo extreme tidal fluctuations. Usually, there are two high tides of unequal height and two low tides of unequal height every day. Sometimes these tidal waters cause currents that can reach speeds of a few miles per hour. As the tide rises, the water flows toward shore as a flood tide, moving into shallow coastal marshes and up streams. During ebb tide, the water moves out, exposing low-lying areas.

Twice daily, the exchange of the nutrient-rich Pacific waters in and out of Puget Sound via the Strait of Juan de Fuca creates dramatic tide differences. A dry mudflat becomes a shallow bay within a few hours. An empty channel transforms itself into a rushing torrent from mid-morning to mid-afternoon. Therefore, you must know roughly what the tide schedules are in order to maximize the birding at your targeted spots. Tide tables are available in the daily newspapers, which list the high and low tides at several locations throughout western Washington.

The best time to bird most areas, from the deepest straits to the shallowest mudflats, is at mid-tide. That is, neither at high tide or at low tide, but somewhere in between. Often, a couple of hours toward the first low tide of the day is best, especially for viewing shorebirds as they feed on mudflats. (When the tide gets too far out, you may not be able to see the birds, they are so far away.)

While watching seabirds in the Strait of Juan de Fuca or Rosario Strait or Haro Strait, look for the disturbance in the water's surface marking the tidal rips and surges so sought after by these birds. Often, the birds will ride along on one of the swift-moving currents, feeding as they go, then get up and fly back to the start of the current and float down once again. Mid-tide is most productive, as the water pulses in and out daily through the narrow waterways, stirring up potential prey.

During your birding in any of the major straits, you may suddenly observe feeding frenzy behavior—when several species of seabirds are attracted to a particular area of the ocean by the schooling fishes in the water below.

Gulls of four or five species may spot the fish first. Diving and squealing they throw themselves into the fray. Landing on the water, they bob and grab at the small fishes. Slurping and wrestling with the food, other gulls join the mob by plunge-diving at the surface of the water time after time.

Soon, they are joined by loons, grebes, cormorants and alcids, which follow the converging gulls in pursuit of the rich windfall. Pigeon Guillemots stick to the edge of the commotion, snatching at left-overs, but the Rhinoceros Auklets come charging in and actually follow the gulls into the middle of the scuffle, going underwater repeatedly to gain their share of the maritime bounty.

The long-necked cormorants, heads held erect like models of dignity in the midst of all the confusion, dive sedately when they can find an opening.

The surface of the water churns with fish, and the birds are dipping, plunging and diving. Sometimes the herring or mackerel jump into the air in a series of leaps, often in an attempt to escape the jaws of larger fish chasing them from below. Once in the air, the smaller fish are eagerly seized by waiting gulls, terns and jaegers.

Feeding frenzy behavior must be visible to seabirds at great distances, and the resultant flocking can include as many as 500 birds. Doubtless an adaptation for communicating food sources amongst each other, the variety of birds and the plunging and pirating is something to behold.

A birder watching from shore cannot fail to get caught up in the excitement of this spectacle, and the chance of spotting numerous birds, including some uncommon species, is a very real one.

A last word about watching waterbirds in Washington: try to obtain a spotting scope before you go. Even though many species can be seen just offshore, positive identification is often difficult or impossible without the extra magnification provided by a scope.

Also, make use of the cliffs and bluffs of the promontories for viewing out into the straits and channels. Whether you have binoculars or a spotting scope, sighting birds offshore becomes much easier if you take up a position well above the waterline at convenient overlooks. By looking down on the birds in the water, you can avoid heat haze distortion, and at the same time see farther out into the straits. Besides, birds flying by will be at eye-level.

The Marbled Murrelet: A Birding Close-Up

"... there are those who enjoy the conflict of the storm even more than [I do]. Above the whining of the waters and the crashing of the prow, come shrill exultant cries, *meer-meer, meer-meer.* The murrelets are in their element, and they shriek to each other across the dancing waters like Tritons at play. Perhaps association will partly account for it, but somehow the note of the Marbled Murrelet seems of itself to suggest piping gales and rugged cliffs beset by pounding surf. It is the articulate cry of the sea in a royal mood. And not a thousand murrelet voices are required to transport the hearer to Alaska forthwith." (W. L. Dawson, *The Birds of California).*

This passage from Dawson introduces one of the smallest members of the alcid family, and one that has been the subject of a true birding enigma—the Marbled Murrelet. This murrelet, *Brachyramphus marmoratus,* (from the Greek *brachys,* meaning short, and *ramphus,* bill; and the Latin *marmoratus* meaning marbled) is a nine-inch stocky seabird with a short neck and a slender bill. You can observe murrelets floating about, often in pairs, diving and fishing just offshore.

In winter, Marbled Murrelets look like typical alcids—generally black and white, but in spring they change to a mottled brown-and-white coat, presumably as camouflage on their nesting grounds. Their breeding range follows that of the coniferous forests up and down the Pacific coast, from central California to Alaska, and therein lies a clue to their mysterious nesting habits.

As recently as 1974, ornithologists in North America had never found a Marbled Murrelet nest. While other members of the alcid group were known to nest in burrows or on rock crevices on offshore islands, Marbled Murrelet nests were never seen among them.

Then, on August 7, 1974, a tree trimmer in Santa Cruz County, on the central California coast, accidentally shook a murrelet chick from its nest 140 feet up in a 200 foot tall Douglas-fir! The tree was in a virgin stand of firs and coast redwoods, and the nest was later described in a scientific report as "little more than a depression or 'bowl' in the bark of a limb and rimmed with moss. It smelled of fish."

Could it be that this tiny seabird, which spends its whole life on the open ocean, comes ashore to nest high in old-growth firs and hemlocks?

Since then, there have been unconfirmed reports of further murrelet nesting sites—all in forests along the coasts of Washington, Oregon and California. (Unknown to Americans at the time of the discovery of the California nest, a Marbled Murrelet tree nest had been found in Siberia in 1963, a similar distance from the sea and in a larch.)

There have, in fact, been clues all along as to the breeding habits of this plump seabird. In the 1920s and 30s, W.L. Dawson in California and Ira Gabrielson and Stanley Jewett in Washington and Oregon, described taking early morning walks in the Coast Ranges, when the sound of whirring wings and the shrill *meer-meer-meer* cries of the Marbled Murrelets rang out through the treetops, but actual nests were never discovered.

Biologists have pieced together what they know, or assume, about the murrelets' secret family life. Oregon biologist David B. Marshall wrote that in the spring and early summer, pairs establish nests and lay a single egg, incubating it for 25 days. Parents take turns on the egg, possibly taking 24-hour shifts, trading places every evening. After the chick hatches, its parents bring it fish to eat, probably only in the morning and at night.

Twenty-eight days after hatching, the chick is ready for its maiden flight to the sea. Launching itself from a high perch, maybe in an old-growth redwood or fir, the young murrelet must find its way to feeding grounds it has never seen—the waters of the Pacific. With short wings beating away and uttering its strange cry, it forsakes the dark forest to live a boisterous life of bobbing and diving in the ocean currents.

Although Marbled Murrelets' nesting has never been confirmed in Washington, a nest was found in nearby British Columbia, and birds with brood patches have been collected off the San Juan Islands. Due to the increased destruction of old-growth trees, biologists and federal agencies are mounting an intensive search for evidence of Marbled Murrelet nests. Recently, the National Audubon Society in conjunction with many other groups, petitioned the U.S. Fish and Wildlife Service to list the Marbled Murrelet as a threatened species in Washington, Oregon and California

If you wish to find Marbled Murrelets, listen for their cries heading inland in the evening or out to sea in the early morning as you bird the dense forests near the coast of western Whidbey Island and San Juan Island. Failing that, murrelets are easily observed floating offshore, particularly in spring and summer. They appear as pudgy, brown-and-white blobs through the binoculars, hardly the sort of bird that could successfully baffle ornithologists for so many years.

NOTES FROM A BIRDER'S DIARY
Western Washington

● May 3, 1988, 4:00 P.M., Whidbey Island: I am sitting on a dock overlooking Penn Cove, contemplating arrival at last in this land of lagoons and inlets, embayments and rocky cliffs and water everywhere. The gray storm clouds pile in the sky after a spring cold front, and the gray is mirrored in the water.

The dark forests—the famous forests of the Pacific coast—shoulder their way to the water's edge, a mix of green shades from darkest fir to brightest maple. Across on the mainland, Mt. Baker and the North Cascades lie completely covered in heavy, fresh snow, their summits cloud-swirled and threatening.

Perhaps I'll grow accustomed to the Bald Eagles circling over the island and perching on the dead snags of Douglas-firs, but it hasn't happened yet. The brown bulky shapes of the huge immature birds appear almost larger than the adult birds, but the adults' dress of white-feathered head and tail commands immediate respect. Whatever their plumage, these magnificent eagles impress a newcomer. I want to stand and shout and show them to someone, but to native Washingtonians, Bald Eagles are nothing out of the ordinary.

The chilly, deep cove lying before me is crammed with loons, grebes and all sorts of sea ducks. Rafts and rafts of White-winged Scoters and Surf Scoters. I have never seen so many White-winged Scoters in one place in my life.

Their plump, black bodies ride the cold northern waters and they look very well-fed. The burgeoning marine life beneath them—the mussels clinging to the rocks and pilings—provide sumptuous meals. Although a commercial mussel venture prospers across the cove, I'll bet it's no match for the hungry scoters. Later, the owner himself tells me so in no uncertain terms.

The flotillas of White-winged Scoters shine black and white and red against the smooth surface of the cove. The males' plumage shows a sloping, feathered forehead coming down to a bright red bill, matched by bright red webbed feet. The fillip of white tear-drop around his eye is in collusion with the white wing patch to make the somber scoter very smart for spring.

Once in awhile, my scope picks up a pair of Black Scoters, a welcome surprise. The orange nubby bill of the Black Scoter is so distinctive, and the head shape is really small and round compared to the other scoters.

The breeding plumage of the familiar seabirds, seen at home in winter drab, is gorgeous to behold in fresh spring molt! The deep green highlights of the Common Loon, black dagger-like bill, tremulo calling, waiting and soon to take off for inland lakes. The outrageously garbed Horned Grebe! Who could have foreseen the orange-poufed hair-do and russet neck and breast, orange eye gleaming in nuptial accoutrements? Outstanding! The plainer appearance of the Red-necked Grebe can't compare, although he looks just fine.

The huge flocks of scoters, and the Western and Red-necked Grebes, talk to themselves as they rest on Penn Cove. Their squeals and grunts, whistles and groans, recall their primordial mission—to fly north to breed. (By the time I was to leave Washington, the far-off calling of the seabirds to each other as they prepared for migration north distilled the essence of birding in the Northwest.)

The tide ebbs slowly, lapping gently at the dock, swirling and draining from the edges of the cove. Without surf and the noisy waves, the constant movement of the tides mark the rhythm here. The water moves quietly in and out, and the birds feed and rest in tune with the tides.

Noticing a small, rocky spit a few hundred yards down the shore, I grab the scope and walk up as close as possible, still a good distance away. I recognize a group of about twenty Black Turnstones, accompanied by five or six Surfbirds, picking tidbits off the freshly exposed rocks. The Surfbirds' copper-colored scapular feathers glisten, as they walk daintily and competently over the barnacle-covered rocks on yellow-green legs.

The Black Turnstones fly up in unison—a blur of black and white—when the rock they feed upon becomes momentarily submerged by a little wave.

But a smaller sandpiper is the one that intrigues me, blending as it does amongst the flock of searching turnstones and Surfbirds. Is it my imagination, or has one of the Surfbirds shrunk? If so, it has also grown a longer bill, and somehow acquired a black smudge across the breast.

My heart begins to pound.

Why is it that we who struggle to learn the birds are so startled when what we suspect might be found turns up?

A Rock Sandpiper. I'd seen only one before, in pure gray winter coat, its head hidden completely under its wing, resting on a surf-washed cliff in central California. What a contrast this bird presents! For one thing, it's in breeding plumage, with a black lower-breast patch and chestnut highlights on its crown and back.

It's also rather uncommon; even in its preferred habitat on Washington's rocky shoreline, the Rock Sandpiper is easy to miss.

Far from its Arctic nesting grounds, this individual bird may have lingered all winter in Penn Cove, but surely now it's headed north.

Silently, I bid the Rock Sandpiper bon voyage.

TRAVELERS' TIPS

Before You Visit: A pamphlet entitled "Destination Washington" available from the Washington State Tourism Development Division tells all about Washington's ferry system, the National Forest Service, private parks/resorts, RV parks, campgrounds, etc. Write to the Washington State Tourism Development Division, 101 General Administration Building, Olympia, WA. 98504-0613 or call toll-free 1-800-544-1800.

The Washington State Department of Transportation, Transportation Building KF-01, Olympia, WA. 98504-5201, publishes an official state highway map.

For state ferry schedules write Washington State Department of Transportation, Marine Division, Washington State Ferries, Colman Dock, Seattle, WA. 98104 or call toll-free 1-800-542-7052. When using the ferry system, remember to schedule your arrival at the ferry dock in advance of departure time; sometimes weekends and holidays are crowded.

For recreation information write State Parks and Recreation Commission, 7150 Clearwater Ln., Olympia, WA. 98504.

Most of the recognized seabird colonies on Washington's offshore islands (notably Protection Island and some of the San Juan Islands) are under the protection of the U. S. Fish and Wildlife Service as National Wildlife Refuges. As such, they are closed to the public unless you receive specific permission for scientific research. For further information write to Fish and Wildlife Service, Nisqually National Wildlife Refuge, 100 Brown Farm Rd., Olympia, WA. 98506.

A portion of Protection Island, the Zella Schultz Seabird Sanctuary, is administered by the Department of Game, 600 North Capitol Way, Olympia, WA. 98504, which may still organize tours to this section of the island. Visits during the nesting season from May to August are discouraged.

For information on chartering a boat for a wildlife cruise in the San Juan Islands area, contact Western Prince Cruises, P. O.

Box 418, Friday Harbor, WA. 98250, (206) 378-5315, or Mark Lewis, P. O. Box 2424, Friday Harbor, WA. 98250, (206) 378-5767. In the Port Townsend/Protection Island area, contact Calm Sea Charters, Point Hudson Marina, P. O. Box 930, Port Townsend, WA. 98368, (206) 385-5288. To avoid disturbing the seabirds, circling refuge islands by boat should be restricted to no less than 200 yards offshore.

The Seattle Audubon Society organizes pelagic birding trips, as well as boat trips in inside waters. Write Seattle Audubon Society, 619 Joshua Green Building, Seattle, WA. 98101, (206) 622-6695.

Flora & Fauna Books, a famous natural history bookstore, stocks a wealth of new and used books about the Pacific Northwest and elsewhere. Be sure to visit them at 121 First Avenue South, Seattle, WA. 98104, (206) 623-4727.

The Seattle Audubon Society's statewide Rare Bird Alert number is (206) 526-8266.

When To Visit: From late August through mid-May, a visit to Washington's inland waterways to view numbers of seabirds, waterfowl and shorebirds is immensely rewarding. A trip timed to coincide with the fall and spring movements of these species adds even more of a variety to the already-high totals of wintering birds.

Western Washington's relatively mild winters mean ideal conditions for observing wintering seabirds and waterfowl, but be prepared for rainy or overcast days and bring snug, waterproof clothing. From late August through October, and from late March through mid-May, migrant waterfowl, waterbirds, and shorebirds add to the excitement. The best time to see the breeding alcids—Common Murres, Pigeon Guillemots, Marbled Murrelets, Tufted Puffins and Rhinoceros Auklets—is May through August.

A visit in late April and early May aims at combining three of the birding aspects mentioned above: 1) some wintering waterbirds are still present, 2) migrant seabirds and shorebirds are moving through, and 3) the colonial nesters on off-shore rocks (cormorants, gulls, and alcids) are visible swimming close to shore. The joy of seeing many species in breeding plumage at this season is offset by the fact that some of the exciting wintering birds, e.g., swans, some ducks, many raptors, have already departed for northern breeding grounds.

On the other hand, a trip in September or October would boast greater numbers of individual birds, plus a chance at unusual migrants, as the throngs of waterbirds, waterfowl, and shorebirds make their way south through the state after successful breeding in Canada and Alaska, some to winter in Washington and others pausing on their way. Pelagic trips along the outer coast are best at this time.

Length of Visit: Any of the destinations in western Washington on this trip can be reached from Seattle in less than a day. Each birding area stands on its own, a sample of Washington's rich bird life. For example, San Juan Island, would make a nice weekend birding visit from Seattle, as would any of the other birding sites.

However, if you wish to string these birding spots together in an organized pattern, allow at least a week. A sample timetable for the trip outlined below might be as follows: Two nights on Whidbey Island, one in Anacortes, two on San Juan Island and two in Port Townsend.

THE BIRDING SITES

Whidbey Island: Take I-5 north of Seattle; at Exit 189 turn left (west) on Washington 526, following the signs to the Mukilteo Ferry. After 4.2 mi. turn right (north) on Washington 525, and go 1.5 mi. to the Mukilteo Ferry (toll) terminal. Approximate crossing time to Whidbey Is. is 30 minutes.

Washington 525, which becomes Washington 20, runs the length of Whidbey Is., and the following locations can be reached from it. Note: If you plan to take the Port Townsend-Keystone Ferry later in your trip, as I did, you may wish to postpone visiting Fort Casey and Crockett's Lake until you return to take the ferry.

CROCKETT'S LAKE: Twenty-three miles north of Columbia Beach, Whidbey Island, take Washington 20 to your left (west) and go 3 mi. to this large, shallow lake. Park along Washington 20 and walk out as far as you can to the edge of the mudflats. Depending upon the water level and the season,

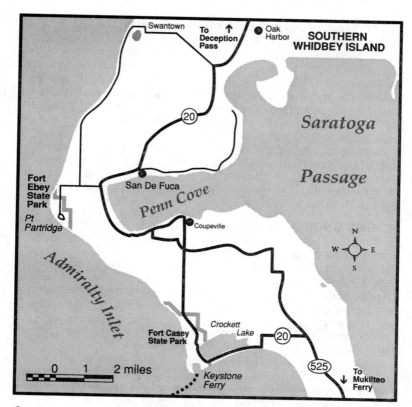

Crockett Lake can be excellent for shorebirds in migration, and waterfowl and raptors in winter. In fall and spring, thousands of Western and Least Sandpipers and Dunlins use it as a stop-over.

FT. CASEY STATE PARK: On the bluff to the west of Crockett's Lake and the Keystone Ferry terminal, Ft. Casey State Park overlooks the Admiralty Inlet. Walk to the edge of the bluffs and scan out over the water for seabirds. The park has nice picnic grounds and an interesting lighthouse.

Ft. Casey State Park and Ft. Ebey State Park, together with the little town of Coupeville, are part of Ebey's Landing National Historical Reserve area. (For an information/orientation exhibit, see the west end of Front St. in Coupeville near the wharf.)

To reach Coupeville from Ft. Casey State Park, take Engle Rd. north 4 mi.

PENN COVE: Follow the sign to Coupeville, north of Washington 20 and proceed straight ahead to the waterfront at Front St., which borders Penn Cove. Park at the base of the pier and scan the south shore of Penn Cove.

The cove is famous for its rocky shorebird habitat (best at low tide), easily viewed from the road. Species to look for are Wandering Tattler, Ruddy and Black Turnstones, Surfbirds, and maybe Rock Sandpiper.

Out in the water, expect to find numbers of Common Loon, Horned, Red-necked, Eared (winter only) and Western Grebes, and a variety of ducks including Greater and Lesser Scaups, Oldsquaw, Black (uncommon), Surf and White-winged Scoters, Common and Barrow's Goldeneyes, and Bufflehead.

To resume your tour around Penn Cove, in Coupeville take Alexander Rd. south from the base of the pier for one block, then turn right on Coveland. At the "Y," bear to your left on Madrona Way, which follows the shore of the cove. Stop at vantage points (respect private property) and scan the bay.

Madrona Way intersects Washington 20 at the west end of Penn Cove. To visit Ft. Ebey State Park, turn left (south) at this junction. To bird the northern shore of Penn Cove, turn right (north) on Washington 20 and proceed to the "Y" at San de Fuca, where you take Penn Cove Road to the right, leaving the highway. Scan the flocks in the cove from Penn Cove Road.

FT. EBEY STATE PARK: This park is reached by taking Libbey Rd. off Washington 20 (just south of the junction where Madrona Way intersects the highway). After a mile on Libbey Rd., turn left (south) to Ft. Ebey State Park. By following the trails along the steep bluffs, with wonderful views across the Strait of Juan de Fuca to the Olympic range, you have an excellent look-out for birds. Many seabirds preferring the open ocean, such as Horned and Red-necked Grebes, Pelagic Cormorant, Harlequin Duck, Pigeon Guillemot, and many gulls can be spied. In spring and summer, look for Rhinoceros Auklets and Marbled Murrelets. Black Oystercatchers frequent the rocky beaches. Bald Eagles soar overhead.

In the woods here, and at other locations on Whidbey Island, look for, among others, California Quail, Rufous Hummingbird, Belted Kingfisher, Western Flycatcher, Violet-green and Northern Rough-winged Swallows, Steller's Jay, Northwestern Crow, Chestnut-backed Chickadee, Bushtit, Red-breasted Nuthatch, Brown Creeper, Golden-crowned Kinglet, Golden-crowned Sparrow (winter), White-crowned Sparrow, Purple Finch, Pine Siskin and American Goldfinch.

SWANTOWN: Swantown is another vantage point, north of Ft. Ebey State Park on the coast. To reach this area, take Washington 20 north of Coupeville 6 mi. to Swantown Rd. Turn left (west) and follow Swantown Rd. until it dead-ends into West Beach Rd. Turn left and proceed to Sunset Beach, just south of a group of resort houses. As with Ft. Ebey State Park, scan for loons, grebes, sea ducks and alcids here and from the bluffs to the south. A marshy area east of the road may be good for ducks and shorebirds, depending upon water level.

WEST BEACH, DECEPTION PASS STATE PARK: Follow Washington 20 north through the town of Oak Harbor. Approximately 10 mi. from Oak Harbor and .5 mi. before Deception Pass Bridge, take the left turn (west) to West Beach, located in Deception Pass State Park. On your left, the road passes by Cranberry Lake, good for wintering waterfowl such as Ring-necked Duck, Common Goldeneye, and Hooded and Common Mergansers.

At the end of the road, park in the lot. Hiking to your right (north) provides a view of the tidal surges in the narrow channel, spanned by Deception Pass bridge. Both here and at Rosario Beach, look for seabirds feeding in the channel and cormorants and gulls resting on the rocks. When feeding conditions are good, look for Red-throated and Pacific Loons, Brandt's and Pelagic Cormorants, Harlequin Duck, Common Murre, Pigeon Guillemot and Marbled Murrelet. Migrating Common Terns and Parasitic Jaegers are a possibility in fall.

Anacortes and vicinity (Fidalgo Island): This island contains a number of good birding spots, many of them at the north end near Anacortes, the jumping-off point for touring the San Juan Islands to the west. The island also connects to the mainland (east) and the Samish Flats area.

ROSARIO BEACH: After crossing over Deception Pass on the bridge, .8 mi. from the West Beach turnoff, go left (west) following the sign to Rosario Beach in Deception Pass State Park. Once in the Park, the road to the beach leads steeply down to the left. Go to the end of the road and park. Walk

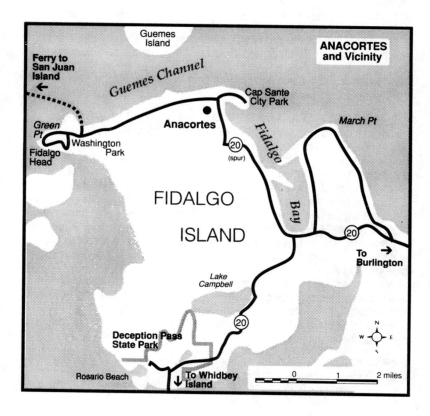

across a grassy area, where trails lead around the cliffs. From here you can look out over Rosario Strait to the west and Deception Pass to the south, scanning for waterbirds.

MARCH POINT: Follow Washington 20 for 5.2 mi. to a "T" junction. A spur of Washington 20 leads to Anacortes on your left. However, to reach March Point, turn right on Washington 20 for .5 mi., then make a left at the sign to March Point.

Immediately after turning left, park the car and scan the expanse of Fidalgo Bay. At mid-tide, the mudflats here host thousands of migrating Western and Least Sandpipers, and Dunlins. These and other shorebirds—Semipalmated Plover, Greater Yellowlegs, and Short-billed and Long-billed Dowitchers—may be seen in spring and fall. In winter and during migration, Merlins and Peregrine Falcons are attracted by the numbers of ducks and shorebirds. Transient landbirds sometimes hide in the shrubbery along the road.

Proceed around the tip of the Point to the oil refineries, stopping wherever the birding looks interesting. To the north and east of March Point, Padilla Bay shelters huge numbers of wintering and transient Brant. Other birds mixed in with the Brant are Red-throated and Common Loons, Horned, Red-necked and Western Grebes, Greater Scaup, Surf and White-winged Scoters, Common Goldeneye, Bufflehead and Red-breasted Merganser, to name a few.

Leaving March Point, cross the railroad tracks, turn left, and after I mi. rejoin Washington 20. Before getting on the highway, park and bird the mudflats here. Turn left on Washington 20 to go to the eastern shore of Padilla Bay and the Samish Flats. Turn right to bird the Anacortes area and the rest of Fidalgo Island.

WASHINGTON PARK, ANACORTES: Take the spur of Washington 20, leading to downtown Anacortes. Follow the signs to the San Juan Ferry, which take you north through town on Commercial Ave. to 12th St. Turn left (west) on 12th St., which becomes Oakes. At the top of the hill, instead of descending to the ferry terminal, keep straight ahead on Sunset Ave., which dead-ends into beautiful Washington Park.

Washington Park features a one-way Loop Rd. circling Green Point and Fidalgo Head. Hiking trails lead to Green Point, where very steep, grassy bluffs overlook Rosario Strait to the west. In spring, a riot of delicate wildflowers cover the bluffs: great camas (tall, blue), poison-camas (white), yarrow (white), western buttercup, spring gold (yellow), sea blush (pink), and blue-eyed Mary.

With the aid of a scope, huge flocks of loons, grebes, cormorants and alcids can be seen feeding in the tide rips in the strait, or flying back and forth to forage in Padilla and Fidalgo Bays.

Views of the San Juan Islands across Rosario Strait in the distance complete the scene.

CAP SANTE, ANACORTES: Another small city park with a marvelous view, Cap Sante is reached by following Commercial Ave. north to 4th St. Turn right (east) on 4th St., and right again on "W" Ave. and drive up the hill to the park at the top. From here, you overlook the eastern end of the Guemes Channel and Fidalgo and Padilla Bays; the Cascades are in the distance. Various wintering waterfowl may be spied, and watch for migrant landbirds in spring and fall.

Padilla Bay/Samish Flats area: From March Point, travel east on Washington 20 toward I-5, crossing the Swinomish boat channel. Turn left (north) at the sign to Bayview State Park. The Padilla Bay shoreline, and the agricultural fields and sloughs along the Bayview-Edison Rd. here, are famous winter habitat for wintering raptors. Peregrine Falcons, and, in certain "invasion" years, Gyrfalcons and Snowy Owls, have been found here. Flocks of Snow Geese and Tundra Swans winter here, too.

BAYVIEW STATE PARK: After 4 mi. on the Bayview-Edison Rd., turn right (east) into Bayview State Park. Make an immediate left and cross under the road to come out at the beach section of the park. In winter and spring, the Brant flocks are easily visible, and huge numbers of other waterfowl can be seen foraging in Padilla Bay. Concentrations of American Wigeons often contain Eurasian Wigeons (winter), and Dunlins and Black-bellied Plovers feed at low tide. Bald Eagles perch along the shoreline.

The Breazeale-Padilla Bay Interpretive Center (.2 mi. north of Bayview State Park), has excellent exhibits and information about the Padilla Bay National Estuarine Reserve area located here.

San Juan Island: All the islands in the San Juan group possess interesting birding spots. Also, the ferry trips provide an opportunity to search for waterbirds. Due to space limitations, only the largest island—San Juan Island—is included here with detailed birding directions (for information on other islands, consult *Birding in the San Juan Islands* by Lewis and Sharpe). The trip begins at the ferry terminal in Anacortes.

FERRY RIDE FROM ANACORTES TO FRIDAY HARBOR, SAN JUAN ISLAND: The ferry ride (toll) takes approximately 2 hours. The route first crosses Rosario Strait, where such species as Pacific Loon, all three of the cormorants, Common Murre, and Rhinoceros Auklet feed. In fall and winter, Parasitic Jaegers, Heermann's Gulls and Common Terns may be seen. At Pointer Island, on the western side of the strait before entering the San Juan archipelago, look to the right for a colony of nesting Glaucous-winged Gulls (spring, summer).

After traveling through Thatcher Pass and proceeding the length of Harney Channel, look on your left for tiny Flower Island, another Glaucous-winged Gull nesting colony. When the ferry stops at Orcas, Lopez or Shaw Islands, look for sea ducks diving for food near the docks, and gulls hovering overhead.

Once in the San Juan Channel, you'll notice an increase in bird activity, as the ferry plies the rich waters here, which attract loons, grebes, cormorants and alcids at all seasons.

Throughout the voyage, be on the lookout for Bald Eagles perched in conifers along the shores of the islands.

FRIDAY HARBOR AND CATTLE POINT, SAN JUAN ISLAND: The best area for birding lovely San Juan Island lies on its south end. However, before you leave the town of Friday Harbor, bird the harbor area, particularly in winter, when various gulls and other seabirds may seek shelter from the storms.

To reach Cattle Point from Friday Harbor, follow the signs from the ferry dock to Spring St., turn left (west) on Spring St. for 2 blocks, then turn left on Argyle St. which becomes Cattle Point Rd. After about 6 mi. you'll come to the American Camp section of San Juan Island National Historical Park, the monument marking the site of Pickett's encampment during the Pig War. Cattle Point Rd. diverges to the left, but you proceed to the right through the historic park, stopping to visit the park headquarters and read the markers if you wish.

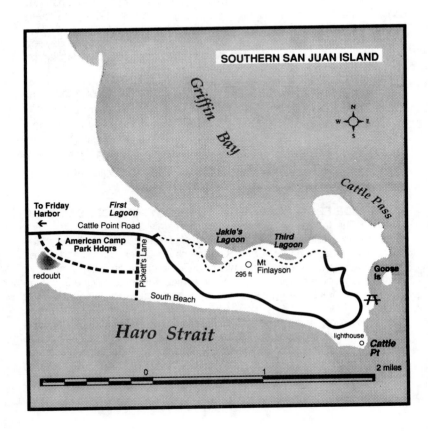

Driving on, scan the downhill slope of grassland to your right (south). This area, from the soldiers' redoubt (encampment) to Pickett's Lane, is the only place in the contiguous U. S. to see breeding Eurasian Skylarks. The introduced population in Vancouver, British Columbia, has colonized here, making it a goal for birders. The best way to locate the skylarks is by listening for their memorable flight song, a lengthy warble given while fluttering high in the sky.

When you come to Pickett's Lane, turn left to continue the tour on Cattle Point Rd., or right to visit South Beach.

Rejoining Cattle Point Rd., turn right and, shortly, left into a small parking lot overlooking First Lagoon and Griffin Bay. By scoping Griffin Bay, you can observe the abundant loons, grebes, bay and sea ducks, gulls and alcids. From the parking lot, Jakle's Farm Nature Trail (pamphlet available) makes a mile loop through the conifer forest. Jakle's Lagoon, reached by walking east either via the nature trail or along the beach, hosts breeding Hooded Mergansers.

Back on Cattle Point Rd. turn left (east) and drive along the steep shoulder of Mt. Finlayson. The grassy bluffs fall off sharply, and pull-outs along the road afford good views of the bird activity teaming in the ocean far below, the Strait of Juan de Fuca. In mid-channel, with the aid of a scope, you can spot such species as Red-throated and Pacific Loons, Horned, Red-necked, and Western Grebes, Pelagic Cormorant, Surf and White-winged Scoters, Red-breasted Merganser, and many more. In late summer and early fall, the large concentrations of birds may produce rarities.

Golden Eagles have bred on Mt. Finlayson, but Bald Eagles are more common at any season.

Follow Cattle Point Rd. to the Cattle Point Picnic Area and the Cattle Point Lighthouse Reservation at the southern tip of the island. Views from this promontory feature Cattle Pass, a narrow stretch of San Juan Channel, and the rocky shoreline may produce Harlequin Ducks, Black Oystercatchers and Black Turnstones, along with views of Goose Island, a Glaucous-winged Gull nesting site in spring.

The clump of willows between the lighthouse and the picnic area is good for landbird migrants. In winter, the grassy fields in the Cattle Point area may yield Horned Larks, Water Pipits, Lapland Longspurs, Snow Buntings and Western Meadowlarks, plus raptors such as Northern Harrier, Rough-legged and Red-tailed Hawks, Short-eared Owl and Northern Shrike.

FALSE BAY: The other outstanding birding spot on the south end of the island, False Bay, is reached by retracing your route on Cattle Point Rd. back to the American Camp area and proceeding north. After a mile, the first road (gravel) to your left (west) is False Bay Rd. (may be no sign). Follow the road 3.5 mi. to False Bay. Anywhere along False Bay Rd. in the woods and shrubbery, unusual migrants may be uncovered in spring and fall.

At False Bay, park and scan the shallow bay, which, particularly at mid-tide, is excellent for shorebirds and gulls. A sampling might include: Black-bellied Plover, Semipalmated Plover, Killdeer, Greater and Lesser Yellowlegs, Least and Western Sandpipers, Dunlin, Short- and Long-billed

Dowitchers, plus possible rarities. Bonaparte's, Mew, Ring-billed, California, Herring, Thayer's, Western, and Glaucous-winged Gulls rest on the mudflats in winter.

To resume your tour of the island, take False Bay Rd. to Bailer Hill Rd. At the intersection turn left (west) and proceed to West Side Rd. which takes you along the west side of San Juan Island. (To explore San Juan Valley, a fertile farmland section with good wintering raptors, turn right (north) on Wold Rd. off Bailer Hill Rd.).

BRITISH CAMP: The British Camp section of San Juan Historical Park at the north end of the island attracts migrating landbirds in spring. A hike up the trail to Mt. Young from the parking lot may produce a variety of western warblers; it's a good way to practice learning their songs in spring. Wild Turkeys are quite easily seen here.

To look at waterbirds, walk down to the historical buildings beside Garrison Bay, or hike out to Bell Point.

Port Townsend area: This charming town filled with Victorian houses is situated at the entrance to the Admiralty Inlet. Due to its location between Puget Sound and the Strait of Juan de Fuca, with

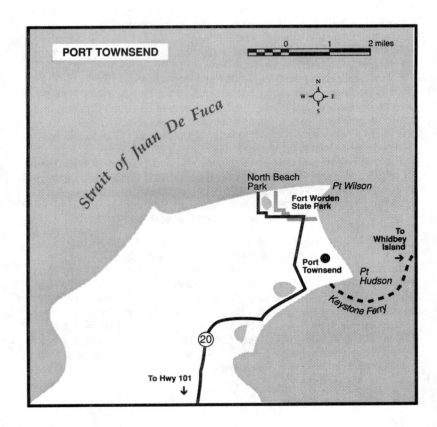

Protection Island several miles offshore, an abundance of bird traffic guarantees good birding from a number of spots.

KEYSTONE FERRY FROM WHIDBEY ISLAND TO PORT TOWNSEND: The ferry (toll) trip across the Admiralty Inlet from Whidbey Island to Port Townsend takes approximately 1/2 hr. and is one of the best ferry routes for birdwatching. Before departing, look at the jetty near the ferry terminal for American Black Oystercatchers.

In spring and summer, large numbers of Rhinoceros Auklets, Pelagic Cormorants, and Tufted Puffins commute between feeding areas in the Admiralty Inlet and their nesting sites on Protection Island. In winter, murres and other alcids are seen along the route, plus gulls, terns, jaegers and phalaropes in migration.

POINT HUDSON: Point Hudson is a beach right in town where numbers of Brant, in spring migration, pause on their journey north. From this little promontory, scope the Admiralty Inlet for alcids, sea ducks, cormorants and other birds. To reach Point Hudson from the ferry terminal in Port Townsend, take a right (east) turn onto Washington St., going for about ten blocks until you reach Monroe. A left turn on Monroe and an immediate right on Jefferson St. puts you on the beach at Point Hudson.

FORT WORDEN STATE PARK: Fort Worden is another location in Port Townsend for watching seabirds in the channel. The tides coming and going around Point Wilson, the eastern-most point of land in the park, generate bird activity. Pelagic Cormorants, Rhinoceros Auklets, Tufted Puffins, Pigeon Guillemots, Marbled Murrelets, and Glaucous-winged Gulls can be found in spring and summer. In winter, look for Brandt's Cormorants, Common Murres, and Ancient Murrelets.

To reach Fort Worden from downtown, turn right (east) on Washington St. at the ferry terminal, turn left (west) on Kearney St., right on Blaine St., and then left on Cherry St. Stay on Cherry St. until it dead-ends into the state park. Entering Fort Worden State Park, follow the signs to Point Wilson and the lighthouse. Park and walk to the beach to scope the channel.

NORTH BEACH PARK: Another, and perhaps the best, of the Port Townsend spots for birding, North Beach Park, is located on the north, rather than the east side of the Port Townsend peninsula. As such, its greater proximity to Protection Island means more chances for good sightings of seabirds, and the best location to look for Tufted Puffins (spring and summer) on this trip. Other birding finds are Harlequin Duck and American Black Oystercatcher on the rocky shoreline here, and Red-throated, Pacific and Common Loons (Yellow-billed a possibility in winter), grebes and cormorants fishing in the waters offshore. Rhinoceros Auklets come and go in huge flocks out in the strait.

To reach North Beach Park from Fort Worden State Park, make a right (west) on "W" St., which curves and becomes Admiralty Ave. At the intersection of Admiralty and San Juan Ave., turn right (north), then left on 49th, and right on Kuhn St. to reach this little beach park.

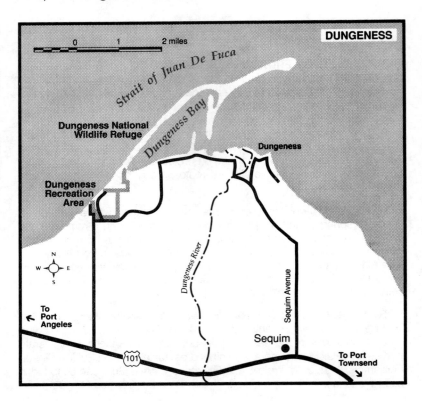

Dungeness area near Sequim: The Dungeness area to the west near the town of Sequim (pronounced Skwim) in Clallam County attracts large numbers of shorebirds and other species, especially in spring and fall migration. To reach Sequim from Port Townsend, take Washington 20 west for 13 mi. to the intersection with U.S. 101. Go north on U.S. 101 for 17 mi. to the town of Sequim.

DUNGENESS SHORELINE AT THE THREE CRABS RESTAURANT: To reach Dungeness, turn right (north) on Sequim Ave. in downtown Sequim, and proceed for 5 mi. (follow the signs for Dungeness Scenic Loop). Turn right on Dungeness Way, which takes you to the shore. Here, at the Three Crabs Restaurant, well-known for its seafood, scan the bay and the shore for all kinds of seabirds and waterfowl. In March through early May, thousands of Brant pause here on their journey north. In the ponds and agricultural fields, keep an eye out for the resident Canada Geese and maybe a Tundra Swan or two.

DUNGENESS RIVER ESTUARY: Retrace your route south and take the first paved road to your right (west), Marine Dr., which follows the coast on the bluffs. After turning onto Marine Dr., cross a bridge over the Dungeness River, and watch for the first spot to get down to the water—a boat launch area reached by driving steeply down to your right (east), where Twinview Rd. intersects Marine Dr. If you see a sign for the Dungeness Oyster Farm, you're in the right spot.

Park and walk to the east, where the Dungeness River drains into the mudflats of the bay. Parts of the beach are private property, but with a scope you can scan the mouth of the estuary and the extensive tidal flats. When tides are right, in spring and fall migration, the exciting numbers of shorebirds here can turn up rarities. Some species to expect are Black-bellied Plover, Semipalmated Plover, both yellowlegs, Whimbrel, Sanderling, Western and Least Sandpipers, Dunlin, and Short-billed and Long-billed Dowitchers.

Out in the bay, every species of commonly wintering waterfowl can be found, including occasional Eurasian Wigeons mixed with the American Wigeons, plus other waterbirds.

To continue the tour, drive back up to Marine Dr. and keep going west along the bluffs, stopping to scope Dungeness Bay below you. Another boat launch area (Cline Spit) can be checked. When you reach Lotzgesell Rd. turn right (west) and then right again on Voice of America Rd. to reach the Dungeness Recreation Area.

DUNGENESS RECREATION AREA: The Dungeness Recreation Area (not good in hunting season October-January) lies adjacent to Dungeness Spit, one of Washington's National Wildlife Refuges. The spit extends for several miles northeast and may be hiked from a trail beginning in the Recreation Area. However, if you don't feel like hiking through the sand on the spit, you can have good views out over the back side (west or north side) of the spit by setting up a scope at one of the picnic areas immediately to your left (west) as you enter the Recreation Area. From this vantage point, you overlook open ocean, preferred by such species as loons, grebes (Red-necked especially), cormorants, Harlequin Duck, Common Murre, Marbled Murrelet and Rhinoceros Auklet, to name a few.

From the Dungeness area, you can either retrace your route back to Sequim, thence to port Townsend or Seattle, or proceed further west towards Port Angeles and Cape Flattery on the Pacific coast.

WASHINGTON'S ISLAND WORLD:
Masses of seabirds and waterfowl
in the Pacific Northwest
Checklist of Common Birds by Habitat

ROCKY SHORELINE
Double-crested Cormorant
Brandt's Cormorant
Pelagic Cormorant
Harlequin Duck
Osprey
Bald Eagle
American Blkack Oystercatcher
Wandering Tattler
Ruddy Turnstone
Black Turnstone
Surfbird
Rock Sandpiper (uncommon)
Marbled Murrelet
Northwestern Crow

**INSHORE WATERS AND
SHELTERED BAYS**
Red-throated Loon
Pacific Loon
Common Loon
Pied-billed Grebe
Horned Grebe
Red-necked Grebe
Western Grebe
Great Blue Heron
Tundra Swan (winter)
Trumpeter Swan (winter, local)
Snow Goose (winter)
Brant
Canada Goose
Green-winged Teal
Mallard
Northern Pintail
Gadwall
American Wigeon
Canvasback
Ring-necked Duck
Greater Scaup

Lesser Scaup
Oldsquaw
Black Scoter (uncommon)
Surf Scoter
White-winged Scoter
Common Goldeneye
Barrow's Goldeneye
Bufflehead
Hooded Merganser
Red-breasted Merganser
Ruddy Duck
Osprey
Bald Eagle
Red-necked Phalarope
Parasitic Jaeger
Bonaparte's Gull
Heermann's Gull (late summer)
Mew Gull
Ring-billed Gull
California Gull
Herring Gull
Thayer's Gull (winter)
Western Gull
CLaucous-winged Gull
Caspian Tern (summer)
Common Tern
Marbled Murrelet
Ancient Murrelet (winter)

**SEABIRD COLONIES AND
SURROUNDING WATERS**
Double-crested Cormorant
Pelagic Cormorant
Common Murre
Pigeon Guillemot
Cassin's Auklet
Rhinoceros Auklet
Tufted Puffin (local)
Glaucous-winged Gull

TIDAL MUDFLATS
Merlin
Peregrine Falcon
Black-bellied Plover
Semipalmated Plover
Killdeer
Greater Yellowlegs
Lesser Yellowlegs
Spotted Sandpiper
WHimbrel
Marbled Godwit
Sanderling
Western Sandpiper
Least Sandpiper
Dunlin
Short-billed Dowitcher
Long-billed Dowitcher
Short-eared Owl
Northwestern Crow

CALIFORNIA'S MOJAVE DESERT

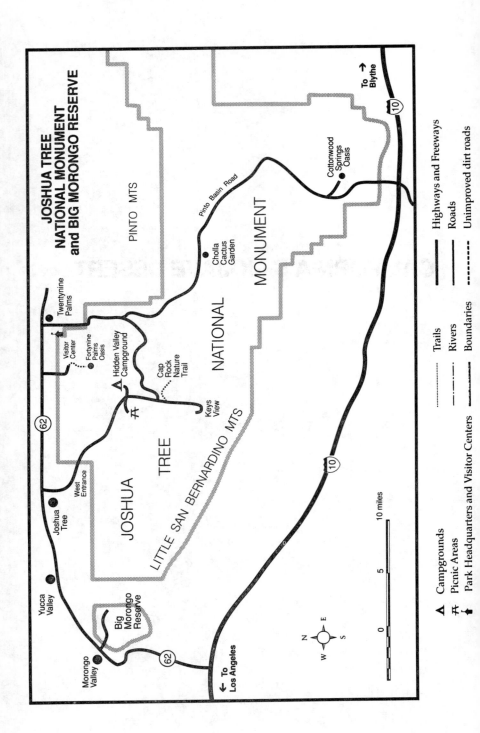

JOSHUA TREE NATIONAL MONUMENT and BIG MORONGO RESERVE

To Blythe

10

Cottonwood Springs Oasis

PINTO MTS

Pinto Basin Road

Cholla Cactus Garden

MONUMENT

Twentynine Palms

Visitor Center

Fortynine Palms Oasis

Hidden Valley Campground

Cap Rock Nature Trail

Keys View

NATIONAL

62

West Entrance

Joshua Tree

JOSHUA TREE

LITTLE SAN BERNARDINO MTS

10

Yucca Valley

Big Morongo Reserve

Morongo Valley

62

To Los Angeles

N
E
S
W

0   5   10 miles

▲ Campgrounds

⌐⌐ Picnic Areas

Park Headquarters and Visitor Centers

·········· Trails

—·—·— Rivers

▬▬▬ Boundaries

━━━ Highways and Freeways

━━━ Roads

- - - - - Unimproved dirt roads

5

CALIFORNIA'S MOJAVE DESERT:
Spring birding amidst lush oases

Contorted Joshua tree silhouettes, their twisted limbs sheaved in dagger-like leaves, symbolize the strange landscape of the wide Mojave Desert. Against a cloudless blue sky, the snow-capped San Bernardino Mountains in the distance, Joshua trees seem to beckon to birders, pointing to the hidden treasures of the desert—the bird species that thrive under the glaring sun, among the jumbled boulders and sparse vegetation of the Mojave.

The peak of wildflower display and spring bird activity in Joshua Tree National Monument falls in April or early May. Then the early mornings and the twilights are cool and pleasant in the desert. In a good year, when the scant rainfall has come just right, wildflowers blanket the sandy washes and dunes. Blooming trees and shrubs attract insects, food for many migrant and resident birds. Bird species are in full song, a few of the most sought-after being Gambel's Quail, Ladder-backed Woodpecker, Verdin, Cactus Wren, LeConte's Thrasher, Scott's Oriole and Black-throated Sparrow.

Desert oases hum with bird life at this season. Migrants are on their way north from Mexico where they've spent the winter. Each night, new swarms of birds from the south stop off at the lush cottonwood and palm oases, drinking their fill and restoring their energy for the journey north to nesting grounds in northern California and beyond. Spring birding at these oases proves rewarding, as intermittent waves of warblers, vireos and sparrows pass through—particularly after a cold front has impeded their normal progress across the surrounding inhospitable desert.

This bird trip commences with a visit to Big Morongo Wildlife Reserve, a surprising island of riparian woodland in the midst of the high Mojave Desert about 25 miles north of Palm Springs. Here, the tangle of willows and cottonwoods attracts numerous birds.

From Morongo, the route goes north through Joshua Tree National Monument, exploring the bird habitats in two desert regions—the Mojave and the Colorado.

The spare beauty of the desert landscape gradually takes hold of a newcomer. The peace and solitude of a quiet spring morning—the cry of the Cactus Wren in the still air, the vivid warblers sipping from the trickle of water at Cottonwood Springs—gives birding here a special quality. You, too, may join the ranks of bird enthusiasts who return year after year to experience the desert springtime.

Climate and Habitats of the Mojave Desert

The deserts of the west fall into three major regions. The largest is the Great Basin Desert, which includes the sagebrush land between California's Sierra Nevada mountains and the Colorado Rockies. The great Sonoran Desert stretches into Arizona and Mexico, characterized by saguaro and cholla cacti. The Mojave Desert, relatively much smaller than the other two, spans an upland region extending into southern California and parts of Utah and Arizona.

Any region with less than ten inches of precipitation a year, whether in the form of rain or snow, qualifies as a desert. In desert climates, the moisture is distributed unevenly throughout the seasons, and much is lost to evaporation and drying winds. The wind and rain combine to erode the naked mountains and broaden the sandy washes and gullies. In summer, flash floods rush through the canyons carrying mud and debris, bringing little relief from the relentless heat. In winter, the freezing night-time temperatures challenge the survival of many desert creatures.

The 560,000 acres of Joshua Tree National Monument sprawl over parts of both the Mojave and Colorado Deserts (the Colorado is the portion of the Sonoran Desert, named for the Colorado River, that reaches into California). The Mojave Desert environment, with its cooler climate and Joshua tree woodlands, occurs in the western third of the Monument. Altitudes here exceed 4,000 feet, and snow often covers the ground after heavy winter storms. The Colorado Desert portions of the Monument, ranging from sea level to 2,000 feet and experiencing hotter temperatures with less precipitation, lie along its eastern third and southern edge. Each has fauna and flora adapted to the extraordinarily difficult conditions imposed by a land of little rain, intense heat and gusty winds.

Desert Oasis: The few green oases scattered over the arid deserts of Southern California act as magnets for resident and migrant bird species which depend on their life-giving water.

Most of the California oases originate from old underground earthquake fault lines which allow the water to bubble up to the surface. Ground water issues from these fissures in the form of pools, streams and springs, allowing plants ordinarily requiring a great deal more water to flourish. Besides the more characteristic plants—mesquite, Fremont cottonwood and willow—the oases have groves of the large, native California fan palm. The immense height and shaggy fronds of these palms provide shade, and nesting and roosting places for birds seeking refuge in their fan-shaped greenery.

The greatest concentration of birds in the desert occurs at the oases during migration. In both fall and spring, but particularly in spring, you can observe numerous western migrant species. On any given day from mid-April to mid-May, flocks of colorful warblers fill the palms and willows. Orange-crowned, Wilson's and Yellow Warblers sip from the shallow pools, flashing shades of yellow as they bathe. A Nashville, Black-throated Gray, Townsend's or Hermit Warbler may suddenly plummet from the sky, intent upon a moment's rest in the welcoming shade.

To acquire a true picture of the desert ecosystem, you will want to include a visit to Big Morongo Wildlife Reserve, the most important desert riparian oasis in southern California, either before or after a trip through Joshua Tree National Monument. Over 200 species of birds have been recorded at this San Bernardino County/Nature Conservancy-owned sanctuary in Big Morongo Canyon.

At an altitude of 2500 feet, Big Morongo Canyon lies in a transition zone, its bird life reflecting a mix of coastal chaparral species—typical of portions of the higher desert—and true desert birds. For example, the Bushtit can be found side by side with the similar Verdin, one building its nest in the willows, the other nesting on the dry hillsides across the canyon. Here, the Nuttall's Woodpecker rubs shoulders with its desert relative, the Ladder-backed Woodpecker. The Blue Grosbeak, a typical desert riparian species, can be found, as well as the California Thrasher, illustrating the blend of desert and coastal influences.

Resident desert birds such as Gambel's Quail, Cactus Wren and Black-throated Sparrow come to drink at Morongo, and White-winged Dove, Long-eared Owl, Costa's Hummingbird, Phainopepla, Yellow-breasted Chat and Scott's Oriole nest in the oasis.

But Morongo Reserve's fame as a birding spot is due in large part to the out-of-range nesting species which extend their westward breeding habitat to include this oasis. These species—Brown-crested Flycatcher, Vermilion Flycatcher, Bell's Vireo, Lucy's Warbler and Summer Tanager—normally nest in central Arizona. Consequently, Morongo is one of the few places in California where birders may be lucky enough to add them to their list.

Due to the precariously small populations of these species (in most cases one or two pairs only), successful nesting is never guaranteed from one year to the next. However, though their tenuous foothold in California may fluctuate, these Arizona birds never entirely disappear from the oasis, or at least they haven't yet. Human encroachment from the burgeoning desert towns nearby threatens to lower the water table in Big Morongo Canyon, which could spell disaster for the variety of birds sustained by its precious moisture.

When you bird Morongo, be sure to walk over to the tiny recreational area, adjacent to the Reserve, known as Covington Park. The dashing black-and-crimson Vermilion Flycatcher takes up its post here every spring, flycatching from the backstop fence of the baseball diamond. A pair of Brown-crested Flycatchers sometimes nests in the hollow pipe that supports the swing set. Lawrence's Goldfinches and Cassin's Kingbirds fly in and out of the giant cottonwoods shading the park's playing fields. While weekenders enjoy the park and picnic grounds nearby, birders eagerly scan the trees above, searching for the bright red male Summer Tanager and his yellow mate.

Representative birding sites:
Morongo Valley: Big Morongo Reserve.
Joshua Tree National Monument: Twentynine Palms Oasis, Forty-nine Palms Oasis, Cottonwood Springs Oasis.

Joshua Tree Woodland: As you enter the Mojave Desert section of the Monument, driving up from the little town of Joshua Tree, your eyes are drawn to the giant rock formations, standing guard at the mouths of the narrow canyons and arranged in huge stacked piles on the ridge tops. Up close, the enormous scale of the boulders overwhelms, but in this sweep of desert they seem as toy blocks remaining from eons ago, stacks of pink and gray and beige quartz granite outlined against the bluest sky imaginable.

The geologic features of the land lie uncovered before you; little vegetation clothes the arroyos and playas, or softens the washes and sinks. The silt washed down from the mountainsides spreads into broad gentle plains at the base of the mountains known as "bajadas." Over centuries, the mountains are slowly being buried in their own debris.

The clear, dry air and warm sun are benign on a day in early April. Later in the season, the sun becomes a relentless force of heat and light, punishing those animals foolish enough to be abroad in the middle of the day. For now, though, this high desert country is pleasant, awakening gradually from the grip of chilly winter temperatures.

If the rainfall has been near normal in this part of the Monu-

ment, the slopes shine in carpets of pale yellow desert dande-
lion and lavender Mojave aster.

At last, the Joshua trees themselves appear, growing in
regular plantations, their twisting branches towering over the
lower shrubs.

Joshua trees were named nearly a hundred years ago, so the
legend goes, when Brigham Young called on Mormon colonies
to join him in Utah. A devout group of Latter-day Saints set out
from San Bernardino, California. They crossed the Cajon Pass
into the Mojave, where they found a weird tree, one that
Captain John Fremont had pronounced earlier as "the most
repulsive tree in the vegetable kingdom." But to the Mormons
it became a symbol, as they progressed northeastward to their
promised land, of the biblical Joshua, standing with arms
uplifted, urging them on across the burning desert.

The tangled shapes of the Joshua tree branches do seem to
point heavenward, terminating in white, columnar sets of
beautiful flowers in spring. The Joshua tree is an unlikely-
looking member of the Lily family and, like other yuccas, has
developed a special arrangement for pollination.

An interdependence, called mutualism, exists between the
Joshua tree and the yucca moth. The yucca moth performs a
vital role, because yucca pollen is too heavy and sticky to be
wind-carried. Collecting a pellet of pollen, the moth carries it
on its head to another blossom and places it on the flower's
stigma for fertilization. Then, crawling down into the blossom,
the female moth punctures the ovary of the flower and inserts
her eggs. When the moth larvae hatch, they feed on some of the
seeds in the flower. Plenty of other seeds mature naturally,
falling to the desert floor. Eventually, the larvae gnaw their way
out of their seedpods, drop to the ground and spin their
cocoons. When spring brings forth new yucca blossoms, the
moths will emerge and the cycle will begin again.

Joshua trees grow almost exclusively in the Mojave Desert,
from 2,500 to 5,000 feet in the cooler, higher parts of the
National Monument. They prefer the bajadas at the foot of the
mountain slopes, where they capture surface and ground water
draining towards them. A Joshua tree takes decades to achieve
a mature height of 40 feet, and some never make it.

Joshua trees are always a center of bird and animal activity. In the upper branches, hawks and owls perch to view the surrounding desert. Ladder-backed Woodpeckers drill nest holes in the trunks of Joshua trees, which, when abandoned, are recycled for use by American Kestrels and Ash-throated Flycatchers. Also, Cactus Wrens are partial to the trees for nesting and perching.

Joshua tree blossoms, fruits and seeds are food for birds, rodents and lizards. Lizards hide during the day under dead limbs or fallen trunks, emerging at night to feed on the termites in the rotting wood and other small insects.

The Scott's Oriole, in a quick burst of black and yellow, is the showiest inhabitant of the Joshua tree woodland. Found in the Monument from the end of March until early September, the Scott's depends upon the Joshua trees for food and nesting. In foraging, it alights on the spines of the tree and works up through them to the flowering and fruiting stalks. The flowers are a source of food and nectar. Fruit, nectar and insects furnish the oriole with sufficient water.

All spring the male Scott's Oriole sings incessantly, a high whistle with a melody similar to the Western Meadowlark's. Even in the silence of the hot noon hours, his clear piping notes will break forth, to the joy of many a birder.

For a nest, this oriole builds a shallow hanging cup of fibers, placed in the shade beneath a cluster of Joshua tree spines, usually about eight feet above the ground. The edges of descending leaves are frayed or notched by the oriole, to serve as an attachment for the threads which support the nest.

If cliffs are near, Red-tailed Hawks, Golden Eagles, Prairie Falcons and Common Ravens establish their territories high above the Joshua tree woodland. Winter snows and chilly nights force most resident birds of this area to migrate far south or withdraw to the milder winter climate of the low desert.

Before you leave the high desert section of the Monument, be sure to visit the Cap Rock Nature Trail, where a variety of typical shrubs of the area can be seen, including paper bag bush, peach-thorn, peach brush, holly-leaf buckthorn, Mormon tea, blackbrush and goldenbush.

Representative birding sites:
Joshua Tree National Monument: Hidden Valley Campground, Cap Rock Nature Trail.

Creosote Bush Scrub: The creosote bush, found on all three of our Western deserts, creates another habitat for birds. Growing throughout the Monument, but mostly in the lower desert sections, these slender-branched pale green bushes stretch in evenly-spaced ranks as far as the eye can see.

Around each creosote bush, a sort of no-man's-land is established, as the shrub releases a toxic substance into the soil. Other plants and seedlings are destroyed, insuring plenty of space for the surface roots of each creosote bush to soak up its own rain supply, should a brief downpour occur. The heavy, shiny coating of the plant's small leaves conserves moisture, and their oily content explains why the creosote bush is often called greasewood. When this shrub is severely deprived of water, it may turn brown and look quite dead, but the slightest rainfall is enough to turn it green once more.

Appearing at first devoid of life, pure stands of creosote bush support a number of desert species. The plants produce seeds needed for the survival of many desert rodents, hunted in turn by Swainson's Hawks, Red-tailed Hawks, American Kestrels, Prairie Falcons, Great Horned Owls, Common Barn-Owls and Common Ravens.

Loggerhead Shrikes thrive in this open scrub. Costa's Hummingbirds sometimes nest here, and Greater Roadrunners scurry along the wide avenues of the desert floor between the bushes.

The Black-throated Sparrow, with its inky black bib and white eye-stripe and whisker mark, hardly looks the part of an extreme in desert adaptation, but it exists daily in exposed, hot areas such as this, never requiring water. Subsisting on a diet of creosote bush seeds, its body is very efficient in extracting metabolic water. Other desert birds share the Black-throated Sparrow's ability to turn the carbohydrates of the seeds they eat into energy, carbon dioxide and water—termed metabolic water.

This little sparrow, sometimes observed singing atop a creosote bush when the surrounding temperatures are near 120 degrees F., must have a special tolerance for above-normal body temperatures, too. Like most birds, whose average body temperature is 104 degrees F., the Black-throated Sparrow is therefore somewhat pre-adapted to desert life. But how it manages to defy the constant heat and desiccating winds of the desert summer is still a mystery.

When birding the lower Colorado Desert section of the Monument, you will encounter the fascinating cacti that flourish there. The cacti come in many sizes and shapes: perfectly suited to resist the harsh desert climate. Substituting spines for leaves, cacti store water within their thick, fleshy stems. The spines also protect the plant from being gnawed by animals, shield the main stem from the sun, and concentrate moisture from brief rainstorms at their tips letting it eventually fall to ground near the base of the plant.

The teddy bear cactus or jumping cholla grows in the Monument at the Cholla Gardens off the Pinto Basin Road, a good place to stop and examine these cacti. Their whitish-yellow spines glisten in the sunlight with a deceptively fuzzy look. Beware! The slightest brush against the plant releases one of its segments into your clothes or your skin—hence the name jumping cholla.

No matter how sharp cholla needles are to human touch, they make ideal nesting places for roadrunners, thrashers and Cactus Wrens. Set deep in the threatening spines, the fledgling birds receive maximum protection from predators and shelter from the hot sunlight.

The ocotillo, a tall shrub with wand-like branches reaching up to 20 feet, is another cactus characteristic of the Colorado Desert. Its long, thin branches, armored with nasty thorns, sprout green leaves every spring. After blooming, the ocotillo looses its leaves as a protection against summer drought.

The crimson-colored blossoms on the tips of the ocotillo branches—a stunning candelabra with vibrant red flames—brighten the somber creosote scrub around them. In spring, and in summer after desert rains, these blossoms attract all sorts of birds. There is no more breathtaking sight than the black-and-orange hued Hooded Oriole sipping nectar from one of the scarlet ocotillo flowers.

Along sandy washes, where the soil holds water from infrequent downpours for longer periods of time, other common desert shrubs growing quite tall include catclaw, palo verde, smoke tree, desert willow, and desert ironwood. Due to the increased plant life there, resident birds choose the washes as nesting areas.

After the blooming season, when the migrants have gone through, resident birds must rely on the fallen fruits and seeds of desert plants for food. Birds feeding on the fallen seeds of desert plants are: Gambel's Quail, Cactus Wren, LeConte's Thrasher, Black-throated Sparrow and Sage Sparrow.

The Phainopepla finds the desert mistletoe a good source of nourishment. Scattered widely among desert trees and shrubs, clumps of mistletoe represent former nest sites of Phainopeplas, where quantities of defecated seeds have clung to the branches and tree trunks, starting new mistletoe colonies.

In the vicinity of Cottonwood Springs, and in many other portions of the Monument, count on watching the little Verdin. The Verdin resembles its chaparral relative, the Bushtit, but, upon closer examination, shows a rufous wing patch and a mustard-yellow head and throat.

Verdins, due to their small size and their great exposure to the sun and wind, would seem vulnerable to the extreme desert conditions here, but the species is highly successful. Their nests, which are also used for roosting, serve as a retreat during the day offering protection from the drying wind and sun. Their insect diet helps, too, for they seldom drink at springs.

Verdins never flock. A pair ranges over a large area, making long powerful flights in the open, especially when they're alarmed or pursued. Verdin nests, placed in a catclaw, smoke tree or other thorny shrub, have a distinct globular shape. The nest is entered by a clever side opening, so that the birds must fly up at an angle and scramble in. The inner part of the finished nest is a softly lined globe protected by a thorny shell. Like some other desert nesters, Verdins may continue to roost in their nests after the breeding season, using them as a shelter from the winter winds and cold.

Its call is a rich *thup* note, surprisingly loud for such a minuscule bird.

Birders who visit the Mojave Desert often come prepared to search for the LeConte's Thrasher, a daunting task but one that may be successful with a little perseverance. These birds, typically found in the lower, hotter creosote bush habitat, do occur throughout the Monument. Though widely spaced and difficult to locate, these shy thrashers are permanent residents here. Their requirements are not so much related to altitude as to terrain. It must be flat with loose soil or sand for the thrashers to run about.

Birders may first discover LeConte's Thrashers by finding their nests, either current or old structures. They look like large bundles made of sticks. The birds need stout, dense bushes to hold and protect their nests, so look for them in cholla cacti, palo verde, mesquite and even sagebrush. Careful perusal of the neighboring terrain may turn up a thrasher.

The LeConte's Thrasher is a pale, clay-colored bird with a long, blackish tail held erect as it runs, showing rusty brown undertail coverts. Very early in the morning, and again late in the day, the male LeConte's will occasionally sing a beautiful, rich song. Otherwise, he is remarkably quiet and unsociable, and can be elusive, disappearing down a desert wash in no time.

Thrashers breed early; one has been recorded sitting on eggs by March 21.

Although most species, like the LeConte's Thrasher, easily tolerate the extremes of desert survival, they may have to relocate during times of prolonged drought. They require no drinking water, but the plants and leaf litter must supply them with insects. If threatened by severely dry conditions, a thrasher colony will move a few miles to a new site, where, presumably, more rain has fallen.

Before you leave the Cottonwood Springs area of Joshua Tree National Monument, take time to walk the nature trail behind the Visitor Center to become acquainted with the typical plants of the Colorado Desert, such as pencil cholla, indigo bush, burroweed, skeleton weed, spiny menodora, prickly pear, buck-horn cholla, silver cholla and barrel cactus. If you visit in early spring, the yellow blooms of bladderpod and brittlebush will line the roads, along with the wonderful red-flowering chuparosa.

Representative birding sites:
Joshua Tree National Monument: Hidden Valley Campground. Twentynine Palms to Cottonwood Springs via Pinto Basin Road: Cottonwood Springs and vicinity.

Watching Western Warblers in Migration

One fascinating aspect of desert birding is the spring warbler migration. These tiny specks of energy fearlessly tackle a desert journey of immense proportions, approximately 700 miles. Flying between their wintering range—chiefly in Mexico from Sonora southward—and their breeding ranges on the Pacific coast and in the mountains to the northwest of the deserts, the warblers follow a southeast/northwest gradient. Locations like Big Morongo near the Little San Bernardino Mountains, and Cottonwood Springs, flanked by Cottonwood Pass, receive the warblers and other migrants as they are funneled in a northerly direction by surrounding mountain ranges.

During the latter part of spring migration, at the end of May and early June, rare vagrants may turn up at Morongo and other oases in the Mojave Desert and farther north. In fact, knowledgeable California birders stage an annual ritual, known in the vernacular as "Memorial Day madness," when they gather to search targeted oases for Eastern vagrants which have become lost or disoriented during their crossing of the vast desert basins between here and Mexico. Oases further north near Death Valley and at the extreme southwest border of Nevada get the most coverage, but Morongo has produced its share of rarities over the years.

An awareness of the challenges posed by a desert journey such as this increases one's admiration for these minute birds. They must obtain a supply of insects to furnish water, and enough vegetable matter for energy, on their way. They will come across periods of severe heat and sun exposure, which they must offset by insect intake, usually from insects that are scarce and which they are unaccustomed to feed upon.

Fortunately, migrant warblers both in spring and fall deposit large amounts of fat before taking off. They can last several days without a normal daily food intake, utilizing the safety supply of fat and gaining metabolic water from it. Still, the journey is exceedingly taxing, particularly in fall, when shade temperatures are above 100 degrees F. on a daily basis.

Thus, Western warbler species must maintain a certain level of fitness not only to live and breed on their summer and winter ranges, but to get back and forth over a desert migratory route. Those that have ineffective fat storage or those that make an inadequate response to the emergencies of a desert crossing, must surely perish.

When warblers migrate, they do so erratically, arriving in waves. Reversals of direction and delays caused by storms or heavy winds are common. For example, a cold day in late March along Cottonwood Pass, south of Cottonwood Springs, saw numbers of migrants battling the fierce wind; birds were perching fearlessly on the ground and in every shrub or bit of greenery, virtually grounded by the chilling north wind following a weather front. It was a birders' dream! However, when the wind subsided, the birds immediately resumed their normal northward progress.

In such fashion, a wave of migrants can develop during spring migration in the desert. At Cottonwood Springs, on May 12 and 13, 1951, as many as 60 warblers were counted in the trees and bushes.

Interestingly, even in migration some warblers show preferences for different types of desert plants. Hermit and Townsend's Warblers, found in conifers on their northern breeding grounds, are usually seen in pinyon pines or junipers on the desert, if any of these are available. Wilson's Warblers favor the lower brushy cover. MacGillivray's Warblers skulk in the desert shrubs and remain close to the ground wherever possible, thereby reflecting their adherence to low, dense thickets on their nesting grounds.

In spring, many warblers are seen at the canyon mouths, and at times on the open desert flats. In fall, migrants cross high over the low-lying areas and tend to follow the ridge tops and windy crests. Little migration occurs before the end of March, and it peaks in mid-April, though birds continue to move through steadily until about May 20.

The Cactus Wren: A Birding Close-Up

The thornier the mesquite and the sharper the cholla, the more suitable they are for the Cactus Wren. Throughout the deserts of the Southwest, from gravelly mesa to yucca flatland, the monotonous cry of this largest of American wrens repeats itself day after day. Of all the birds of the desert, the Cactus Wren fits most neatly into its environment of cacti, heat and dust.

The Cactus Wren is not a subdued member of the desert community; as soon as you begin birding here it will get your attention. At first glance, this wren might even be mistaken for a small thrasher, as it sings perched—tail hanging straight down, unlike the cocked tails of typical wrens—at the top of a bush or pole or even a building on the outskirts of town. The male's song is noisy and unmusical, having a rather grating, throaty quality, often described as *chuh-chuh-chuh-chuh* repeated over and over. Still, he appears to be very content with his desert surroundings, and his voice itself sounds like a boastful conversation, not in the least mournful.

The Cactus Wren's behavior may remind you of a thrasher, because it's a swift runner, though it takes wing when necessary. Like thrashers, Cactus Wrens forage on the ground. Coming upon a leaf or piece of debris, the wren will poke its bill under one side and peer underneath, then snatch up the bugs, ants or weevils it finds there.

Cactus Wrens appear uninterested in drinking water from a birdbath; the only liquids they need are gained from eating the fruit of the prickly pear cactus and desert insects.

Both male and female Cactus Wrens are brownish above with white markings; they have a bold white eye stripe over each eye, and their underparts are pale with heavy spots on the breast. This wren often fans its tail in flight, when the black-and-white barring on the outer tail feathers becomes easily visible.

As you drive through the desert, watch for the conspicuous, flask-shaped nests of the Cactus Wren, particularly in the chollas. Time after time, this bird will choose the devilish-looking cholla cactus as a nesting site, wedging its bundle of sticks between the spines.

The elaborate nest of the Cactus Wren serves not only as a receptacle for the young birds, but as a home throughout the winter, and a protection against daytime storms and nighttime predators. The adult wrens work constantly at repairing and rebuilding the nest. When the young reach adulthood, they too will begin building their own nests to shield them from the oncoming winter.

In 1922, Florence Merriam Bailey, a pioneer in early Western bird observation, wrote: "In form, the Cactus Wren's nest suggests a retort [a bulb of glass with a bent beak used in laboratories], having a large globular chamber about 6 inches in diameter approached through a long passageway or entrance, the whole normally about 12 inches in length, the mouth of the entrance being about 3 inches above the base of the globular chamber. This nest chamber in course of years becomes a thick, felted mass of gray, weathered plant fibers so hard that saucer-like sections sometimes crack off from the back, showing the solid bottom of the nest. The entrance, on the contrary, is made of long straw-like plant stems, which may easily get blown about and so often need replenishing."

In constructing their nests, Cactus Wrens first lay a flat bottom, then fashion the domed upper part, and finally construct the tunnel. The tunnel usually slopes steeply down into the interior of the nest, which is lined with downy feathers. The pointed spines of the cholla segments embrace the nest and its entrance portal so skillfully that only the Cactus Wrens themselves can come and go freely.

Initially, it was believed Cactus Wrens nested in colonies; every year so many new nests would appear in groups. Upon closer examination, ornithologists have observed many of these nests used as winter shelter by single birds or wrens in groups of twos and threes. Some of the wintering nests lack the workmanship of the true nests, and are often open to the elements at the top.

When spring arrives, the wintering nests undergo renovation, or an entirely new nest may be constructed. By March or April, a clutch of four or five salmon-colored eggs is laid.

Few birds embody the spirit of the desert like the Cactus Wren. Birders will have no difficulty in spying this garrulous fellow. Equally at home singing from a backyard on the edge of town or a roadside Joshua tree in the middle of nowhere, the Cactus Wren has adapted perfectly to life in the desert.

NOTES FROM A BIRDER'S DIARY
Joshua Tree National Monument

● April 1, 1987, 9:00 P.M. Late in the day, I began hiking the dusty, rocky trail over the ridge to Fortynine Palms Oasis. The sun was beginning to get low over the jutting rocks of the barren mountainsides, but I was sure the oasis could be reached before nightfall.

I walked fast, following the steep path as it climbed upward. Pausing to look back over the immense view of the Mojave Desert, I saw the town of Twentynine Palms lying in the late afternoon shadows far below.

After that, the narrow canyon walls closed in. The creosote bushes, the saltbushes, and every manner of gray, thorny shrub dotted the hillsides of this winding canyon. Most spectacular were the fat barrel cacti. Thick and robust, they thrust their plump forms entwined in curved spines from beside the trail. Their rusty color and cylindrical shape gave an ominous touch to the surroundings, as the canyon wound deeper and deeper into the mountains.

The afternoon sun had long since left the steep rock walls, but I pushed on, a feeling of anticipation in every step.

At last, from a far-off cul-de-sac in the chalky cliffs, the green, fan-shaped fronds of the tall, native palms—an incongruous green here—rose into view. Aware of the oncoming darkness, I hurried faster.

Up and down the sandy escarpments and pebbled ledges I ran. The fan palms loomed ever closer in the dusky light, guarding the water oozing out of the ground beneath them. Finally, the sound of water trickling over rocks met my ears.

With no warning, the oasis emerged around the next corner. The nearby wasted hillsides, where struggled the typical desert plants, gave no clue to a thirsty, weary traveller that rest and liquid refreshment was imminent.

Nature here is full of surprises, supreme in the ability to keep you guessing. You begin to think you can read the landscape of this arid country, but the more you think you know, the more inscrutable the desert becomes.

Distances are deceptive, too. After twice the estimated time to reach the oasis, I finally stood in the twilight near the towering palms. Their untrimmed, long blond skirts rustled in the breeze.

"Whew ... whew ...," a low whistle caught my ear and I turned around.

"Whew!" Again, the low whistle came, so human in its utterance that a cold chill began to creep up my spine. Four people had been hiking out as I came in. Was somebody left behind, hiding?

Then, a coal-black bird with white flashes in the wings flew right over my head and landed in a cluster of mistletoe covered with red berries. The bird began feeding—a final morsel for the evening—and at last I discerned the curved top-knot and the blood-red eye of the Phainopepla. A glossy black male, soon joined by the female in her all-gray garb, was giving his quiet whistle, an ever-present sound in our Southwestern deserts.

This Phainopepla pair seemed to assume the role of guardians of the oasis. Perhaps their fluttering, graceful flight and inimitable presence would protect the wild spirit of the oasis from civilization.

The trickle of life-giving water flowing out of the rocks at my feet created two shallow pools. Birds were flying back and forth everywhere. The onset of evening had hastened their search for a resting spot for the night, a drink and a bath. Besides the desert-dwelling birds, such as the tiny Costa's Hummingbirds, the Verdins and the beautiful Hooded Orioles, a sprinkling of migrant birds sparked my interest. Marking this green oasis from high up in the sky and knowing it spelled relief from the heat and parched landscape all round, the birds must have alighted just before dusk.

An Ash-throated Flycatcher, Townsend's Solitaire, Black-throated Gray Warbler, Common Yellowthroat, Wilson's Warbler and White-crowned Sparrow, unlikely birds in this desert habitat, were perching in the low shrubs which clung to the rocks. From here the birds descended to bathe and drink.

Gazing at the tiny, bright warblers, I reflected on the distances they might have flown that day. How many barren, treeless miles had they crossed? In the waning light, they preened and drank in the shelter of the welcoming palms. A thin slice of moon rose above the bleak canyon walls.

Lulled by the soothing sound of the running water and the sight of the birds, all sense of time was suspended. But, realizing I was alone, and without food or flashlight, I goaded myself into making the necessary journey back.

As I scrambled over the rocks and climbed away from the greenery, the low hoot of a Great Horned Owl bid me a lone farewell. Even the Phainopeplas were silent.

Up and up and twisting and turning, the trail led homeward. An inadvertent slip of my hiking boot could send me headlong into any one of those well-placed barrel cacti.

Nearing the end, the view out over the desert spread to the horizon. Lights twinkled from the towns and ranches, but they were almost lost in the vast space. Forever, the gentle skirts of pale gravel drifted down from volcanic peaks. Forever, the miles lay across the Mojave, now bathed in near-darkness. I looked north towards Death Valley, and thought of the early settlers and their ordeals.

There are still places to go where the desert's spell lingers . . .

The hike to Fortynine Palms Oasis is one of them.

TRAVELERS' TIPS

Before you visit: Before visiting Big Morongo Canyon Preserve, send for a bird checklist to Big Morongo Canyon Preserve, P. O.

Box 780, Morongo Valley, CA. 92256. The phone number of the Preserve Manager is (619) 363-7190. Motels (see below) are the same as for Joshua Tree National Monument.

Joshua Tree National Monument has nine campgrounds and several day-use picnic areas. There are no motels, restaurants, or gas stations in the Monument, but these are easily found in nearby towns. For information, a bird checklist and a map of the Monument, write Superintendent, Joshua Tree National Monument, 74485 National Monument Drive, Twentynine Palms, CA. 92277 or call (619) 367-7511. Camping facilities can be crowded on spring weekends.

Joshua Tree National Monument lies 140 miles east of Los Angeles, and can be approached from the north at the towns of Joshua Tree and Twentynine Palms and from the south at Cottonwood Springs via I-5. At the Twentynine Palms entrance, the Oasis Visitor Center has an extensive collection of books, maps, field guides and some very nice, inexpensive pamphlets on desert fauna and flora. The Cottonwood Springs entrance has a small Visitor Center with books and information. The Joshua Tree entrance has no visitor center, but driving maps are available there.

Motel accommodations can be procured at Palm Springs (which is 50 miles away) or at the smaller towns of Yucca Valley, Twentynine Palms, and—close to the Cottonwood Springs entrance—Indio.

When to visit: Due to high summer temperatures, the best time to visit the Monument is October through May. To enjoy the spectacle of the spring bird migration at the oases, and to assure that the summer residents, such as the Scott's Oriole have arrived, time your visit to occur after April 1.

The Colorado Desert portions of the Monument, particularly around Cottonwood Springs, may show a wildflower display as early as March, depending upon the previous winter's rains. However, the cooler, Mojave sections are often quite chilly in March, and the birds may still be at lower elevations, or not arrived from more southerly climes. Although storms are unlikely this late, cold winds can sweep the desert at any time in the spring.

From early April to mid-May, the presence of blooming Joshua trees, colorful wildflowers, and resident and migrant birds make the Mojave desert a truly delightful spot. This is also the best time to visit Morongo Reserve.

Length of Visit: A birding trip to Joshua Tree National Monument can be made in a day from Palm Springs, but from the Los Angeles area and beyond, a one-night stay in the area is suggested, especially if you plan on including Big Morongo in your itinerary.

Do yourself a favor and spend most of a morning at Big Morongo. Then, drive to the cooler parts of Joshua Tree National Monument for a picnic. A hike in the evening to Fortynine Palms Oasis, or a stroll around the oasis at Twentynine Palms would complete the day.

Staying in Yucca Valley or Twentynine Palms can facilitate an early start the following morning. Be sure to bird the Pinto Basin area and Cottonwood Springs by the middle of the morning or in late afternoon. Save your wildflower explorations for mid-day, when the birds are less active.

THE BIRDING SITES

Morongo Valley: To reach Morongo Valley, go north at the intersection of I-10 and California 62 and proceed for 10.5 mi., climbing through the Little San Bernardino Mountains up to the plateau of the Mojave desert.

BIG MORONGO RESERVE: At the town of Morongo Valley, turn right (east) on East Drive and go three blocks to the Reserve. Park your car and bird the paths of the Reserve that lead through the moist willows and cottonwoods of the oasis, much of it on a boardwalk above the seeping water and around a tule-lined pond. Expect to see a number of western migrant species including flycatchers, vireos, warblers and orioles in the dense thickets.

Across the way, you'll see the playing fields and swing sets of Covington Park, best known as the home of the Vermilion Flycatcher. Bird the little Park and scan the cottonwoods everywhere for Brown-crested Flycatcher, Cassin's Kingbird and Summer Tanager.

Joshua Tree National Monument — from West Entrance to Twentynine Palms: From Morongo Valley, go 8 mi. north to the bustling town of Yucca Valley, a good place to stop for gas or food.

After another 8 mi., the little town of Joshua Tree marks the turn-off point to the Monument. Watch closely for an unobtrusive brown sign on your right that says Joshua Tree National Monument. Turn right (east) here onto Park Blvd. After the turn, the Monument lies 5 mi. ahead.

This portion of the trip includes the heart of the Joshua tree woodland, representing the Mojave Desert segment of the Monument. Stop and get out of your car anywhere along the road to observe the wildlife. Walking out among the Joshua trees, you may see and hear more birds than are obvious from the moving car.

HIDDEN VALLEY CAMPGROUND: Nine miles into the Monument you will come to Hidden Valley Campground, the first of several dry campgrounds. Watch for Prairie Falcons, White-throated Swifts, and ravens on the boulders that loom above you. LeConte's Thrashers have nested in the area, and you may be lucky enough to spot one. Otherwise, just enjoy the Scott's Orioles, which often perch in the Joshua trees nearby, and the Black-throated Sparrows singing everywhere.

CAP ROCK NATURE TRAIL: About a mile beyond Hidden Valley Campground, take the Keys View Road turn-off to your right, go .25 mi., and turn left into the Cap Rock Nature Trail parking lot. Walking the trail here should turn up some high desert birds, and will certainly enhance your botanical knowledge of the typical shrubs of the area.

KEYS VIEW: Proceed 5.6 mi. along the road to Keys View for a visit to one of the highest points in the Monument. From this 5,185 ft. overlook, you see the Colorado Desert spread out below you, as it slopes far away to the Salton Sea. The snow-topped peak to the west of Palm Springs is Mt. San Jacinto, rising from the desert floor to over 10,000 ft.

Notice the pinyon-juniper habitat in this high corner of the Monument. Small populations of Mountain Quail, Scrub Jay, Plain Titmouse, Bushtit, California Thrasher and Rufous-sided Towhee exist here, and occasionally a Pinyon Jay or Gray Vireo, may be discovered.

TWENTYNINE PALMS OASIS and VISITOR CENTER: Retrace your route from Keys View back to the main road and turn right (east) toward the intersection with Pinto Basin Rd.(9.7 mi.). En route, you may wish to stop at Sheep Pass or Jumbo Rocks Campgrounds to explore.

At the junction with the Pinto Basin Rd., turn left (north) and follow the signs to Twentynine Palms and the Visitor Center (8.1 mi.). The Visitor Center will be to your left as you enter the town of Twentynine Palms. Be sure to spend some time here to acquire books and a bird checklist of Joshua Tree National Monument, if you have not already done so. The interesting exhibits and information offer a good background for your desert trip.

The little trail that meanders through the original oasis, which contained 29 palms, is a good birding spot for Gambel's Quail, Cactus Wrens, Verdins and Phainopeplas.

If you spend the night in the town of Twentynine Palms, revisit the oasis the next morning. It is accessible even if the Visitor Center is not open yet.

Fortynine Palms Oasis hike: This moderately steep hike is lovely in the early morning or late afternoon. Aside from Lost Palms Oasis (near Cottonwood Springs and a much longer hike), Fortynine Palms is the only natural oasis in the Monument retaining the remote quality of the desert. In spring migration, unusual birds may be encountered—particularly warbler species—but the hike is recommended more for a close-up of the desert landscape and oasis' setting than for high numbers of birds. Round trip distance is 3 miles.

To reach the trailhead to Fortynine Palms Oasis, go left (west) 4 mi. on California 62 (from its intersection with Utah Trail Rd. just north of the Visitor Center). Turn left (south) off California 62 at Canyon Rd., where there's an animal hospital on the corner, and follow Canyon Rd. 1.8 mi. to its end at the National Park Service parking area. (You are once again in Joshua Tree National Monument here).

Twentynine Palms to Cottonwood Springs via Pinto Basin Rd.:
From the Twentynine Palms Visitor Center in the town of Twentynine Palms, retrace your route back into the Monument. It is 36 mi. from the Twentynine Palms Visitor Center to Cottonwood Springs. After 7.7 mi., bear left at the intersection and follow the signs to Cottonwood Springs via Pinto Basin Rd.

Driving along the Pinto Basin Rd., you gradually descend from the Mojave Desert plateau to the lower Colorado Desert sections of the Monument. En route, visit the Cholla Cactus Gardens and take the self-guided nature trail.

COTTONWOOD SPRINGS: As you approach the Cottonwood Springs complex of campground, oasis and Visitor Center, pull off to your left (east) and stop at the Visitor Center first. The building here contains only a small selection of books and pamphlets, but the Nature Trail around it is definitely worth walking. A pair of Bendire's Thrashers (very uncommon in the Monument) has nested near the Visitor Center for the past several years.

Cottonwood Springs can be crowded, especially on spring weekends, but if you visit on weekdays and get there early in the day, this desert oasis is the best birding spot in the Monument. It boasts a bird checklist of over 200 species, 80% of which are migrants and vagrants.

After stopping at the Visitor Center, continue east about a mile to the springs. From April 1 to mid-May, it pays to simply take up a post near the springs and watch while the birds—a variety of migrants and desert residents—come in to the pools to bathe and drink. Wander further down the wash and look for birds and blooming wildflowers. Costa's Hummingbirds, Phainopeplas, Verdins, and Black-throated Sparrows abound, plus all the Western warbler species in migration.

On your way back from the springs to the Visitor Center and Pinto Basin Rd., stop and turn right (north) into the campground. A pair of LeConte's Thrashers once nested on the edge of the campground here, in spite of their reputation as one of the most shy and elusive of desert species. If the campground isn't packed with people, explore the area for birds.

Any of the dry, sandy washes that cross the road en route from the springs back to the Visitor Center are worth birding.

To reach I-10, the main highway back to Indio, turn left (south) outside the Cottonwood Springs Visitor Center, and go 5.9 mi. on the Pinto Basin Rd. as it winds down through Cottonwood Pass. The dry washes and desert vegetation by the roadside often hold numerous birds in migration, since Cottonwood Pass is a recognized thoroughfare for birds passing north from Mexico.

CALIFORNIA'S MOJAVE DESERT:
Spring birding amidst lush oases
Checklist of Common Birds by Habitat

DESERT OASIS
Gambel's Quail
White-winged Dove
Mourning Dove
Common Barn-Owl
Western Screech-Owl
Long-eared Owl (uncommon)
Anna's Hummingbird
Costa's Hummingbird
Ladder-backed Woodpecker
Nuttall's Woodpecker (local)
Northern Flicker
Western Wood-Pewee
Western Flycatcher
Black Phoebe
Vermilion Flycatcher (local)
Ash-throated Flycatcher
Brown-crested Flycatcher (local)
Cassin's Kingbird
Western Kingbird
Scrub Jay
Verdin
Bushtit
White-breasted Nuthatch
Bewick's Wren
Cactus Wren
Ruby-crowned Kinglet (winter)
Black-tailed Gnatcatcher
Townsend's Solitaire (winter)
Swainson's Thrush
Hermit Thrush (winter)
American Robin
Northern Mockingbird
California Thrasher (local)
Phainopepla
Bell's Vireo (rare)
Solitary Vireo
Warbling Vireo
Orange-crowned Warbler
Nashville Warbler
Lucy's Warbler (rare, local)

Yellow Warbler
Yellow-rumped Warbler
  (Audubon's)
Black-throated Gray Warbler
Townsend's Warbler
Hermit Warbler
MacGillivray's Warbler
Common Yellowthroat
Wilson's Warbler
Yellow-breasted Chat
Summer Tanager (local)
Western Tanager
Black-headed Grosbeak
Lazuli Bunting
Rufous-sided Towhee
Brown Towhee (local)
Black-chinned Sparrow
  (uncommon)
Black-throated Sparrow
Song Sparrow
Lincoln's Sparrow (winter)
White-crowned Sparrow
Dark-eyed Junco
Hooded Oriole
Northern Oriole (Bullock's)
House Finch
Lesser Goldfinch
Lawrence's Goldfinch

JOSHUA TREE WOODLAND
Turkey Vulture
Red-tailed Hawk
American Kestrel
Prairie Falcon
Mountain Quail (rare)
Common Barn-Owl
Western Screech-Owl
Burrowing Owl (rare)
Lesser Nighthawk
Common Poorwill
White-throated Swift

Ladder-backed Woodpecker
Northern Flicker
Horned Lark
Western Kingbird
Scrub Jay
Pinyon Jay (local)
Common Raven
Plain Titmouse
Verdin
Rock Wren
Cactus Wren
Canyon Wren
Black-tailed Gnatcatcher
Western Bluebird
California Thrasher (uncommon)
LeConte's Thrasher
Phainopepla
Gray Vireo (rare, summer)
Black-throated Sparrow
Western Meadowlark
Hooded Oriole
Scott's Oriole
House Finch

CREOSOTE BUSH SCRUB
Turkey Vulture
Swainson's Hawk
Red-tailed Hawk
American Kestrel
Greater Roadrunner
Common Barn-Owl
Great Horned Owl
Costa's Hummingbird
Gray Flycatcher (rare, winter)
Common Raven
Sage Thrasher (winter)
LeConte's Thrasher
Phainopepla
Loggerhead Shrike
Black-throated Sparrow
Sage Sparrow (winter)

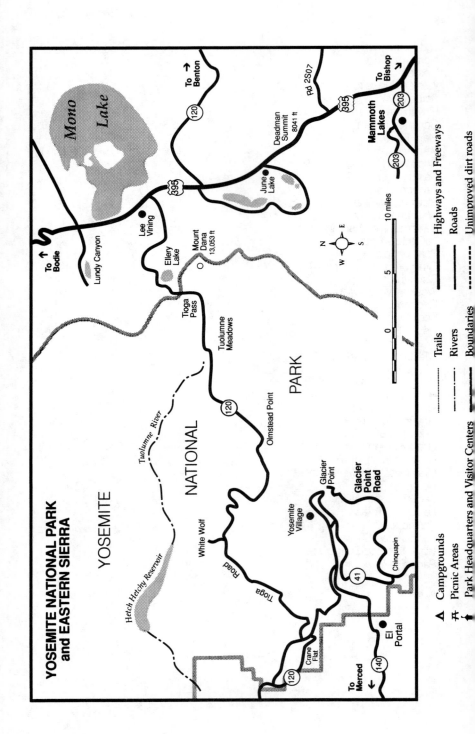

YOSEMITE NATIONAL PARK and EASTERN SIERRA

YOSEMITE NATIONAL PARK

Mono Lake

To Bodie

To Benton

To Bishop

Lundy Canyon

Lee Vining

Ellery Lake

Mount Dana 13,053 ft

Tioga Pass

Tuolumne Meadows

Deadman Summit 8041 ft

Rd 2S07

395

203

203

Mammoth Lakes

June Lake

120

Olmstead Point

120

Tuolumne River

Hetch Hetchy Reservoir

NATIONAL

PARK

White Wolf

Tioga Road

Yosemite Village

Glacier Point

Glacier Point Road

Chinquapin

41

Crane Flat

El Portal

120

140

To Merced

N
W E
S

0   5   10 miles

············· Trails
—··—··— Rivers
━━━ Boundaries

━━━ Highways and Freeways
─── Roads
------- Unimproved dirt roads

▲ Campgrounds
🏕 Picnic Areas
🚩 Park Headquarters and Visitor Centers

6

FROM YOSEMITE TO THE EAST SLOPE:
Birding the splendors
of the Sierra Nevada

Yosemite National Park has enthralled birdwatchers ever since John Muir first extolled its natural wonders over a hundred years ago. Lying like a jewel in the midst of the Sierra Nevada range—that great 400 mile-long chain of mountains bordering California on the east—Yosemite is a gateway to the forested slopes and lush meadows of the Sierra Nevada. It is here, on a scenic journey seldom equaled anywhere in the West, that birders can venture from the shade of the giant sequoias in Yosemite up over the crest of the Sierran summit, and descend to the sagebrush plains beyond, a trip encompassing an enormous variety of habitats filled with birds.

The specialty birds of the western slope of the Sierra, and those of the Great Basin country adjacent to its eastern escarpment, entice even the most experienced birders to repeat this trip often, and at various seasons. But for the first-time visitor, late spring through mid-summer is the best time to appreciate the glory of this mountain range and its plethora of bird life.

In Yosemite's forests, the rare Great Gray Owl lurks in isolated meadows. The Black-backed Woodpecker drills the bark of lodgepole pines, and the Pine Grosbeak hides in willow

163

thickets beside little creeks. The American Dipper frolics at the base of breathtaking waterfalls. Mountain Quail, Black Swift, Calliope Hummingbird and Townsend's Solitaire: the list of montane species here reads like a guide to some of the most avidly-sought birds of the West.

Continuing over the crest of the Sierra Nevada, the birds of the Great Basin beckon from a landscape of stark beauty. Your first views of the tiny Brewer's Sparrow, the wonderful, chartreuse Green-tailed Towhee, or perhaps even a flock of Pinyon Jays raucously calling overhead, should convince you of the bird finding opportunities offered by several locations on the eastern slope.

The route traverses one of the most famous birding transects in California, due to the variety of bird habitats encountered. You leave the agricultural fields of the Central Valley, ascend the foothills, and finally enter the dense coniferous forests of Yosemite National Park. Following Tioga Road on its lovely route through the high Sierra, you then proceed down the steep eastern slope to visit the Mono Lake area. Here, snow-capped spires give way to aspen-lined creeks and scented sagebrush.

Mono Lake is the breeding ground of about 50,000 California Gulls, as well as numerous Snowy Plovers. Thousands of Red-necked and Wilson's Phalaropes use the lake as a stop-over in migration. South of Mono Lake, our trip will conclude at the town of Mammoth Lakes, an excellent spot—less well-known to birders than Yosemite but equally productive—to acquire any mountain birds you might have missed.

In the space of a mere 80 miles as the crow flies, a trip across the Sierra Nevada will take you from near sea level to heights of 10,000 feet (14,000 if you scale one of the peaks!) and back down. Join me as we embark on a birding trip that has become a universal favorite, a classic introduction to much of California's fauna and flora.

". . . no temple made with hands can compare with Yosemite. Every rock in its walls seems to glow with life. Awful in stern, immovable majesty, how softly these rocks are adorned, and how fine and reassuring the company they keep: their feet among beautiful groves and meadows, their brows in the sky, a thousand flowers leaning confidingly against their feet, bathed in floods of water, floods of light, while the snow and waterfalls, the winds and avalanches and clouds shine and sing and wreathe about them as the years go by, and myriads of small winged creatures—birds, bees, butterflies—give glad animation and help to make all the air into music."

The above passage appears in *The Yosemite* by John Muir. Published in 1912, this volume contains some of his finest writing on the Yosemite area.

It was John Muir, the explorer, naturalist and writer, who influenced Congress to create Yosemite National Park in 1890. Muir's love of Yosemite's natural beauty inspired his writings, helping to popularize the high Sierra. Writing articles on the geology, weather, trees and other aspects of Yosemite's natural history, Muir became one of the first true conservationists in the West. His spiritual leadership of the environmental movement remains as a legacy to all of us who treasure Yosemite and the Sierra Nevada.

Muir's description of the American Dipper, entitled "The Hummingbird of the California Waterfalls" (originally published in *Scribner's* magazine in 1878) stands as an example of keen bird observation and has been called the finest bird biography ever written.

Muir spent six years actually living in Yosemite Valley and was the first person to explain the glacial origin of this segment of the park. A classic U-shaped valley formed by a glacier which scooped out the Merced River canyon thousands of years ago, Yosemite Valley is now nearly one mile wide and almost a mile deep in some places, flanked by cliffs and cascading waterfalls. The Merced River flows down the center of the valley floor. Tributary streams flowing into the Merced River did not carve their valleys as deep as that of the Merced, and thus their canyons have been stranded high above the valley floor. The streams pour out of the canyon mouths, known as hanging valleys, and join the Merced in leaping descent into Yosemite Valley.

After exploring the valley floor, wind your way upwards along the Glacier Point Road. At the end of the road, the view from Glacier Point gives a feeling for the geologic forces that molded this famous valley. It is one of the most unforgettable vistas in the world.

Watching Birds in Yosemite: Even without knowing the concept of vegetation zones, birders in the Sierra Nevada quickly begin to observe that different types of vegetation are frequented by different birds. In mountainous country, such as the Rocky Mountains of Colorado, the "Mexican mountains" of southeastern Arizona and the Sierra Nevada, these habitats or vegetation zones are compressed into very short distances. As the elevation changes, so do the birds that live there. Bird finding in Western mountains produces a great variety of birds in a relatively short period of time.

You will see the term "life zones" in books about the fauna and flora of the West. Biologists in the past have used latitudinal zones to describe climate belts. In other words, climbing a mountain was likened to traveling from south to north, ecologically speaking. C. Hart Merriam, the famous biologist who originated the concept, described the lowest elevations as Sonoran (typical of Mexican climate). Then, he proceeded up the mountain by identifying the Transition Zone (central U.S.), Canadian (northern U.S. and southern Canada), Hudsonian (Hudson Bay region) and the Arctic Zone.

Nowadays, however, biologists prefer to give these habitats names more accurately describing the vegetation that grows there. Instead of the terms Sonoran and Transition Zones, they use the terms foothill chaparral zone and ponderosa pine zone.

As you cross the Sierra Nevada, the dramatic changes in vegetation are obvious. The chaparral-covered foothills give way to oak woodlands, which merge into the pine forests, and so on. Although climatic changes accompany this upward progression, they are no longer used as descriptive terms.

Vegetation zones are more useful, because they are not always strictly tied to elevation. A cool north-facing slope could support a dense forest of mixed conifers, while the sunny south-facing slope at the same elevation might have a quite different ponderosa pine forest. Mini-habitats are thus created, each with their respective bird life.

As a birder, you might find it helpful to learn in a general way the appearance of the plants or trees frequented by the birds you seek, especially when traveling the mountain ranges of the West. Although the boundaries between habitats are not always clear-cut, they exist as a rough guide to aid you in planning your bird trip. Just as you would not look for Black-backed Woodpeckers in the oak woodland, nor Mountain Quail above 10,000 feet, learning the preferences of your targeted birds saves time and assures a great trip.

Climate and Habitats of the Sierra Nevada

The Sierra Nevada range rises like a tilted block, with the gently sloping side facing west towards the Pacific Ocean and the steeply vertical side facing east towards Nevada. Due to structural uplift and earthquake faulting, the eastern escarpment of the range rises high above the flat Owens Valley, creating lofty peaks along its backbone.

The Sierra Nevada was christened "the snowy range" by early explorers, who spied the snow-capped mountains of the western slope from far away. The range is covered with a deep snowpack in normal winters. It receives much precipitation from Pacific storms that blow in during the winter and, as these air masses are forced upward and cool, they dump heavy snowfall. The lush coniferous forests, wet meadows and rushing streams—so typical of Yosemite—are a result of these moist, cool winters.

In contrast, the arid eastern side of the Sierra Nevada is closer in vegetation and bird life to that of the Great Basin, with its pinyon-juniper stands and sagebrush flats. The eastern slope gets little precipitation from Pacific rain clouds, lying as it does in the rain shadow of the Sierra's great peaks, which receive most of the moisture. An exception to this is Mammoth Pass in the vicinity of Mammoth Lakes, which allows Pacific storms to spill over to the eastern side, bringing heavy snows to the town of Mammoth Lakes and the adjacent popular ski area.

The Sierra Nevada is a young range, geologically speaking. Volcanic cones, earthquake faults and hot springs, so visible among the sagebrush plains bordering the eastern slope, attest to this. Mono Lake, formed more than a million years ago as a result of the uplifting of the Sierran escarpment, is in a geologic "bathtub," a result of the downwarping of the Mono basin.

Foothill Woodland and Chaparral: Traveling east on California 120, 140, or 41 towards Yosemite, you pass first through the rolling agricultural fields and grasslands of the San Joaquin Valley and then meet the chaparral-covered foothills. In the chaparral, blue oaks and interior live oaks are interspersed with gray pines (formerly known as digger pines). The multi-branched trunks of the gray pines, draped with long greenish-gray needles and clasping large tan cones, cling to even the hottest hillsides. Gray pines are the first pines to appear on the western Sierra slope, standing out against the background of chamise, manzanita and buckbrush that constitute the chaparral here.

In March and April the foothills begin to come alive. The new green on the oaks and the magenta bloom of the redbud trees greet the cool, windy days of spring. White popcorn flower and blue lupine are a mass of blooms along the roadsides.

This is the time to bird the foothills. Resident and migrant species of birds are in full song. The trill of the Bewick's Wren and the haunting call of the Wrentit echo from the canyons. Scrub Jays and Plain Titmice scold from the oaks.

By mid-summer, however, the foothills are hot and pretty empty of bird life. When the heat comes, some foothill bird species straggle upslope to forage in cooler climes. You may find them at higher elevations in the Sierra in July and August.

Since the birds occurring in California's chaparral habitat are handled in detail in Chapter Seven, a lengthy discussion is superfluous here.

Representative birding sites:
Turn-outs along California 120, 140 or 41 en route to Yosemite National Park.

Ponderosa Pine Forest: At about 5500 feet, the warm chaparral-clothed hillsides give way to the first ponderosa pines. (They are also known as yellow pines, and this is sometimes called the yellow pine belt.) With their thick bark divided into orange plates and their tall, open branches, the ponderosas are on the leading edge of the true conifer forest, welcoming the eager visitor to the clean air and piney fragrance of the Sierra.

The ponderosa, a sun-loving pine found on mountainsides in nearly every Western state, adapts well to the snowy, moist winters and long, hot summers of the western side of the Sierra. Its look-alike, the Jeffrey pine, sticks to the drier, more open countryside, such as that around Mammoth Lakes and along U.S. 395.

Ponderosa pines and Jeffrey pines are often indistinguishable at a distance: both are tall, sturdy-looking pines with platey bark and longish needles borne in clusters of three; but, if you examine the cones you can always identify the two. Ponderosa cones are smaller than those of the Jeffrey and the spines on the scales point outward, pricking your hand when you pick them up. Jeffrey pine cones are considerably bigger and their spines point inward, making handling easy. The phrases "gentle Jeffrey" and "prickly ponderosa" may help you remember this in the field.

At moister sites, ponderosas are joined by a host of other conifers, such as sugar pine, Douglas-fir, incense-cedar and white fir. Deciduous California black oaks are sprinkled throughout this green forest, and they turn a lovely yellow-orange in autumn.

On the forest floor, a shrubby member of the rose family, known as the kit-kit-dizze grows. Perfuming the air with its pungent aroma, this shrub has earned the name of "mountain misery," due to a tar-like substance exuded from its stems and leaves.

The ponderosa pine forest is exceptionally rich in bird species. In late spring, the trees resound with bird song.

Hairy Woodpeckers and White-headed Woodpeckers are both common here, often located by their calls. The Hairy gives a sharp single-noted *peek,* while the White-headed gives a double-noted *ick-ick.* Some birders remember this difference by comparing the Hairy and White-headed calls to those of the Downy Woodpecker and Nuttall's Woodpecker in the lowlands. That is, the single-syllable squeak of the Hairy Woodpecker resembles the call of the Downy, and the double-noted call of the White-headed sounds similar, at times, to that of the Nuttall's.

Speaking of sounds, differentiating the lovely warbling song of the Black-headed Grosbeak from that of the Western Tanager often puzzles birders. The jaunty grosbeak song is faster and crisper than that of the tanager. Think of the grosbeak's clear notes as sounding like "a tanager who has got rid of his hoarseness," as Thoreau put it.

Singing forth in slower cadence, not as melodious as the grosbeak, the Western Tanager does not need to call attention to himself. Almost a symbolic bird of the Western montane forests, his gorgeous red and yellow plumage is an arresting sight high in the boughs of ponderosas and Douglas-firs.

The male Olive-sided Flycatcher perches on a treetop singing his *Quick, three beers,* staking out his territory and proclaiming availability to passing female Olive-sideds. Their near carbon copy, the smaller Western Wood-Pewee, is quieter, but more widespread. The pewee is the most abundant flycatcher in the Sierra. Both Olive-sided Flycatchers and Western Wood-Pewees share a preference for open edge situations created by meadows, open woods or streams. Their insect-eating flights need the airspace in which to sally forth and nab their prey.

Pileated Woodpeckers, their crow-like forms maneuvering through the trees, may be glimpsed fleetingly. Large rectangular holes drilled in the bark of the ponderosas signal the presence of one of these huge woodpeckers in the area, probably on nesting territory.

If you have had difficulty spotting Mountain Quail further down the mountain, watch for them in this zone, particularly in areas where manzanita grows. The smooth sienna trunks and bluish leaves of the manzanita shrubs, often burgeoning to good-sized trees, give the quail coveys nice protection.

The Northern Pygmy-Owl hides in the ponderosa forest, sitting quietly in the early morning hours on the branch of a nearby tree. Sometimes looking remarkably like a pine cone—one with a sparrow-sized tail protruding from it—the pygmy-owl frequently hunts and calls during daylight hours. The owl may be coaxed to answer an imitation of its call, thus revealing its presence.

Whether or not the pygmy-owl responds to yours, or a tape's, imitation of its low, halting whistle, other small birds of the forest will react swiftly. Pygmy Nuthatches, Brown Creepers, and several species of warblers will soon fill the surrounding trees, scolding and calling. This mob of stirred-up little birds attracts other bird species, curious about the fracas. Meanwhile, the guilty birder finds him or herself immersed in a flock of frantic bird activity, with plenty of time to examine and identify each of the attackers. (As always, use tape recorders with discretion in these forests. All the birds are there, you just need to be patient.)

Representative birding sites:
Yosemite Valley area: Yosemite Valley floor, Bridalveil Fall Picnic Area.
Glacier Point Road area: Chinquapin.
Crane Flat area: Foresta, Tuolumne Grove.

Mixed Conifer Forest: This verdant forest, as its name implies, contains a rich mixture of beautiful cone-bearing trees. White fir, Douglas-fir, incense-cedar and sugar pine grow above the cool forest floor. The sunnier slopes of the ponderosa pine country are left behind, as you climb up the Sierran range into the heart of the montane forest.

Around areas such as Crane Flat, the tall spires of the silver-barked white firs dominate the forest, forming deep woods adjacent to grassy meadows. White and red firs are the only true firs in the Sierra. Their cones furnish food for chickarees, little squirrel-like fellows which give a high-pitched whinnying call when alarmed, a familiar sound throughout the Sierra and one often mistaken for a bird. Busily the chickarees cut the green cones and let them fall to the ground, stashing them for the long winter, when they will have plenty of time to shuck the seeds.

The sugar pines, with their graceful, spreading limbs, are the ones with the long, pendant cones dangling from the tips of their branches. The clever Steller's Jays have figured out how to make intelligent use of the cones. They choose a tall sugar pine and fly up to one of the long cones, knocking a seed loose. As the dislodged kernel falls, the jay swoops down and retrieves it in mid-air!

Incense-cedars, white firs and sugar pines—huge trees in their own right—seem dwarfed in comparison with the giant sequoias. These big trees are confined to a series of 75 groves scattered along the western slope of the Sierra, mostly between the 5000 and 7000 foot level. Giant sequoias are so perfectly proportioned that when you gaze up at one, it is hard to comprehend just how massive its bulk is. Old growth giant sequoias average 10 to 15 feet in diameter and 250 feet in height, the world's largest living things!

A visit to the Tuolumne or Mariposa groves in Yosemite will give you a chance to view these stupendous trees. From the damp forest floor around the base of the giant sequoias, look for a Winter Wren or two hopping about.

The mixed conifer forest contains a number of bird species desirable to the first-time visitor. The light sound of a wood-pecker's tapping should be explored, in the hopes of locating a Red-breasted Sapsucker. (Its relative, the Williamson's Sap-sucker, is usually found at higher elevations in the Sierra.) The key to locating woodpeckers and sapsuckers is to listen for the high-pitched whining of the juvenile birds as they beg for food in June and July. They will do this from the nest hole even when the adult isn't present, and afterwards, when they are fledged, for several weeks. This begging noise should alert you to a possible family group in the vicinity, the adult birds usually being pursued by a few hungry youngsters.

Birders can expect to find several species of the "gnat kings," as David Gaines calls them in his excellent *Birds of Yosemite and the East Slope:* "Some of the small Sierran flycatchers, especially the five species of the genus *Empidonax,* the 'gnat kings,' are so similar that most birdwatchers despair of telling them apart. When Theodore Roosevelt met John Muir, he reputedly asked, 'How does one distinguish the Hammond from the Dusky Flycatcher?' Muir, who knew more about rocks than birds, probably had no idea. Yet these gnat kings and their relatives differ enough in voice, behavior, habitat and plumage to be recognizable to the cognoscenti, especially in their breeding haunts."

Watch for the unobtrusive Hammond's Flycatcher on moist meadow edges bordered by huge white firs. In the late afternoon, the Hammond's can be spotted as it perches on a low branch, nervously flicking its tail and uttering its *peek* call. Eventually, the bird will dash out from the low perch and snap up one of the thousands of insects hovering around mountain meadows at this season. The Hammond's Flycatcher breeds on the western Sierra slope only, shunning the more arid eastern slope. In contrast, the Dusky Flycatcher, another member of the *Empidonax* group, breeds in the drier forest zones, amongst the ponderosas, jeffrey pines and lodgepole pines, on both sides of the crest.

The beautiful notes of the Hermit Thrush, considered by many to be North America's finest singer, can be heard caroling up and down the scale. The bird is difficult to find, as it holds forth from a quiet hiding place, but its song carries clearly in flute-like tones through the tall trees.

Representative birding sites:
Crane Flat area: Crane Flat, Tuolumne Grove.

Red Fir Forest: The stately brown-barked red firs, festooned with chartreuse-colored lichen, require a well-drained, moist habitat. Red firs flourish in the colder elevations on the western slope, where the snowpack lies deep and undisturbed for many months. At Badger Pass in Yosemite, a lovely forest of red fir cloaks the hillsides south of the Glacier Point Rd. Red firs occur only occasionally on the eastern slope, with the exception of a fine stand near the town of Mammoth Lakes.

Due to the shade of the red fir monoliths and the short summer growing season, the forest floor here is practically devoid of shrubbery. Most birds spend their lives foraging high in the canopy of the firs, or up and down the furrowed bark of the tree trunks, seldom feeding near the ground.

Although birds may seem scarce in the red fir forest, perhaps the difficulty of spotting the bird activity high in the canopy has something to do with it. Mountain Chickadees, Golden-crowned Kinglets, Yellow-rumped Warblers, Hermit Warblers, and Pine Siskins move through the treetops, the thin lisping notes of their calls wafting down to the listening birder.

Evening Grosbeaks relish the cones of the red fir, and their chunky, finch-like shape can be espied in the crowns of the trees. When they fly, the grosbeaks give a very unmusical *chew* call and also a muffled *brrr* note by which they communicate with each other. Watch for the white patches in their wings, a good field mark visible as they fly over high above in small flocks.

Representative birding sites:

Glacier Point Road area: Badger Pass.
Mammoth Lakes area: Twin Lakes Campground, Canyon Blvd.
area.

Lodgepole Forest: Anyone who has hiked the high country of the Sierra recalls the erect, slender little pines that line the wilderness trails in close-ranked formation—the lodgepoles. John Muir called them "Tamarack pines," confusing them with the eastern larch, or tamarack. This explains why there are so many "Tamarack Lakes" scattered throughout the Sierra. On snowier, north-facing slopes, lodgepoles are joined by mountain hemlock, and on very high exposed ridges by the whitebark pine, whose seeds form a staple in the diet of several montane birds.

Red heather, pinemat manzanita, and labrador tea grow in the understory, providing shelter for White-crowned Sparrows and food for Rufous Hummingbirds.

The bird species of the lodgepole forest are often the most prized by birders. Sites along Glacier Point Road and Tioga Road swarm with bird life in early summer. Here, bands of Red Crossbills invade the tree-tops, their loud *kip-kip* call giving them away to the alert observer. With a perfectly-adapted bill, the Red Crossbill pries apart the closely twined whorls of the cones and extracts the seeds with its tongue.

Male Red Crossbills are a nice brick-red, but the females and young are sometimes more difficult to recognize, like heavy-bodied brown finches with varying amounts of yellow on them.

The criss-cross shape of their strange bill is not easily visible unless the birds alight nearby.

Crossbills are joined by the noisy Clark's Nutcracker at this elevation. The nutcracker, which looks like a smartly dressed black and white crow, is actually a member of the jay family. With raucous call and swooping flight, the nutcracker plays about the trees at timberline, seeking the cones of the whitebark pine.

The Clark's Nutcracker has a masterful approach to the problem of survival over the long, Sierra winter. If the cone crop of the whitebark pine is good, the nutcracker harvests the seeds with its chisel-like bill and stashes them in selected spots in its territory. Buried safely underground and covered with a blanket of snow, the pine seeds help the birds subsist throughout the long winter and spring.

In order to retrieve the seeds, the nutcrackers must remember the exact locations of their particular caches from season to season, even beneath the winter snows. Ornithologists are still studying just how these birds re-locate their seed stores, but they theorize that perhaps a sophisticated system of triangulation, using certain landmarks, enables the birds to go right to the correct spot.

The Black-backed Woodpecker, one of the rarest of Sierran birds, nests in dead lodgepoles here. Like the Three-toed Woodpecker in Colorado, this bird prefers burned-over or beetle-infested patches of forest, where it raises a brood in a hole about 20 feet off the ground. Clinging to the tree's bark, the Black-backed makes a soft tapping when foraging. When they drum, however, the noise is very loud and hollow, carrying for more than a mile.

The Northern Goshawk, the large accipiter hawk of the mountains, soars high above the forest, or dashes swiftly through the trees, bent on pursuing an unwary warbler or sparrow. More easily observed on the eastern slope of the Sierra, the Northern Goshawk is never an expected bird. Keep your eye out for the goshawk flying above the hillsides of some of the narrow canyons such as Lundy, McGee and Rock Creek off U. S. 395.

Blue Grouse are a possibility anywhere in this zone. In the

spring, the males utter a muffled booming noise while perched high in a conifer, not on the ground. Due to the ventriloquial nature of the very low-pitched booming, it is difficult to tell the origin of the sound. With careful listening and an arduous search, you may be able to find the male Blue Grouse at his treetop post during late May or June. A more reliable method is to hunt for Blue Grouse a little later in the season, when flushing a female and a group of young will reveal their location. Note where they alight, usually high up in a pine, and approach quietly.

The Townsend's Solitaire, that gray, thrush-sized phantom of the Sierra, haunts steep canyons and cascading waterfalls. A retiring bird, never found in flocks, the solitaire quietly rests on a limb, waiting for you to discover its presence in the forest. But if you should chance to be hiking beside a rushing stream, or scrambling up the trail between granite slabs, a sudden outpouring of liquid notes will issue from the throat of a mysterious singer. Above the roar of the water rushing down the chasm, the clear song of the Townsend's Solitaire carries pure and sweet. Focus your binoculars on a dead snag protruding from a nearby tree or even on the top of a well-placed boulder to locate the singer.

The Pine Grosbeak, another elusive species that birders hope for in subalpine meadows and lodgepole forests, may appear in front of you when you least expect it. The bird's habits are difficult to predict, but they sometimes feed in streamside thickets on young willow buds, and, later in the season, on the berries of a variety of shrubs.

In the breeding season, the Pine Grosbeak is found in pairs—the strawberry red male and the less colorful female with her olive head and rump. In late summer, Pine Grosbeaks gather in large groups of female and immature birds, which appear very grayish in plumage, with a touch of dull olive on their heads. These flocks wander widely, and have been seen at Twin Lakes Campground and at Sotcher Lake on the eastern side of the Sierra, as well as in Westfall Meadow in Yosemite.

Representative birding sites:
Glacier Point Road area: Summit Meadow, McGurk Meadow,

Bridalveil Creek Campground (including Peregoy Meadow, Westfall Meadow).

Tioga Road area: Siesta Lake, White Wolf, Olmsted Point, Tuolumne Meadows.

Mammoth Lakes area: Twin Lakes Campground, Lake Mary, Lake George, Canyon Blvd. area, Devil's Postpile National Monument (Agnew Meadows and Sotcher Lake).

Alpine Arctic: Even from the heights of Tioga Pass and Minaret Summit, you can gaze upward still at the barren talus slopes and precipitous snow banks of the peaks above timberline. To fully absorb the alpine flora and fauna of the Sierra, you will have to leave your car and hike up one of the many trails to gain an elevation of 10,000 feet. Here, the rocky slopes and huge boulders shelter a number of gorgeous wildflowers, hidden like jewels in crevices and crannies of the mountainsides.

But the Sierran alpine landscape is much drier than that of the Rocky Mountains. The regular summer rains irrigating tundra vegetation in the Rockies do not occur to the same extent on Sierran peaks. The combination of poor soil due to recent and prolonged glaciation and the absence of drenching summer rains explains the paucity of tundra plants in the Sierra Nevada, compared to that of the Rockies.

Still, the Sierran alpine zone does possess some unusual plants related to Pacific coastal varieties, a few of which have been able to ascend the mountains by developing alpine races. Also, you will come across plant species native to the arid Great Basin that have crept up the mountains from the east or risen with them when they were uplifted by earthquake faulting.

Be on the lookout for the hardy birds breeding at this altitude, such as the Horned Lark, Rock Wren, Water Pipit, White-crowned Sparrow and the Gray-crowned race of the Rosy Finch. As for the White-tailed Ptarmigan, it was introduced from the Rockies into remote areas of the Sierra Nevada in the early 1970s, and is infrequently encountered. (For more on alpine birds, refer to Chapter Two.)

Representative birding sites:

Tioga Road area: Ellery Lake, Saddlebag Lake, hike toward

summit of Mt. Dana from Tioga Pass.
Mammoth Lakes area: Take gondola to top of Mammoth Moun-
tain, hike toward Duck Pass from Lake Mary.

Jeffrey Pine, Pinyon Pine and Juniper Forest: Birding the eastern slope of the Sierra is a fascinating contrast to the Yosemite Sierra. This is the start of the Great Basin country, where range after range of rugged mountains dotted with Jeffrey pines, pinyon pines and junipers advance eastward into Nevada and Utah.

In the steep canyons and on the pumice-drained flats along U. S. 395, the Jeffrey pines welcome you to a different kind of forest. Shorter than the ponderosas, and with stouter trunks, the well-spaced Jeffreys provide delightful birding. While walking through a Jeffrey pine forest, take time to pause and sniff the aroma of vanilla that issues from their thick bark. It is particularly pungent in the heat of the day and on warm nights.

Vivid turquoise Mountain Bluebirds perch on the lower branches of Jeffrey pines, especially where the pines border open meadows. The bluebirds fly down and hover above the ground—legs dangling, tail outspread—before pouncing on a bug and retreating to another low vantage point.

Pygmy Nuthatches hang from the clumps and search the needles for tidbits, chattering all the while in high calls. They form the nucleus of flocks of small birds in late summer, which may include Mountain Chickadees, White-breasted Nuthatches, Orange-crowned Warblers and Dark-eyed Juncos.

The understory here is a mix of mountain mahogany, bitterbrush and sagebrush. At the mouths of steep canyons such as Lundy and Lee Vining, this habitat is the home of the Green-tailed Towhee. On the west slope, Green-tailed Towhees are outnumbered by Fox Sparrows, with which they often mingle, but east of the crest the Green-tailed Towhee rules the thickets of snowberry and desert mahogany. With its bright rufous head and chartreuse upperparts, it is hard to miss as it scuffles in the brush, or alights on a boulder to sing its cheerful, lilting song.

Occasionally, the Lewis' Woodpecker, an uncommon breeder in the Jeffrey pine forest, will show itself as it hawks for insects from a utility pole or dead branch. Unlike other woodpeckers, this woodpecker feeds on insects not in the bark but on the wing. It will fly out from a good scanning post, then follow the movements of the insect in mid-air until it captures the prey in its mouth, almost in the manner of a flycatcher. To return to its original lookout, the Lewis' Woodpecker uses a flapping wing-beat, not the undulating flight typical of the woodpecker family. In fact, this bird is sometimes mistaken for a small black crow from a distance, because of its regular flight and dark coloration.

On the lower slopes in poor soils, smaller bluish-gray pines scatter among the sagebrush. These are the pinyon pines, whose little cones contain the pine nuts which many Indian tribes harvested every autumn. Pinyon pines, especially where they exist in the company of junipers, are prime habitat for Gray Flycatchers and Pinyon Jays.

Pinyon Jays have evolved a beneficial relationship with pinyon pines. The pines depend upon the jays to harvest and transport their seeds to communal cache areas in the fall. During the following season, the jays will not reclaim all the buried seeds, so some are left to germinate in the soil, insuring the propagation of young pinyon pines.

Pinyon Jays gather only the most healthy pine seeds. Experiments have shown that the jays collect the good, brown-shelled seeds, not the light-brown empty ones. To ascertain this, the Pinyon Jay tests the soundness of a seed by bill clicking. While the seed is in its bill, the jay rapidly opens and closes its mandibles on the seed. Bad seeds have a hollow sound to them, while good, meaty ones do not. Clark's Nutcrackers also use this method to test the seeds of the whitebark pine.

Pinyon Jays, though highly coveted by birders, are difficult to locate because of their nomadic tendencies. The jays move in social flocks, and if the pinyon pine crop is poor, they will move around considerably from one year to the next. Listen for their nasal *mew* sound as a flock flies over.

Representative birding sites:
Lee Vining area: Bodie, Lundy Canyon, Mono Lake County Park, California 120 to Benton, Deadman's Summit.

Sagebrush Scrub: The expanse of blue sky and wide sagebrush plain lend a flavor of the old West to birding here. The semi-arid high desert is covered with waist-high sagebrush scrub, well-suited for the hot summers and freezing winters accompanied by little precipitation. Walk out into the midst of the sagebrush, until you are completely surrounded by these gnarl-stemmed shrubs. The sweet fragrance of the gray sagebrush mingles with the vinegar-like aroma of the rabbitbrush.

This is the home of the Sage Grouse, the Sage Thrasher and the Brewer's Sparrow. In the early morning, patient scanning of the tops of the sage bushes should produce the tiny, pale Brewer's Sparrow trilling its buzzy song. A Sage Thrasher may hop up from time to time, after which it will retreat in order to forage by running from one sage clump to another, staying for the most part on the ground.

If the object of your search is the handsome male Sage Grouse in display, time your visit for late March and April, when the grouse joins other males to perform his marvelous strutting ceremony before the females on a lek northwest of Crowley Lake. Otherwise, in mid-summer, the females and young Sage Grouse can often be seen on the outskirts of Bodie, where they forage on grasses to fatten up before the long winter.

Representative birding sites:
Lee Vining area: Bodie, California 120 to Benton.
Mammoth Lakes area: Crowley Lake.

Rivers, Lakes, Meadows, Cliffs: Certain special habitats for birds exist throughout the Sierra Nevada, occurring at intervals in many of the vegetation zones discussed above.

Red-winged Blackbirds, Marsh Wrens and Common Yellowthroats live on lake margins, marshes and streams. Every swift-moving Sierran stream boasts a resident pair of American Dippers. California Gulls, en route to and from their breeding grounds at Mono Lake and beyond, can be seen cruising high above Sierra lakes.

The narrow stretches of riparian habitat that formerly lined foothill streams on the western slope, now more and more scarce due to development and agriculture, harbor Willow Fly-catchers, House Wrens, Warbling Vireos, Yellow Warblers, Wilson's Warblers and Lazuli Buntings. Here, where cottonwoods, sycamores and willows still line the streams, these species raise their broods.

Mountain meadows throughout the Sierra are special. These meadows were glaciers eons ago, and gradually became isolated lakes. The lakes slowly filled with sediment and became meadows, which will one day be overtaken by the forest. Exquisite displays of wildflowers adorn the moist Sierran meadows in the summer months, after the winter snow has finally melted.

Montane meadows come alive with birds in late spring. Marshy meadow edges are full of mosquitoes and other insects. Flycatchers and warblers feed on these, while enjoying the protection of the nearby forest for nesting and perching. Lincoln's Sparrows and MacGillivray's Warblers prefer the moist meadow thickets, as do Calliope Hummingbirds, Chipping Sparrows, Purple Finches and many other species.

Calliope Hummingbirds are the only breeding hummers of the Sierra Nevada, yet they are not particularly easy to find. They pause on the tops of low willows to survey their mountain meadow kingdoms, then feed eagerly wherever columbines, scarlet gilias, and currants invite these minuscule hummers to their colorful blooms.

On the cliffs and rock faces of the Sierra, White-throated Swifts, Golden Eagles and, sometimes, Prairie Falcons and Peregrine Falcons nest. Black Swifts nest at Bridalveil Fall. Golden Eagles may be found almost anywhere from the foot-hills to the high country. Tuolumne Meadows is a good place to watch for them overhead.

Lifestyles of Sierran Birds

Not only do Sierran birds select certain vegetation zones, each follows its own lifestyle attuned to the rhythm of the seasons: some are year-round residents, some are long-distance migrants and some short-distance migrants.

Resident birds, such as chickadees, nuthatches and woodpeckers, remain throughout the winter even at high elevations, withstanding the freezing Sierran winters as long as the pine seed crop is good, and the insect supply under the bark adequate. In the occasional year when pine seeds fail to sustain them, Clark's Nutcrackers, Pinyon Jays and Red Crossbills will make visits to the lowlands, sometimes even to the coast. These montane invasions happen only sporadically and when they do, they represent unexpected wide-scale "irruptions" of mountain bird populations in lowland areas of California.

The insect-eating birds, those which feed on bugs in the air, migrate the greatest distances to avoid the winters of the Sierra Nevada. Arriving in the mountains in April and leaving by the end of August, species such as nighthawks, swallows, flycatchers and some warblers journey to Mexico and Middle America and, in some cases, even to South America to spend the winter.

The short-distance migrants, those birds which are ground-feeders, or those which depend on sap or fruit for food, winter in the lowlands of California or other areas in the Southwest or northern Mexico. Red-breasted Sapsuckers, American Robins, Dark-eyed Juncos and many species of sparrows desert the Sierran forests where they breed to forage in the foothills and chaparral of warmer climates during the winter.

Although you would think short-distance migrants would simply leave Yosemite and move to locations in lowland areas of California, studies show it's not that simple. Most of them will leapfrog further south to Arizona or northern Mexico, because many of the California wintering spots are already occupied with populations of birds arriving from Alaska and Canada. For example, the two most common subspecies of the White-crowned Sparrow which winter in southern California, the *gambelii* and the *pugetensis,* nest in Canada and the Northwest, while the subspecies of the White-crowned nesting in Yosemite and the Sierra moves to southern Arizona and Mexico to spend the winter.

Sierran birds have evolved the above lifestyles to take advantage of the abundant summertime food sources available in the high mountains, a feast which ends for many of them with the start of the winter snows. Weeks before the first snow flakes fall, the birds have obeyed their urge to migrate to warmer climes, an age-old pattern which perpetuates itself season after season, handed down instinctually from one generation of the species to another.

The Great Gray Owl: A Birding Close-Up

The largest North American owl, a bird with a wingspan of nearly five feet, the Great Gray Owl is a primary lure for birders to Yosemite. This owl is also one of California's rarest resident birds. Probably only 30 or 40 individuals remain in the Sierra, most of which are found in meadows of Yosemite's fir forests.

The Great Gray Owl, normally a denizen of circumpolar forests, is at the southernmost tip of its range in Yosemite. It is found sparingly, as well, in the Cascades and the northern Rockies.

Great Gray Owls may not even nest every year. Recent studies indicate the few breeding pairs occupying Yosemite's moist meadow systems may breed only in years when there is an above-average density of prey, in particular meadow voles and mice. In other years, the owls will skip nesting.

When a Great Gray Owl pair does set up housekeeping, it chooses a dead fir stump or an abandoned hawk's nest. The female lays up to three eggs in May, but usually only the two chicks that hatch first will survive. Like many birds of prey, sequential hatching of the young spreads out the food demands, assuring that at least the first-born will be able to thrive, should food supplies dwindle later in the season. The youngest owlet has the poorest chance for survival, because the older and stronger fledglings monopolize the prey brought by the adult.

For the first three weeks after the young hatch, the female feeds them by tearing up food delivered by her mate. Then, when the young are larger, the male takes over by bringing food to the nest. After the young leave the nest, the female owl vacates the immediate nesting area, leaving the male to watch over the fledged owlets.

At first this appears a hardship on the young owls, but research has shown that Great Gray Owls are cooperative, frequently feeding young that are not their own offspring. Their sense of territory is restricted to the immediate nest site, and, beyond this area, an adult will respond to a begging owlet, whether it is their own or their neighbor's. Thus, orphans are adopted and cared for, should something befall one or both of their parents.

Great Gray Owls have extraordinarily acute hearing, which perfectly adapts them for hunting in the long grass of Yosemite's meadows. Even a thick blanket of snow does not hinder their ability to detect the slightest noise of a mouse or vole tunneling underneath the grass.

Fortunately, Great Horned Owls, which also breed in Yosemite in a variety of habitats from the foothills to the higher forests, eschew the lush meadows of the mixed conifer forest, preferring to hunt in shorter grass in more open surroundings. They leave the moist, long grass meadows to the Great Gray, which is just as well since Great Horneds will attack and kill young Great Grays, given the opportunity.

Although Great Gray Owls are an endangered species in California, they will probably maintain a stable colony in Yosemite, if left in peace by over-zealous birdwatchers. Do not expect to elicit nest site information from local birders; these locations are secrets closely guarded by biologists studying the owls.

The owl can be very elusive, gliding silently above the meadows at dusk, or perching perfectly hidden on the meadow's edge at dawn. Listen for the scolding of American Robins and Steller's Jays as a clue to the owl's possible whereabouts. Visiting the meadow complexes listed below, especially from June through September when the owls are on territory, is your best chance to see this magnificent bird. Sometimes, the owl acts quite tame and approachable. Please do not get too close or harass the bird!

Some meadows where Great Gray Owls have been known to breed in Yosemite include Crane Flat (north of the Chevron gas station, on both sides of Tioga Road), Peregoy Meadow, McGurk Meadow, and Westfall Meadow, among others.

NOTES FROM A BIRDER'S DIARY
Yosemite National Park

- October 14, 1980, 7:00 P.M. It has been snowing and raining off and on all day—the first storm of the season. Now the evening is settling in, as a dozen of us walk quietly through the snowy woods.

We are on the trail to McGurk Meadow, high up in Yosemite's fir forest. As we approach the meadow, the snow begins falling faster and faster. The dark trees make dim silhouettes bordering the large meadow, and a tiny creek runs through the middle of it.

The birdwatchers hug their ponchos tightly around them; hoods go up and mittens get pulled on. We begin our vigil.

Fruitlessly, our leader stomps bravely around the upper and lower portions of the meadow. It is so quiet... The quiet and the snow flakes provide a mystical setting as we wait in readiness for the appearance of this boreal owl.

Our little band of birders hovers without much hope, licking the snow flakes from our faces and stamping our feet softly to keep warm. I cup my hands behind my ears straining to hear the faintest sound.

"Whoo... whoo... whoo..."—the deep, muffled hooting comes floating towards us from across the dark woods. And again, the low-pitched, eerie sound telling us the owl is close.

We stand, transfixed. This is the hunting call of the Great Gray Owl.

Nobody moves a muscle. All we need is a form to take shape and glide over that snowy clearing. We wait and wait. Visibility at last becomes impossible.

As a faint moon rises, we turn and head back up the cold mile to Glacier Point Road. We whisper to each other, each moved in his own way by the phantom presence of the owl.

That night, I mark an "H" (for "Heard Only") by Great Gray Owl on my life list. I am still mesmerized by that frozen Yosemite meadow and the aura of mystery surrounding the unseen owl. It was, in a way, a more dramatic experience than if the owl had actually appeared.

● August 20, 1986, 6:00 P.M.: It has been six years since I last stood in the falling snow in McGurk Meadow. Six years of imagining what it would be like to finally see the Great Gray. I am almost afraid of being disappointed, should I see the owl. Could it live up to the fantasy bird, the hidden hunter of the chill forest that had been so tantalizingly close on my last attempt?

This time I am earlier in the season, and camped at Crane Flat Campground. I had heard that the owl was being seen regularly in the large meadow behind the Chevron gas station at the intersection of Tioga Road and Big Oak Flat Road.

I shoulder my scope and proceed cross-country to the road, arriving at the gas station. The cars and people milling about seem incongruous with my purpose, but I walk over to the north side of the station for a good view of the meadow. It stretches for nearly a mile, enclosed by dense firs and pines. The long meadow grasses are bent and yellowish-brown this time of year. They harbor the little voles and mice which the Great Gray is so fond of eating.

It is only 6:00 P.M. Plenty of light left.

Looking through the scope, I carefully examine the first object I come to, a felled log with a series of dead branches sticking up from it. The log is about 200 yards away. Is it my imagination or does one of those dead snags have a gray oblong extension to it?

My heart starts beating faster and the adrenalin is pumping. Of course . . . it's a Great Gray Owl.

There's its perfect perch. It can look down closely and comfortably into the meadow. An immobile statue of an owl, peacefully hunting on this late summer evening.

And I'm having a fit! A bird I have wanted for six years! I must get closer, but how?

Every birder with a conscience is aware of the pressures on the Great Gray Owl these days. There are horror stories of birdwatchers harassing these owls so they desert their territories. The ideal solution would be to sneak up on the bird and not disturb it, camouflaged by the surrounding trees.

Car engines are accelerating around me and the traffic at the nearby intersection is busy, but the owl continues to sit imperturbably on its snag.

Circling to the east side of the meadow, I make a giant detour, running and walking and stepping up to my ankles in boggy places, using the woods as cover. Quietly approaching the forest edge, about even with the owl, I hold my breath. What if it has flown?

The owl has gone. I watch and wait and scan the margins of the meadow. I know that Great Grays, when hunting, will not fly deep into the forest. How could it have disappeared?

Just then a slight movement transforms a lichen-draped stump into a Great Gray Owl. Through the scope, at this range, the view is incredible. I can see the gray head swivel slowly, revealing the thick down feathers of the owl's neck. The large, facial discs that comprise this massive head are centered each with a formidable yellow eye. In my mind, those eyes seem to reflect the inner fire of some Arctic forebear; I feel honored to be in the presence of a living thing so wild and free, fierce and functioning.

The prominent white mustachio markings at the base of the facial discs give the owl a grizzled, bearded look. They echo the whitish pattern of the dead lichen clinging to the firs here. His body is pure, gray fluff, flecked with lighter gray-and-white markings.

By now the owl is pretty relaxed. It scratches its head with a long stretch of feathered anklet. It blinks those yellow eyes several times in seeming boredom. But it is far from bored.

All at once, the owl is swooping swiftly from 20 feet up, wings outstretched, down, down to the meadow. Its powerful talons snatch a small, furry object and the owl is off.

Just as it does in the boreal forests of the far north, the Great Gray Owl has hunted successfully tonight. The difference was that tonight there was an observer. An observer who walked elatedly back to camp and erased the "Heard Only" from beside the species named Great Gray Owl on her life list.

TRAVELERS' TIPS

Before You Visit: Eating facilities, stores, and lodgings are available in Yosemite National Park at Yosemite Valley, Wawona, El Portal, Tuolumne Meadows, and White Wolf. Reservations for accommodations are recommended, and should be procured far ahead of your visit. Write to Yosemite Park and Curry Co., Yosemite National Park, CA. 95389, or call (209) 373-4171. For general information and a map write to Superintendent, Yosemite National Park, CA. 95389. Some campgrounds remain on a first-come, first-served basis, and others, such as those on the valley floor, must be reserved through Ticketron up to eight weeks in advance. For campsite reservation forms write to Yosemite Information Office, National Park Service, Yosemite CA. 95389 or call (209) 372-0302, or write Ticketron Reservations, P.O. Box 2715, San Francisco, CA. 94126.

Publications about the park are available by writing to Yosemite Natural History Association, Box 545, Yosemite National Park, CA. 95389.

On the eastern slope, for information on accommodations in Mono County, write the Mono County Chamber of Commerce, P.O. Box 514, Bridgeport, CA. 93517, and in the Mammoth Lakes area, write Mammoth Lakes Chamber of Commerce, P. O. Box 123, Mammoth Lakes, CA. 93546. Usually, lodgings are easy to come by in the non-skiing (summer) season at Mammoth Lakes or nearby June Lake.

For information about campgrounds, trails and maps for the Toiyabe National Forest in Mono County, write Bridgeport Ranger Station, Bridgeport, CA. 93517, and for Inyo National Forest, write Supervisor's Office, Bishop, CA. 93514.

If this is your first visit to Yosemite National Park, you may wish to spend some time at the museum and Visitor Center in Yosemite Village on the valley floor. Keep in mind that the crowds are greatest in this section of the Park, so any birding in the valley should be started very early in the day. Fortunately, there are numerous birding sites in the less crowded areas of the Park, but the earlier you start your day, the better.

On the eastern slope, be sure to visit the headquarters of the Save Mono Lake Committee in Lee Vining, P. O. Box 29, Lee Vining, CA. 93541, phone (619) 647-6386. This little shop, located on the west side of U.S. 395 in Lee Vining (the sign says

Visitor Information), has a good selection of books on nature subjects, the proceeds of which go to preserving Mono Lake.

When To Visit: This tour of the Sierra Nevada, including Yosemite National Park and the eastern slope, was planned with a summer visit in mind. From late May through mid-August, most Sierra birds will either be nesting or will have fledged young, making them easier to see. Road closure could be a problem until early June, if the snowpack is heavy at higher elevations. From the first snowfall, usually in late September, and throughout the winter, Glacier Point Road is closed past Badger Pass, and Tioga Road is closed from Crane Flat to Lee Vining

All in all, a summer trip to the Sierra Nevada will maximize your chances of seeing the greatest variety of bird species on both sides of this glorious range. Although this is also the time when Yosemite National Park is at its most crowded, if you plan your days wisely you can arrange to bird before the sightseers really get going. On the eastern slope, crowds are seldom a problem, but the warm summer days dictate an early start here as well, because bird activity in the lowlands subsides by late morning.

Length of Visit: If you choose to follow the full route—from Yosemite to Lee Vining to Mammoth Lakes to Crowley Lake—plan on spending four or five days. At least two of those nights should probably be spent in Yosemite, accompanied by two full days of birding. It takes a day to do the Bodie/Lee Vining/Mammoth Lakes stretch, and then another couple of days to fully explore the Mammoth Lakes area and Crowley Lake.

Although the roads through the high country of Yosemite National Park are well-maintained, they are winding, narrow and steep in places. In order to bird them, stopping at the suggested locations, takes time and patience. Once arrived at U.S. 395, you can go more rapidly, but there's more distance to cover and the stops are further apart. A five day trip, easily split into smaller segments should you decide to bird only Yosemite or only the eastern slope, should provide sufficient time for plenty of birding and a chance to get to know this unbelievably beautiful country en route.

THE BIRDING SITES

Yosemite Valley area: From El Portal (accommodations are often easier to come by here, because it's just outside the Park) on California 140, travel east approximately 7.5 mi. to Yosemite Valley floor.

YOSEMITE VALLEY FLOOR: To make a loop of the valley floor, follow the signs to Yosemite Village. Along the way, bird the picnic areas and along the banks of the Merced River and its tributaries. Some species to watch for are: Steller's Jay, American Robin, Western Tanager, and Dark-eyed Junco. Look for Pileated Woodpecker above Mirror Lake and Acorn, Hairy, Downy and White-headed Woodpeckers elsewhere. Along the water courses, Spotted Sandpiper, Belted Kingfisher, and American Dipper are present; streamside vegetation may attract Swainson's Thrush, Warbling Vireo, Yellow, MacGillivray's and Wilson's Warblers. Be sure to gaze up at the face of El Capitan from below—a breathtaking sight!—and search the cliff face for Peregrine Falcon. Other valley species are: Band-tailed Pigeon, Great Horned, Northern Pygmy, Spotted (rare) and Saw-whet Owls, Western Flycatcher, Western Wood-Pewee, Olive-sided Flycatcher, Mountain Chickadee, White-breasted and Red-breasted Nuthatch, Brown Creeper, Golden-crowned Kinglet, Solitary Vireo, Yellow-rumped Warbler, Purple Finch and Chipping Sparrow.

BRIDALVEIL FALL PICNIC AREA: Park your car at the Bridalveil Fall Picnic Area on the south side of Yosemite Valley and walk the short distance to gaze at this amazing 620 foot-high stream of water.

Visiting Bridalveil Fall early in the morning or in the late afternoon and evening will increase your chances of seeing the Black Swifts that nest on the cliffs. Black Swifts, like the White-throated Swifts found here in abundance, forage for miles away from the falls during the daytime. You will see White-throated Swifts on the edges, but watch for the Black Swifts directly underneath the waterfall. There are only a few pairs of Black Swifts here; their steadier glide and large, coal-black appearance should distinguish them from the White-throated Swifts.

Glacier Point Road area: To reach the Glacier Point Road, take California 41 south from Yosemite Valley to Chinquapin (9.3 mi.), then bear to your left (east) on the Glacier Point Road towards the Badger Pass Ski area.

CHINQUAPIN: Instead of turning east at Chinquapin, stay on California 41 for .4 mi. and turn right (west) down a road that says Yosemite West. Anywhere along the road, park and bird the area, keeping a lookout for ponderosa pine forest birds; watch for Mountain Quail.

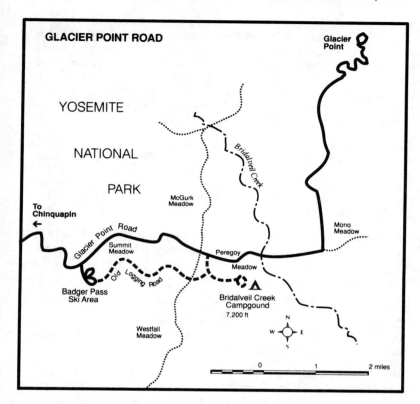

GLACIER POINT ROAD

YOSEMITE NATIONAL PARK

To Chinquapin

SUMMIT MEADOW: Return to the Chinquapin intersection and go 6.8 mi. along Glacier Point Road until you come to a meadow on your right called Summit Meadow (a mile before you get to Bridalveil Creek Campground). Here you can find all the Western warblers, including Hermit, Nashville, and Wilson's. Black-throated Gray Warblers and Lazuli Buntings have been seen, as they move upslope in late summer.

Summit Meadow is especially good for woodpeckers. Both Red-breasted and Williamson's Sapsuckers, plus a family group of Black-backed Woodpeckers, have been found.

McGURK MEADOW: Halfway between Summit Meadow and the entrance to Bridalveil Creek Campground, on Glacier Point Road, a trail leads to your left (north) to McGurk Meadow (1 mi.). All the birds of the high fir and lodgepole forests are possible here, including Great Gray Owl.

BRIDALVEIL CREEK CAMPGROUND AREA: This campground is 7.8 mi. from Chinquapin. Bird the entrance road into Bridalveil Creek Campground, and the surrounding meadow complex (called Peregoy Meadow); both are great places for high country birds. The lodgepole forest may contain everything from Black-backed Woodpeckers to Dusky Flycatchers. To reach

Westfall Meadow, another productive spot, take the old logging road which leaves the campground to the southwest (to the right of a telephone booth). After a short distance, the trail to Westfall Meadow leaves the logging road to your left (south) and reaches the meadow in less than a mile. Species to look for include: Blue Grouse, Great Gray Owl, Williamson's Sapsucker, Black-backed Woodpecker, Ruby-crowned Kinglet, Cassin's Finch, Pine Grosbeak, Evening Grosbeak and Red Crossbill in Westfall, Peregoy and McGurk Meadows.

GLACIER POINT: After birding the Bridalveil Creek Campground area, drive to Glacier Point (8 mi.) for a view of Yosemite Valley far, far beneath you, and the whole backcountry of the Sierra Nevada in the distance. The Glacier Point area has produced Northern Goshawk, Blue Grouse and Northern Pygmy-Owl. On the way to Glacier Point, you may wish to stop at Mono Meadow, approximately 3 mi. from Bridalveil Creek Campground.

Crane Flat area: This part of the route begins at the juncture of the Big Oak Flat Rd. (California 41) and California 140 at the exit from Yosemite Valley. Just before you make this turn-off (follow signs to Crane Flat), park your car and walk over to the little dam on the Merced River there, where an American Dipper is usually found.

FORESTA: Once on the Big Oak Flat Road, watch for the sign to Foresta (3.4 mi.) on your left (west). You may wish to make a side trip here, where typical ponderosa pine belt bird species abound.

CRANE FLAT AREA: About 10 mi. from Yosemite Valley, at the intersection of the Big Oak Flat Rd. and Tioga Rd., you will see a Chevron gas station, to the north of which, on both sides of Tioga Road, a large meadow complex exists. Try to visit here in the early morning or late afternoon, to scan the meadows for Great Gray Owls. In mid-day, the owl retreats into the deeper forest. Vaux's Swifts can be seen hunting over the meadows early and late in the day. Watch for Hammond's Flycatchers.

The Crane Flat Campground is good for other birds found in the mixed conifer forest.

In Tuolumne Grove, at the beginning of the one way Old Big Oak Flat Road, Pileated Woodpeckers, White-headed Woodpeckers, and Red-breasted Sapsuckers are often seen.

Tioga Road area: Proceed onto Tioga Road (California 120) for the trip up over Tioga Pass and down to Lee Vining.

SIESTA LAKE: About 13 miles from Crane Flat, pull over at the turn-out for Siesta Lake. Around Siesta Lake, look for Pine Grosbeak, Williamson's Sapsucker, Red Crossbill, Dusky Flycatcher, and Black-backed Woodpecker. A pair of Black-backed Woodpeckers have nested in an area 1/4 mi. east of the lake on the south side of Tioga Road.

WHITE WOLF: About .9 mi. after Siesta Lake, follow the signs to White Wolf, turning left (north) off Tioga Rd. White Wolf Lodge is a good place for breakfast (summer only; no lunch). Bird the entrance road to the Lodge and stables complex. The meadows around the stables and the Lodge may hold Pine Grosbeak, both Kinglets, Black-backed Woodpecker, Williamson's Sapsucker, and Townsend's Solitaire.

OLMSTED POINT: About 14 miles further along Tioga Rd. at Olmsted Point, which is beyond the turn-off for May Lake, stop and pull off the road. Take the trail down the hillside to the lowest meadow, where there are several large western white pines growing. In early summer, you may hear the deep booming sound of the male Blue Grouse. Later in the year, look for family groups of grouse. Also, you can see Clark's Nutcracker, Townsend's Solitaire, and White-headed Woodpecker here.

TUOLUMNE MEADOWS: Hike any of the trails out of the meadows to see subalpine bird species. Rosy Finches have been seen high up on Mt. Lyell.

ELLERY LAKE: At Ellery Lake, just outside the Tioga Pass entrance station to the Park, you may wish to search for Rosy Finches (Gray-crowned race). If it has been a heavy snowfall year, and you are visiting from late May to early July, the finches may be seen feeding around the rocks after you cross the dam. Otherwise, you will have to hike to higher elevations, such as Saddlebag Lake, northwest of Ellery Lake, or the slopes of Mt. Dana (a trail from Tioga Pass).

Lee Vining area: After leaving Yosemite National Park, follow California 120 to its intersection with U.S. 395 (12.1 mi.). If you wish to make a side trip up to the ghost town of Bodie, turn north (left) on Highway 395 and drive 11.6 mi. to the Bodie turn-off.

BODIE: Turn east (right) at California 270 and follow the Bodie road for approximately 13 miles to Bodie State Historic Park. This road is snow-covered and impassable in winter months.

Great Basin species to be watched for here include Prairie Falcon, Pinyon Jay (along California 270), Sage Thrasher, Vesper Sparrow, and Brewer's Sparrow. Watch for the Mountain Bluebirds that nest in the deserted buildings, and, in late summer, look for female Sage Grouse and their young. This is the best place to add Sage Grouse to your list, unless you visit in March and April to see their strutting dance near Crowley Lake.

LUNDY CANYON: Return to U.S. 395 and go 11.6 mi. south to Lundy Canyon, a right (west) turn off the highway. This gorgeous canyon that snuggles into the Sierra has good birding. Look for Green-tailed Towhee and Calliope Hummingbird among others.

MONO LAKE COUNTY PARK: From the Lundy Canyon turn-off, go south 2.5 mi. on U.S. 395 and turn left (east) on Cemetery Road to Mono Lake County Park. Situated along a small stream, this park is a good picnic spot, and a place to view Mono Lake. The preservation of Mono Lake has become a major conservation issue, since the Los Angeles' water district's lowering of the water level has endangered the health of the gull colony here and made the lake increasingly saline. Walk toward the lake and look for Spotted Sandpiper, American Avocet, Common Snipe, Snowy Plover and California Gull which breed here. Beginning in July, migration brings thousands of Wilson's and Red-necked Phalaropes and Eared Grebes.

CALIFORNIA 120 to BENTON: Past the town of Lee Vining on U.S. 395, travel south (5 mi.) until you come to California 120, which takes off to the left (east) to the town of Benton and Benton Hot Springs. Immediately after making the turn, stop and park off the road on California 120. Birding the sagebrush plains east of the intersection here can produce Gray Flycatcher, Sage Thrasher, and Brewer's Sparrow.

Resuming the drive east on California 120, turn left at the sign leading to the Mono Lake Tufa Reserve. Follow the signs along the dirt road for about a mile to the main parking lot. From here you can see the columnar groups of tufa deposits, tower-like structures formed from calcium carbonate underwater when the lake level was much higher.

Continuing east on California 120, you will come to a pine grove approximately 5.7 mi. from the U.S. 395 intersection (.5 mi. from Tufa Reserve turn-off). On the edge of this forest, there is a pull-out where you can park (100 yards past the "Use Ashtray" sign). Here, check the trees and adjacent scrub for Pygmy Nuthatch, Green-tailed Towhee and Blue-gray Gnatcatcher. Listen for the descending nasal call of the Pinyon Jays, as they roam in flocks through the pines. The Lewis' Woodpecker has nested here in the past, but it is uncommon.

DEADMAN'S SUMMIT: About 3.2 mi. south of Deadman's Summit on U.S. 395, Road 2S07 turns left (east) toward Arcularius Ranch and Long Valley. After 2 mi. on this road, you will come to Big Springs Campground. Turn left here and cross the rushing Owens River, born just upstream from beneath a rock formation. Downstream from the bridge over the river, a pair of American Dippers are resident. Watch for birds of the Jeffrey pine and pinyon-juniper zones.

Back on U.S. 395, .1 mi. further south, a rest area on the right (west) side of the highway is worth a stop for further Jeffrey pine forest birds.

Mammoth Lakes area: To reach the town, turn west (right) on California 203 off U.S. 395, and proceed up the hill.

TWIN LAKES CAMPGROUND: Driving in to Mammoth Lakes on California 203, you'll see the Visitor Center/Ranger Station on your right, good for nature publications and maps of the area. When 203 veers to the right further up the hill, keep going straight. You are now on the Lake Mary Road. Follow this road until you come to Twin Lakes Campground (about 3 mi. from downtown Mammoth Lakes).

Turn off to the right (west) and follow the campground road until it comes to a bridge that crosses between the two lakes. Park here, and walk across the bridge; bear to the left after you cross the bridge. Past the campsites, and before you reach the cabins, a wet "meadow" filled with scrubby willows

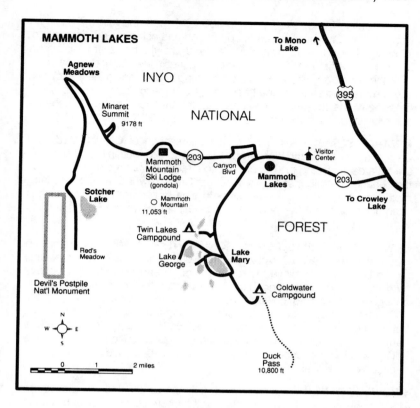

MAMMOTH LAKES

appears on your right. It is surrounded by red firs and nestled against a steep slope. Here, in the willows and surrounding forest, can be found many of the birds of the red fir and lodgepole forest communities, including Northern Goshawk, Red-breasted Nuthatch, Brown Creeper, Ruby-crowned Kinglet, Orange-crowned, Yellow-rumped, Hermit, MacGillivray's and Wilson's Warblers, Lincoln's Sparrow, Pine Grosbeak, Cassin's Finch, Red Crossbill and Pine Siskin.

LAKE MARY and LAKE GEORGE: Retracing your route to the Lake Mary Road, turn right (south) and wind your way up to beautiful Lake Mary. A walk around Lake Mary and the higher Lake George should yield more species such as Calliope Hummingbird, Dusky Flycatcher, Wilson's Warbler, Cassin's Finch, and Red Crossbill, to name a few.

The Lake Mary Store on the far southern edge of the lake has hummingbird (watch for Calliope Hummers) and seed feeders. Across the road, at the Coldwater Campground, you can drive to the trailhead for the Duck Pass trail (Rosy Finches inhabit the talus slopes near the pass; the hike is fairly strenuous).

CANYON BLVD. AREA: Returning to the intersection of California 203 and the Lake Mary Road, take California 203 left (north) and turn left again on Canyon Blvd. Canyon Blvd. leads up through one of the residential areas of Mammoth Lakes to the big ski facility at the end of the boulevard; it is also in the midst of the fir forest. This is good birding (not in the height of ski season). Walk the streets anywhere in the area listening and scanning the treetops. In late summer and early fall, the trees here are sometimes besieged by Red-breasted Nuthatches, Red Crossbills, Cassin's Finches, Evening Grosbeaks and other birds that feed on the plentiful cones.

MINARET SUMMIT: Returning to the intersection of Canyon Blvd. and California 203, follow the highway up to Mammoth Mountain (about 5 mi.). At the ski area, try taking the gondola up to the top of Mammoth Mountain, on the chance you might see Rosy Finches (Gray-crowned race). Past Mammoth Mountain Ski Area, there will be a sign to Minaret Summit, which is often good for birds. The view out to the west of the Minaret Range and the watershed of the San Joaquin River is stupendous.

DEVIL'S POSTPILE NATIONAL MONUMENT: From Minaret Summit you may wish to visit Devil's Postpile National Monument. In the summer months, shuttle buses are employed to ferry visitors up and down the precipitous road to the Monument and back. If you enter the restricted area early enough in the morning, however, you can drive your own car.

There are several good birding places along the road to the Monument, but the best are at Agnew Meadows and Sotcher Lake. Sotcher Lake is particularly productive, and a walk around the established nature trail there will net a number of species, including Pine Grosbeak and possibly Black-backed Woodpecker.

CROWLEY LAKE: After birding the Mammoth Lakes area, drive south on U.S. 395 about 5.3 mi. to the turn-off for Whitmore Hot Springs and Benton Crossing (Road 2S84). A little green church sits by itself at the turn-off. Turn left (east) here and go 1.2 mi., when you'll see a dirt road that bears off to your right. Follow it to the shore of Crowley Lake, stopping often to scan the sagebrush for typical Great Basin species such as Sage Thrasher and Brewer's Sparrow. In early spring, the Sage Grouse males establish a lek amidst the sagebrush on the northwest edge of Crowley Lake.

In late summer, Crowley Lake is good for migrating shorebirds. In addition to the spot mentioned above, you can see shorebirds by returning to Road 2S84 and continuing on beyond where the road crosses the Owens River at Benton Crossing (approximately 6.7 mi. from the original U.S. 395 turn-off). Proceed 3.9 mi. after Benton Crossing to where the road makes a sharp left curve to the east. At this curve, you'll turn right (west) and go on the dirt road leading .7 mi. to the lakeshore. Scanning with a scope should turn up a good number of species, particularly migrant shorebirds.

FROM YOSEMITE TO THE EAST SLOPE:
Birding the splendors of the Sierra Nevada
Checklist of Common Birds by Habitat

**FOOTHILL WOODLAND
AND CHAPARRAL**
Mountain Quail
Common Poorwill
Black-chinned Hummingbird
Anna's Hummingbird
Nuttall's Woodpecker
Scrub Jay
Plain Titmouse
Wrentit
Bewick's Wren
Blue-gray Gnatcatcher
Orange-crowned Warbler
Black-throated Gray Warbler
Rufous-crowned Sparrow
Sage Sparrow
Black-chinned Sparrow
House Finch

PONDEROSA PINE FOREST
Northern Goshawk
Peregrine Falcon (rare)
Mountain Quail
Band-tailed Pigeon
Northern Pygmy-Owl
Spotted Owl (rare)
Black Swift (local)
White-throated Swift
Hairy Woodpecker
White-headed Woodpecker
Pileated Woodpecker
Olive-sided Flycatcher
Western Wood-Pewee
Dusky Flycatcher
Western Flycatcher
Violet-green Swallow
Steller's Jay
Mountain Chickadee
White-breasted Nuthatch
Pygmy Nuthatch
Brown Creeper
Winter Wren
American Dipper

American Robin
Western Bluebird
Townsend's Solitaire
Solitary Vireo
Warbling Vireo
Nashville Warbler
Yellow-rumped Warbler (Audubon's)
Hermit Warbler
Western Tanager
Black-headed Grosbeak
Dark-eyed Junco
Chipping Sparrow
Brown-headed Cowbird
Purple Finch
Evening Grosbeak

MIXED CONIFER FOREST
Northern Goshawk
Blue Grouse
Great Gray Owl (rare)
Vaux's Swift
Red-breasted Sapsucker
Hairy Woodpecker
Pileated Woodpecker
White-headed Woodpecker
Olive-sided Flycatcher
Western Wood-Pewee
Hammond's Flycatcher
Mountain Chickadee
Red-breasted Nuthatch
Brown Creeper
American Dipper
Hermit Thrush
American Robin
Solitary Vireo
Warbling Vireo
Yellow-rumped Warbler (Audubon's)
Hermit Warbler
Western Tanager
Chipping Sparrow
Fox Sparrow
Lincoln's Sparrow
Dark-eyed Junco

Purple Finch
Evening Grosbeak

RED FIR FOREST
Blue Grouse
Williamson's Sapsucker
Hammond's Flycatcher
Mountain Chickadee
Red-breasted Nuthatch
Brown Creeper
Golden-crowned Kinglet
Hermit Thrush
Yellow-rumped Warbler (Audubon's)
Hermit Warbler
Purple Finch
Pine Siskin
Evening Grosbeak

LODGEPOLE PINE FOREST
Northern Goshawk
Golden Eagle
Red-tailed Hawk
Blue Grouse
Calliope Hummingbird
Rufous Hummingbird (late summer)
Williamson's Sapsucker
Hairy Woodpecker
Black-backed Woodpecker
Olive-sided Flycatcher
Western Wood-Pewee
Dusky Flycatcher
Violet-green Swallow
Clark's Nutcracker
White-breasted Nuthatch
Townsend's Solitaire
Hermit Thrush
American Robin
Ruby-crowned Kinglet
Yellow-rumped Warbler (Audubon's)
Chipping Sparrow
White-crowned Sparrow
Dark-eyed Junco
Brown-headed Cowbird
Pine Grosbeak
Cassin's Finch
Red Crossbill
Evening Grosbeak

ALPINE ARCTIC
Prairie Falcon
Common Raven
Horned Lark
Rock Wren
Mountain Bluebird
Water Pipit

White-crowned Sparrow
Rosy Finch (Gray-crowned)

JEFFREY PINE, PINYON PINE AND JUNIPER FOREST
Common Poorwill
Lewis' Woodpecker
Williamson's Sapsucker
Dusky Flycatcher
Gray Flycatcher
Western Wood-Pewee
Steller's Jay
Pinyon Jay
Clark's Nutcracker
Common Raven
Mountain Chickadee
Bushtit
White-breasted Nuthatch
Pygmy Nuthatch
Brown Creeper
American Dipper
Mountain Bluebird
Townsend's Solitaire
Orange-crowned Warbler
Green-tailed Towhee
Fox Sparrow
Dark-eyed Junco
Cassin's Finch

SAGEBRUSH SCRUB
Golden Eagle
Sage Grouse
Great Horned Owl
Common Poorwill
Common Nighthawk
Say's Phoebe
Gray Flycatcher
Horned Lark
Black-billed Magpie
Common Raven
Mountain Bluebird
Sage Thrasher
Loggerhead Shrike
Green-tailed Towhee
Brewer's Sparrow
Vesper Sparrow
Sage Sparrow
House Finch

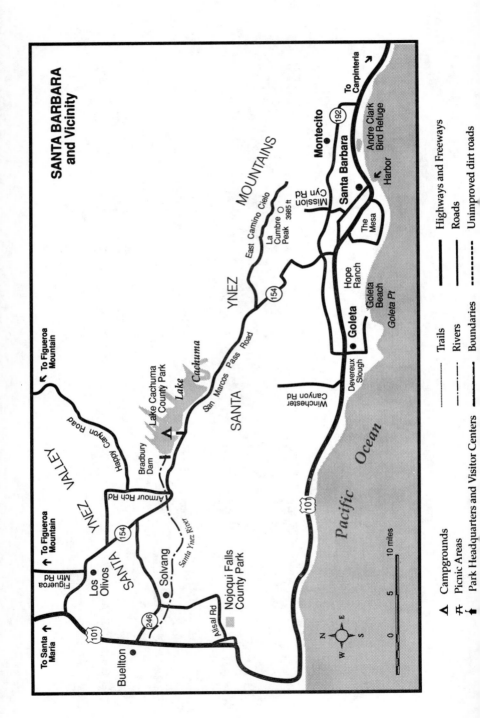

SANTA BARBARA and Vicinity

Legend:
- Highways and Freeways
- Roads
- Unimproved dirt roads
- Trails
- Rivers
- Boundaries
- ▲ Campgrounds
- ⚲ Picnic Areas
- ⛟ Park Headquarters and Visitor Centers

7

SANTA BARBARA:
Birding a famous winter hot spot

Santa Barbara is a birders' paradise. Situated on a narrow coastal shelf between the chaparral-covered Santa Ynez Mountains and the blue Pacific Ocean, this Spanish-style resort town has always been famous for its beautiful setting and rich bird life. An amazing 430 different kinds of birds have been recorded in the Santa Barbara area!

With marine, foothill and montane habitats all close by, Santa Barbara has earned its reputation as a birding hot spot, not only because of its variety of birds, but because the birds are so plentiful during the winter months. Santa Barbara is usually in the top five in the nation in number of bird species seen during the annual Audubon Society Christmas Count held every December. Birds, as well as people, choose to winter in Santa Barbara's pleasant, Mediterranean climate.

Santa Barbarans are justly proud of their beautiful environment, and have attempted to preserve it through the years, frequently taking the leadership in environmental causes. Although the pressures for development increase daily in Southern California, Santa Barbara's diverse bird habitats are still holding their own—at times somewhat tenuously—bolstered by rigid zoning codes and an enlightened populace.

The influence of early California naturalists who headquartered here and helped establish the superb Santa Barbara

Museum of Natural History, such men as William Leon Dawson and Ralph Hoffmann, may account for the strong interest in natural history that has always thrived in the community. The area continues to attract birders and naturalists who take up residence, stimulating bird finding accuracy and turning up countless new bird records.

Doubtless each of these catalysts for birdwatching in the Santa Barbara region has nurtured the others, and we, the birders of Southern California, and those who visit us, are the beneficiaries.

The first part of the chapter features one of North America's most unusual habitats for birds, and one that many Californians take for granted—the chaparral. Those dull looking, brush-clad hillsides hold a precious, hidden community of bird species. The California Quail, Bushtit, Bewick's Wren, Wrentit, California Thrasher, and Rufous-crowned Sparrow are a few of the species revealed to the birder who takes time to stop and listen to the chaparral birds.

The second part of the chapter concentrates on other good birding spots in the Santa Barbara area. Resident species such as Acorn Woodpeckers, Nuttall's Woodpeckers and Hutton's Vireos enliven the oak woodlands. The harbors, lagoons and lakes provide resting places for wintering waterfowl. In the oak woodland/savanna of the adjacent Santa Ynez Valley, the Yellow-billed Magpie—with the condor's demise, now the only endemic California bird—is easy to observe.

From harbors to lagoons, and from creeks to oak woodlands and chaparral, this charming town and its environs invite a birding visit anytime. However, from December through March, when the rest of the country is shivering, Santa Barbara can provide impressive totals of wintering species for an exciting bird trip.

As early as 1929, Santa Barbara was conducting winter bird counts. Led by avid ornithologist William Leon Dawson, Santa Barbara established its fame as a haven for wintering birds by tallying 104 different kinds of birds in a 24-hour period that year, reportedly the highest of all the towns competing in the United States.

Today, the tradition continues. Known as the Audubon

Christmas Count, this annual census of wintering species occurs on a pre-arranged date (rain or shine) in December or early January. The birds must be seen within a prescribed count circle, which has a radius of 15 miles. Over 1500 Christmas Counts are conducted every year, representing communities throughout North America, and Santa Barbara has consistently been one of the front-runners in the number of species recorded. These days the totals of the top contenders are usually from 205 to 220 different species observed, with the highest numbers counted being in communities in California or Texas.

Although the chief value of the Christmas Counts lies in their important contribution to our knowledge of winter bird populations and their movements, an informal rivalry often arises between neighboring towns, intensifying the search for unusual species within each count circle.

During the Santa Barbara Christmas Count, local birders often find interesting species which remain to spend the winter. These, added to the regularly wintering birds, make the birding here even more fruitful.

Climate and Habitats of the Santa Barbara area

Only three percent of the earth's land surface is composed of regions with Mediterranean climates. All have shrubby plant life similar to California's chaparral, and all are located on the western borders of continents in a strip between 30 degrees and 45 degrees north or south latitude.

Santa Barbara's balmy Mediterranean climate has temperate, wet winters and long, warm summers. The region receives about 17 inches of rain per year, most of it between November and March. Summer temperatures are rarely too hot near the coastal strip, due to the cooling fogs borne by sea breezes from the Pacific.

The Santa Barbara region is considered by botanists and, to a lesser degree, by ornithologists, to constitute a watershed between Northern and Southern California. Elna Bakker in *An Island Called California* terms the Santa Ynez Mountains the "Hadrian's Wall" of California flora: north of this range, the fauna and flora assume a more northerly character, while south of the mountains, on the coastal plain encompassing the town of Santa Barbara, species more typical of Southern California prevail. Looking at a map of the California coast along this stretch provides a partial explanation. The coastline turns the corner at Pt. Conception, changing from a north/south direction to one that is east/west. North of Pt. Conception, weather patterns and ocean currents have more of an affinity with those of Northern California, while south of the Point, Santa Barbara, with its sheltered beaches guarded by the Channel Islands, receives a decidedly southern influence.

As illustration, the Chestnut-backed Chickadee, the Nuttall's race of the White-crowned Sparrow, and the Yellow-billed Magpie reach the southernmost tip of their ranges north of the Santa Ynez Mountains. In the same way, numbers of the more southern species such as the Costa's Hummingbird, Phainopepla and Hooded Oriole fall off dramatically in areas to the north of Santa Barbara County.

The habitats described below are located largely south of the Santa Ynez Mountains, because the coastal plain surrounding the city of Santa Barbara attracts the most birds and receives more birder coverage during the winter months.

However, there are a few locations in the Santa Ynez Valley, less than an hour's drive north of Santa Barbara, that have been included as well.

Chaparral: The Santa Ynez Mountains rise steeply behind Santa Barbara reaching a high point of almost 4000 feet at La Cumbre Peak. Looking up at the mountains from below, you notice that, aside from the pale sandstone outcroppings, the whole range is covered by an inhospitable-looking grayish-green mantle of shrubbery. From a distance, this mass of bushy vegetation looks very uninteresting. It also looks hot and dry, for the strong California sun bears down directly on the south-facing mountain slopes here.

Chaparral is the name given to the collection of woody shrubs that flourish in these foothills. When riding horseback through the brush-choked canyons of California, early Spanish settlers gave the term *el chaparro* to the scrub oak they encountered, similar to one that grows in Spain. The word *chaparro* plus the *al* suffix which means "the place of" in Spanish, is today used to designate a plant community that grows on coastal and interior slopes stretching from Oregon to Baja, and includes far more than just the scrub oak after which it was named.

Chaparral holds up well under the prolonged dryness of the summer season in a Mediterranean climate. The individual plants are tough and springy, with many branches. Their leaves are small and usually stiff; some are resinous. Most shrubs are evergreen as well. To reduce water loss, some have hairy leaves and others have leaves that assume a vertical orientation to the sun, so that they don't receive sunlight directly.

Chaparral is classified into two general types—hard chaparral and soft chaparral. Soft chaparral, often called coastal sage scrub, is found at lower elevations in the Santa Ynez Mountains, and consists of low shrubs such as California sagebrush, coyote brush, poison oak, California buckwheat, and the white, purple and black sages.

Hard chaparral is composed of the woodier, darker green shrubs that grow so thickly on the higher mountain sides as to render passage between them virtually impossible. These thorny, small-leafed plants can grow as high as 20 feet, and their dense canopies serve as protection for the birds and other animals that forage in the hidden tunnels beneath them.

Chamise is by far the most common and widespread species in the hard chaparral. It is a member of the rose family and has tiny needle-like leaves that grow in bundles, and delicate white blooms on wispy spears. The reddish-brown seed pods of the chamise remain on the shrubs for much of the year, giving chamise-dominated chaparral its characteristic rusty color. Due to its high oil content, chamise burns intensely when ignited by a wildfire.

Another dominant plant in hard chaparral is the ceanothus or wild lilac. Occurring in numerous varieties, ceanothus spreads its sweet-smelling blue or white blossoms over Southern California foothills in winter and early spring. In early February, the south-facing slopes of the Santa Ynez Mountains are strewn with the white-flowering variety of ceanothus, *Ceanothus megacarpus*.

It is joined by several kinds of manzanita at higher elevations, and by, of course, the scrub oak, whose scratchy leaves
and impenetrable growth gave the early Spanish cowboys such
a hard time.

On the mountain slopes above Santa Barbara, other species
accompany the wild lilacs and manzanitas. Holly-leaf cherry,
chaparral pea, toyon, yucca, bush poppy, prickly phlox, and
mountain mahogany are some of the most frequently found. At
shady springs, bigleaf maples and western sycamores grow,
making splashes of bright green against the gray-brown background of the chaparral.

After the long summer, the chaparral shrubs become brittle
and tinder-dry, susceptible to wildfires. These fires, ignited by
lightning or human carelessness, can rage out of control for
days, fuelled by the thick, resinous shrubs of the chaparral, and
fanned by Santa Ana winds.

Paradoxically, fire is necessary to the chaparral. In the
natural way, chaparral would burn on a cycle of perhaps 25 or
30 years. Recently, ecologists have concluded that controlled
burns are necessary (as the Chumash Indians discovered
centuries ago) to prevent catastrophic fires and to renew the
chaparral.

Many chaparral plant species are well-adapted to fire: they
can stump-sprout from crown roots, or bear seeds and fruits
that open only after heat stress. Fire is a regenerative force and
often does not kill the entire shrub; many areas return to near
normal within ten years.

Fire thins out the chaparral, allowing new species of plants to
flourish, and creating more food in the way of seeds, grasses
and forbs for the birds and mammals that live there. After a
chaparral burn, the slopes are covered with "fire-followers,"
beautiful wildflowers that only bloom after a fire, their seeds
having lain dormant since the last fire.

Bird species benefit from fires, too. For example, the Lazuli
Bunting nests in areas that have been recently burned. It
prefers tall perches above low vegetation, and the dead stalks of
chaparral shrubs work perfectly, protruding above the burned-
over grassy places.

Despite the great diversity of plant types in the chaparral, the shrubs and bushes seem a monotonous collection at first glance. The bird life, too, can seem unexciting and predictable—until you learn how to listen for the chaparral birds, and take time to study their secretive lifestyles.

You notice at once that most of the birds found here are drab in color. Their subdued tones of brown and gray, buff and cinnamon, reflect the muted colors of their chaparral surroundings, and help camouflage the birds. It is important for these species to blend in with their background, for many dwell on or near the ground, within easy reach of predators.

Birds living in the dense brush are also good ground-foragers. Protected by the chaparral canopy, they can locate food in the leaf litter or on low branches, and, rather than fly from one spot to another, they run or hop.

John Davis and Alan Baldridge in *The Bird Year* cite interesting studies showing that an unusually large proportion of the resident chaparral birds have short, rounded wings and long tails. Birds inhabiting this type of vegetation make only short flights and don't require strong wings; many never migrate. Wrentits, for example, have very short wings and a weak flight; they are reluctant to cross even fuel breaks or wide trails in the chaparral.

The California Thrasher uses its long tail as a rudder, steering the bird upwards or sideways as it climbs through the brush. Rather than fly, the thrasher runs underneath the closely entangled twigs of the chaparral, counterbalanced by its long tail. The Greater Roadrunner, Scrub Jay, Bushtit, Bewick's Wren, Rufous-sided Towhee and Brown Towhee all have proportionately short wings and long tails, enabling them to negotiate the chaparral tangles.

Although the variety of species in the chaparral is not great, bird numbers are high here. Particularly in winter and early spring, the shrubs are loaded with food consumed by mammals and birds. Buds, berries, cherries, bulbs, corms, and flower seeds, as well as a healthy insect population, provide the birds with nourishment. Should this food supply dwindle or become sparse due to lack of rainfall in a particular year, some chaparral birds will not nest. The California Quail, for example, will reproduce only in years when the available food is sufficient for their needs, and those of their dozen or more chicks.

Spring in Southern California's chaparral begins soon after the first rains, which can arrive any time between November and January. Overnight, what was once a wasteland of dead leaves and desiccated stalks erupts in new green shoots. By mid-winter, wildflowers have begun to bloom. Prickly phlox, golden yarrow, fiesta flower and Indian pink line the trails behind Santa Barbara. The aroma of the black and purple sages combines with the honey-like fragrance of the ceanothus to make a walk through the chaparral a pure delight.

American Robins, Cedar Waxwings, and Hermit Thrushes descend on the toyon bushes, stripping them of their scarlet berries. These birds, as well as Fox Sparrows, Ruby-crowned Kinglets and Yellow-rumped Warblers, use the chaparral as a pleasant place to spend the winter. On the edges of the shrubbery, and at feeders in foothill neighborhoods, White-crowned and Golden-crowned Sparrows sample Santa Barbara's mild climate.

By late January and early February, Anna's Hummingbirds feast on the bright red fuschia-flowering gooseberry bushes in the chaparral. The Anna's Hummingbird, the resident chaparral hummer, nests as early as December, and the nectar of the gooseberry blossoms provides the sustenance it needs. At the same time, the hummer helps to pollinate the gooseberry bush.

Resident chaparral birds begin to display courting behavior by February. Bushtits leave their flocks and separate into pairs, searching for a good spot to hang their pendant nest. Brown and Rufous-sided Towhees, ever-present in suburban gardens bordering the chaparral hillsides, become more visible now, as they scratch in the leaf litter with their special two-step: feet-together forward and feet-together backward. The male California Quail, his sleek black head plume shaking, assumes a position of prominence atop a post or bush, performing the duty of sentinel for his hidden mate. And the first warbler song of the spring issues from the Orange-crowned Warbler. In a pretty little trill that rises and gently fades away, the Orange-crowned assures the California birdwatcher that spring is here, even though the rest of the country may be deep in snowdrifts.

Although spring really commences with the first rains and continues to the end of the rainy season in early April, the main growing season in the chaparral occurs between late March and May, which may be likened to summer elsewhere. Food supplies are at their peak and the nesting birds take advantage of it.

By mid-April, summer visitors to the chaparral such as Costa's Hummingbirds, Ash-throated Flycatchers, Blue-gray Gnatcatchers, Lazuli Buntings, Black-chinned Sparrows and Sage Sparrows procure territories away from the coast. On the road known as East Camino Cielo, which runs along the crest of the Santa Ynez Mountains, look for the bright blue-and-orange Lazuli Buntings as they sing from atop a bush on the edge of one of the grassy clearings. Ash-throated Flycatchers flash their rufous tails and flycatch actively from shrub to shrub. Black-chinned Sparrows and Rufous-crowned Sparrows may be found on the rockier outcroppings, where they forage on the ground beneath the chaparral.

June and July might be considered autumn in the chaparral. Some birds which are summer visitors, and even some of the resident birds, may drift upslope to search for food and moisture in the cooler climates of the higher forests. Thus, certain chaparral birds like the Ash-throated Flycatcher, Lazuli Bunting or Costa's Hummingbird—all summer visitors—might be considered to migrate three times in one year. In spring, they fly north from their wintering grounds in Central America; in summer, they move upslope from their chaparral environs to higher elevations in the mountains; and in fall they migrate south once again to Central America.

The hot, dry months of August, September and October are a time of dormancy in the chaparral. Some of the resident birds will remain in the chaparral during these months, but many will visit adjacent oak woodland or creekside areas in search of food and water. At this season, the slopes lie fallow and lifeless, waiting silently for the awakening that will take place once again with the first rains.

Representative birding sites:
Mission Canyon area: Rocky Nook Park, Botanic Garden.

Montecito area: San Ysidro Trail.
Santa Ynez Valley area: East Camino Cielo Rd.

Oak Woodland and Oak Woodland/Savanna: The oak woodland in the Santa Barbara area is comprised of close stands of
coast live oak, its twining gray trunks and shiny evergreen
leaves sheltering a wealth of birds. A profuse supply of acorns
provides resident and wintering species with a fine source of
food, and the oaks themselves are often the receptacle for
storing the acorns. Acorn Woodpeckers, Plain Titmice and
Scrub Jays harvest the acorns, the jays sometimes burying the
acorns which sprout into oak seedlings. Nuttall's Woodpeckers,
Plain Titmice, White-breasted Nuthatches and Hutton's Vireos
depend upon the oaks for nesting cavities and foraging. On the
ground, Brown Towhees and Rufous-sided Towhees pick at the
left-over acorn bits discarded by other birds.

In the Santa Ynez Valley, the oaks form a habitat known as
oak woodland/savanna, where the understory is grassland and
the trees are widely spaced. Here, coast live oaks become more
scattered, clinging to shady hillsides, while the majestic valley
oaks predominate on the valley floor. Yellow-billed Magpies,
their long pointed tails accentuating the blue-green sheen of
their stunning plumage, strut about beneath the valley oaks,
retrieving acorns as they chatter. In winter, Western Bluebirds,
American Robins, and Cedar Waxwings feed on the berries of
the mistletoe, which hang in clumps in the bare oaks.

In both the oak woodland and the oak woodland/savanna,
species numbers are augmented with the arrival of winter
visitors. In Santa Barbara's coastal woodlands, such as at Rocky
Nook Park in Mission Canyon, towhees, juncos and other
sparrows feed on the ground. Townsend's Warblers and Orange-
crowned Warblers join the masses of Yellow-rumped Warblers
searching the oaks. Hutton's Vireos and Ruby-crowned Kinglets, looking so similar as to warrant careful scrutiny, bounce
about in the canopy of oak branches.

In the Santa Ynez Valley and at Lake Cachuma, wintering
raptors add zest to the birding. Northern Harriers, Ferruginous
Hawks and Golden Eagles are a possibility, and near the lake,

Bald Eagles perch. Lark Sparrows and Western Meadowlarks flock in the open fields.

Representative birding sites:
Mission Canyon area: Rocky Nook Park, Santa Barbara Museum of Natural History, Santa Barbara Botanic Garden.
Santa Ynez Valley area: Happy Canyon Rd., Nojoqui Falls Park, Lake Cachuma.

Coastal Creeks: White alders, black cottonwoods and California sycamores constitute a deciduous forest along the streamside corridors of creeks draining Santa Barbara's coastal plain, attracting a number of bird species. In this semi-arid climate, the mere presence of water draws birds, and many species breeding in the oak woodland and chaparral visit the creeks for drinking and bathing.

Although these creeks are primarily birded in fall and spring, due to migrants' stopping there to rest and refuel, they lure birds to remain throughout the winter as well. The insect population, though greatly reduced from the summer months, may be sufficient for certain warblers, and even a flycatcher or two, to eke out a living in the thickets along the creekbed.

Along the coastal plain, at places in Goleta like Atascadero Creek and San Jose Creek, unusual species may elect to winter along the creeks, whether or not they might normally breed in such riparian habitats. The fallen leaf litter holds worms, beetles and spiders, enough to induce several out-of-the-ordinary birds to overwinter every season, and help boost the Christmas Count total.

Representative birding sites:
Goleta area: Atascadero Creek, San Jose Creek, Winchester Canyon.

Freshwater Lakes: Santa Barbara has several important freshwater lakes, which serve as wintering sites for a variety of waterbirds. Lake Cachuma in the Santa Ynez Valley is the largest, but both the Andree Clark Bird Refuge in Santa Barbara and Lake Los Carneros in Goleta serve as examples of this type of habitat. Bordered by cattails, tules, and sedges, these lakes are

winter homes to large numbers of ducks. An assortment of
herons and egrets feed at their margins, and gulls often rest
nearby. At the Bird Refuge, one of the chief pleasures of winter
birding is a chance to study at close range the array of gulls that
preen and perch there.

Lake Cachuma, the extensive inland lake formed behind
Bradbury Dam, possesses several species not found elsewhere
in the Santa Barbara area: Greater Scaup, Common Goldeneye,
Hooded Merganser, and Common Merganser which winter on
the lake. Bald Eagles and Ospreys arrive in December to spend
the winter months on Lake Cachuma, too.

Representative birding sites:
Santa Barbara area: Andree Clark Bird Refuge.
Goleta area: Lake Los Carneros.
Santa Ynez Valley area: Lake Cachuma.

Harbors, Sloughs and Beaches: At Santa Barbara's harbor, at
Devereux Slough and at Goleta Beach, birders will find a
number of marine habitats like those described in detail in
Chapter Eight. From ocean to sandy beach to estuarine salt
marsh, many locations for wintering seabirds and shorebirds in
the area offer excellent birding.

By December, most of the wintering loons, grebes and sea
ducks have arrived to loaf in the sheltered offshore waters of
Santa Barbara's channel. The Double-crested Cormorants and
Brown Pelicans that rest on the buoys in the harbor are
accompanied by as many as nine different kinds of gulls. The
most common are Heermann's, Ring-billed, California, and
Western Gulls, but Bonaparte's, Mew, and Glaucous-winged are
easily found, too. Occasionally, a Herring Gull (more common
inland at Lake Cachuma) shows up at the harbor, and immature Thayer's Gulls sometimes visit the Bird Refuge.

Devereux Slough remains as one of the precious examples of
salt marsh habitat in the area. Depending upon water levels,
Devereux Slough can be crammed with ducks, shorebirds and
herons. Raptors—Sharp-shinned Hawks, Merlins, and an occasional Peregrine Falcon—lurk in the treetops with watchful
eyes cast upon the shorebirds and ducks. Above the coastal

scrub surrounding the slough, Northern Harriers and Black-shouldered Kites hover in search of prey.

Representative birding sites:

Santa Barbara area: Santa Barbara Harbor.
Goleta area: Goleta Beach Park, UCSB Lagoon/Goleta Point, Devereux Slough.

Man-made Habitats: Santa Barbara birders have discovered that often interesting or rare species choose to overwinter in the well-planted residential sections of the city. Gardens and parks in suburban sectors of town—such as Montecito, Hope Ranch, the Riviera and the Mesa—are planted with ornamental trees and shrubs, providing blossoms and berries for wintering birds.

The tall eucalyptus trees lining many of the streets burst into bloom in December and January, attracting hundreds of Yellow-rumped Warblers. Mixed in with the warblers, you may find an occasional tanager, oriole or grosbeak which has chosen to winter here, rather than undertake its traditional migration to Mexico.

Luxuriant vines and other subtropical plantings embellish the streets of these neighborhoods, sometimes luring vagrant hummingbirds or warblers. Walking the streets on a winter afternoon can turn up unusual birds, which, enticed by the abundant food and pleasant climate, will linger for the winter, and perhaps the Christmas Count.

Due to the irregular occurrence and great diversity of bird species to be found in man-made habitats, no checklist has been provided at the end of the chapter. Consult local birders and call the Santa Barbara Rare Bird Alert for current information.

Representative birding sites:

Santa Barbara area: The Riviera, The Mesa, Hope Ranch.
Montecito area: Manning Park.

Recalling the Condor

"... an adult condor soars in from the southeast, circles above us at 300 feet and lands on the Twin Roost. Sits alone, looking around and preening. Seems the voyaging bird has returned ... Now it chases away a raven, lands and then goes after a hawk. Condor from below joins it in air and now both are soaring ... truly magnificent! Coming together in the air, we can see their white underwings clearly as they circle, legs down, bouncing in air as they obviously hit an air pocket. I'm watching upper bird, Monty [watching] the lower one through binoculars.

"Now they are crisscrossing—BEAUTIFUL—spiralling above this canyon bottom, rising in an airlift here and there. Absolutely fabulous to see them soar. Beautiful birds moving so very slowly, majestically ..." (From a June 15, 1976, entry in *Condor Journal* by Dick Smith, well-known Santa Barbara photographer and condor observer.)

Until 1987, the Santa Barbara area was famous for another bird, which, although not a resident of the chaparral, soared high above the rugged, chaparral-covered mountains of Santa Barbara's backcountry. The first condor sanctuary ever to be established, back in the 1930s, was created in a remote canyon of the San Rafael Mountains. The steep cliff faces and secret waterfalls of the surrounding wilderness were visited by California Condors, perhaps since Pleistocene times.

On April 19, 1987, the last wild California Condor was captured and brought to the San Diego Wild Animal Park to join the captive breeding program for this highly endangered species. There are less than 30 California Condors in the San Diego and Los Angeles Zoos, representing a large enough gene pool, biologists hope, to successfully breed and re-introduce these majestic birds into the wild by the early 1990s. Bird-watchers everywhere were heartened by the hatching of the first California Condor egg to be conceived in captivity in the spring of 1988. This event may mark the long journey back from near-extinction for this incredible bird.

Another step towards the condor's future was the acquisition of the 11,500 acre Hudson Ranch in Kern County by the U.S. Fish and Wildlife Service. This huge cattle ranch was a mecca for condors, and they would come from time to time to feed on a carcass there, especially during calving time. From a viewpoint a few miles from the ranch, birdwatchers from all over the world were able to glimpse the few remaining condors as they gathered in the sky above the golden hills of the southern San Joaquin Valley.

Indeed, the Hudson Ranch, now renamed the Bitter Creek National Wildlife Refuge, will figure prominently in the condor's re-introduction—a prime parcel of future habitat for the great birds.

Several female Andean Condors have been released in an adjacent portion of the condor's former range. If the Andeans fare well, after two or three years they will be recaptured and replaced by the California Condors, all zoo-hatched birds. These carefully monitored, yet highly controversial, methods of restoring the condor to Southern California's skies represent our only hope of re-introducing a viable condor population.

Who knows . . . maybe a new generation of birders will have the chance to gaze at the awesome sight of a California Condor circling once again over Santa Barbara's backcountry.

Listening to Chaparral Birds

Fortunately for birders, chaparral birds are very vocal. Although they may be difficult to see, some of the species give forth remarkably loud and beautiful songs, plus characteristic calls. As the birds move through the chaparral, they advertise their presence to each other. The alert birder can soon recognize the sounds of chaparral birds and eventually identify most of them by call only, or at least get a clue to the whereabouts of the unseen singer.

The California Thrasher, the Wrentit and two species of wren, the Bewick's Wren and the Canyon Wren, dominate the chaparral with their loud calls and fine songs. The thrasher scoots up to the top of the highest shrub around and bursts forth in a measured cadence—a mixture of chirrups and guttural slurrings—less musical than that of the Northern Mockingbird, but just as energetic. Its boisterous song has been described by Florence Merriam Bailey as *kick'-it-now, kick'-it-now, shut'-up shut'-up, dor'-a-thy dor'-a-thy*... As he throws his head back and enunciates these thrasher syllables, his long, sickle-like bill opens and shuts vigorously. On and on, the thrasher declaims his position as the "mockingbird of the chaparral" in preparation for springtime.

The Bewick's Wren has a repertoire of at least three or four different songs. This wren can drive birders crazy with its snatches of songs, beginning phrases of songs, and partial endings of songs. Also, the Bewick's has about five or six call notes, all with a wren-like quality but none easily distinguished from the House Wren, which also frequents the chaparral, but mostly along its borders. Listen for the loud, petulant *breck, breck, breck* of the Bewick's Wren, which the House Wren lacks. Bewick's Wrens may be vociferous, but they are sometimes quite cagey about coming out in the open. A Bewick's will only appear for a split-second, hardly long enough for you to see its characteristic white eyebrow line, before retreating into a brush pile.

The Canyon Wren, creeping about the rock walls of the steeper canyons, gives a marvelous cascading trill—the notes rapidly descending the scale in sweet, bell-like tones. The Canyon Wren prefers areas with rock faces or creekside boulders, where it can build its nest underneath an overhanging rock or wedge it into a hole. Sometimes Canyon Wrens will even show a liking for human habitations, and they will sing from the roofs of houses situated near the chaparral.

The Wrentit: A Birding Close-Up

"Even those who ordinarily have no ear for bird songs often comment on a loud, ringing voice from the chaparral-covered hillsides in the foothills that repeats the same staccato note, finally running the series rapidly together. This is the Wrentit, heard a hundred times before it is seen." (Ralph Hoffman's field guide, *Birds of the Pacific States*, written in 1927, has delightful descriptions of many California birds and is especially good on bird calls.)

The Wrentit and its echoing song have come to symbolize the chaparral. No hillside is too overgrown with the brushiest of scrub for the Wrentit. The hot, close, impenetrable thickets of mature chaparral, draped with clematis and buttressed by poison oak, are the home of the little Wrentit.

Pause long enough in your stroll through the chaparral and you will discover the Wrentit. A quivering shrub, a disappearing brown tail and a perky bird staying hidden in the shrubbery are telltale signs.

In every season and in almost every corner of the chaparral, the Wrentit lives out its sedentary life, its only companion being a mate, which it chooses for life. The males and females are constantly together, flitting quickly and quietly from one twig to another in the densest bushes, never perching up to sing like other birds. Together they travel the unknown passages of a secret landscape, one that looks thoroughly uninviting to humans, but one for which the Wrentits are perfectly fitted.

Male and female Wrentits look alike: small, round-bodied birds with a long tail held cocked at an angle. The Wrentit's upperparts are grayish-brown and its breast, faintly streaked, is washed with cinnamon. The bird's distinctive white eye is visible at close range.

The Wrentit doesn't venture more than a few miles from the place of its birth, and it spends most of its life on a home territory of about two acres. Loath to fly in the open, when it finally does, the Wrentit pumps its tail and flutters its short wings, as though even crossing distances of 10 or 20 feet is too much of an effort.

The Wrentit's nest is usually placed in a bush, sometimes quite near a pathway. The nest is built by both birds, and resembles a deep cup; four pale green eggs are laid within it.

After the breeding season, the adult birds remain together. They make a soft *tik-tik-tik* noise to communicate with each other when traveling through the chaparral. Wrentit pairs also reportedly preen each other, and "roost together, leaning against each other with feathers interlaced and inner legs

drawn up, appearing as one ball of feathers", to quote Terres in
The Audubon Encyclopedia of North American Birds.

Once heard, the *pit-pit-pit-pit-tr-r-r-rrr* song of the male
Wrentit, reverberating from the hillsides and carrying far up the
canyon, is not soon forgotten. Though the bird gives fragments
of the song throughout the year, the spring version issuing
across the sweet-smelling ceanothus slopes haunts your
memory.

You may grow accustomed to the Wrentit's song, but it never
looses its wild, solitary feeling. Hiking down the trail late in the
afternoon, the view stretching out over Santa Barbara to the
ocean, the shadows lengthening over the chaparral into a
purple haze, the Wrentit's cry breaks the serenity of the
evening. It is at once near and far, bearing a note of vague
uneasiness. Perhaps the Wrentit's song evokes a simpler, more
natural Southern California, a place where the sunny foothills
lay undisturbed beside the Pacific, and the footsteps of the
Chumash Indians were the only intrusion upon the Wrentit's
world.

NOTES FROM A BIRDER'S DIARY

Santa Barbara, California

● January 1, 1988: American Bittern, Snowy Plover, Ruddy
Turnstone, Northern Pygmy-Owl, Short-eared Owl, Greater
Roadrunner, American Dipper, Varied Thrush, Hermit Warbler,
Vesper Sparrow and so on . . . Anxiously, I scan the list of birds
that will be hard to get during tomorrow's Christmas Count. So
much depends upon our luck and good weather. The realization hits me that in another 24 hours it will all be over—Santa
Barbara's Christmas Count will be history and my job of
helping to organize this giant census will be finished.

The more competitive birders in our territory are going
around with long faces, predicting a low finish for the Santa
Barbara Count this year. For one thing, we seem to have fewer
participants. (Silently, I castigate those whom I know are on
bird trips elsewhere!) Also, right here in California, our neighboring Counts in Ventura and Morro Bay have already collected

impressive totals of 206 and 211 species on their respective surveys, behind top-ranked Freeport, Texas, with 215 this year.

Forget being Number One. Now that I'm chairman for the first time, let's just finish respectably.

• January 2, 1988: 10:00 A.M. Count Day at last! Very cold, but calm and dry. On a tree-lined street in Montecito, I stroll along making a mental note of the bird numbers as I walk. A flock of American Robins flies out of a pyracantha bush across the way, close to 100 of them. They were feeding with Cedar Waxwings, Purple Finches, and White-crowned Sparrows on the succulent red berries.

As I walk beneath a large eucalyptus tree, the chorus of *tchips* from the Yellow-rumped Warblers increases; they're feeding on the whitish blossoms. I perk up my ears, hoping to hear the rough chatter of a Northern Oriole or the *thrrrup* call of a Western Tanager. Who knows what good birds can hide in eucalyptus trees this time of year?

But soon it's time to move on to the next spot. I have three birds targeted in my particular area: a vagrant Black-and-white Warbler in a sycamore stand; a pair of Scott's Orioles I found last week up near the foothills; and, most important of all, for its NINTH consecutive year on our Christmas Count, the visiting Grace's Warbler.

"Amazing Grace," or "Gracie," as this bird is sometimes called, has become famous all over Southern California. Countless birders have gazed up at this pretty warbler, which decided to come to Santa Barbara one winter instead of going to Mexico like others of its kind, and has been coming back ever since to a group of pine trees bordering a Montecito lane.

However, as the morning passes, and still no Grace's Warbler appears, I begin to feel a shadow of doubt about the bird. It hasn't been seen recently, and the extremely cold and windy weather we've been having could have been too much for the warbler.

• Noon: I can't believe it! As of check-in time, when most of the birding groups meet to compare notes and find out what species are still missing before the afternoon hours, we tally 183 species. Although there are still some regrettable gaps in the list, such as Long-billed Curlew, Lesser Yellowlegs, Thayer's

Gull, American Dipper, and Greater Scaup—not to mention the staked out Hepatic Tanager in Rocky Nook Park and "my" Grace's Warbler—we have made a good showing thus far.

But it is the extra rarities, the birds that turn up unexpectedly, which make the difference. Without them, we can't break through the 200 mark.

And so the afternoon unfolds. The skies are becoming increasingly threatening. Hour upon hour, standing or pacing up and down the block, I wait and hope for the Grace's Warbler's return. I dare not leave my post. My stake out duty watching for this precious warbler is too important to warrant leaving the spot even for a short time.

● 7:00 P.M.: The moment of truth has arrived. All participants are gathered in the Bird Habitat Hall of the Museum of Natural History for the potluck dinner and compilation countdown. The mood is high; old birding friends greet each other; everybody has had a good day. Bird lists and envelopes full of participants' fees are littered over the tables, along with paper plates heaped with food.

Most of the birders are keeping their secrets close, though. I want to run up to the leader of the group which covered the harbor and shout, "Well, did you get the Wandering Tattler or not?" To another, I want to ask his luck with Mountain Quail and Townsend's Solitaire. But I restrain myself. It's not good form to get too excited about the outcome of the Count.

*　　　*　　　*

When all the numbers had been added up and all the species checked and validated, Santa Barbara's Count total that year was 212! Respectable indeed! Even though there were mutterings of "Always a bridesmaid, never a bride", most birders were elated at the thought of finishing third (behind Coastal Orange County and Moss Landing) in California, and fourth nationwide—Freeport being number one, of course.

Easterners will cringe when they learn that the "best" bird on the Count was a Common Grackle—a first county record for Santa Barbara—found scrounging around the dump. Also discovered were a Vermilion Flycatcher, a Tropical Kingbird, a

Black-throated Blue Warbler, as well as four Summer Tanagers, a Clay-colored Sparrow and a Peregrine Falcon.

An unprecedented invasion of montane species helped. Remarkable this close to the coast, such species as White-headed Woodpecker, Mountain Chickadee, Pygmy Nuthatch, and Red Crossbill were found in numbers.

There was one bird, alas, that was missing. Despite my efforts, the Grace's Warbler never appeared. For the first time in nine years, Gracie wasn't on the Santa Barbara Count.

So ends the saga of how Santa Barbara gained some good birds and some fancy totals, but lost amazing Grace . . !

One year later, in January 1989, Santa Barbara reclaimed its title as Number One in the nation with a whopping 218 species totaled on the Christmas Count. Of this remarkable sum, 35 of the species were represented by only one individual bird, testimony to the skill of local birders. Santa Barbara's position as a top winter birding spot appears stronger than ever.

TRAVELERS' TIPS

Before You Visit: For information about accommodations in Santa Barbara, write to the Chamber of Commerce, Visitor Information, 1 Santa Barbara St., Santa Barbara, CA. 93101. Phone (805) 965-3021. Information about county park campsites (Lake Cachuma and others) can be obtained from calling (805) 568-2460, or writing the County Parks Administration at Rocky Nook Park, 610 Mission Canyon Rd., Santa Barbara, CA. 93105. They also have information about the eagle tours around Lake Cachuma.

For state park information about campsite reservations, call 800-446-7275 (Gaviota, El Capitan, Refugio and Carpinteria State Beaches).

Maps of the Santa Barbara area are available at the Chamber of Commerce, the Museum of Natural History and the Botanic Garden. Compass Maps, Inc., P.O. Box 4369, Modesto, CA. 95352, issues one of the best.

The Channel Islands National Marine Sanctuary, which includes the nearshore and offshore waters around the Channel Islands, is administered by the National Oceanic and Atmospheric Administration in conjunction with the Sea Center (a branch of the Santa Barbara Museum of Natural History). The Sea Center is located at 211 Stearns Wharf, Santa Barbara, CA. 93101, and houses interesting displays about marine birds and mammals of the Santa Barbara Channel. Next door, the Nature Conservancy at 213 Stearns Wharf administers the largest island privately held within Channel Islands National Park, Santa Cruz Island.

One place you must not miss is the Santa Barbara Museum of Natural History, an outstanding regional museum, and one of the finest on the West Coast. The Museum has two excellent bird halls, and other fine exhibits on the area's animals, plants, geology, and early Indian tribes. The bookstore stocks local bird checklists (including *Birds of Santa Barbara and Ventura Counties, California* by Webster, et al.), maps and other items of interest to nature lovers. The museum is located at 2559 Puesta del Sol, Santa Barbara, CA. 93105. Phone (805) 682-4711.

The Santa Barbara Botanic Garden, 1212 Mission Canyon Rd., Santa Barbara, CA. 93105, phone (805) 682-4726, is definitely worth a visit. A lovely canyon planted with native shrubs and wildflowers, the Garden attracts numerous birds. It has an excellent bookstore, which sells a good bird checklist of the Garden, among other items.

The Santa Barbara Audubon Society is located at 300 N. Los Carneros Rd., Goleta, CA. 93117. Phone (805) 964-1468. The Rare Bird Alert number for the Santa Barbara area is (805) 964-8240.

When To Visit: The pleasant climate makes Santa Barbara a perfect spot for a winter vacation. Day-time temperatures are warm, but nights are chilly. Although this is the rainy season the winter storms never last for long, and sunny, smog-free days are a bonus.

Remember, Southern California's spring—at least for chaparral birds and many other resident species—commences in February and is over by the end of May. The wildflowers and hiking trails are beautiful at this time of year, and you can catch part of the spring landbird migration, if you stay through April.

Santa Barbara is known for its birding year-round, and fall, too, has its advantages, with numbers of transient landbirds appearing at coastal creeks.

Length of Visit: A visit to Santa Barbara for bird finding can be limited to a day or two, or can stretch into a month or more, if you decide to join the birds and spend part of the winter in Southern California.

Santa Barbara is less than two hours' drive from Los Angeles and vicinity. By getting an early start, you can make an easy day of birding in selected spots in Santa Barbara County, and be back for a late dinner in Los Angeles.

THE BIRDING SITES

Mission Canyon area: This northwestern section of Santa Barbara derives its name from the Old Mission which sits on a low hill overlooking the city. The mixture of sycamores and live oaks, combined with shrub and tree plantings around the residences nearby, afford prime oak woodland and chaparral habitat for resident and wintering birds. In spring, Western migrants such as flycatchers, warblers, tanagers, grosbeaks and orioles frequent the birding sites listed.

To reach Mission Canyon, exit U.S. 101 east on Mission St., go 4 blocks to State St., turn left (west) on State St., go 2 blocks, turn right (east) on Los Olivos for 4 blocks, proceeding past the Mission. Just after the Mission, a fork in the road (bear to your left) takes you to Mission Canyon Rd.

ROCKY NOOK PARK: Stay on Mission Canyon Rd. for 2 blocks, and, after crossing a bridge, you'll see the sign to Rocky Nook Park on your right. Drive all the way in to the northeastern parking spaces and bird the park, which extends further north into good oak woodland. A Hepatic Tanager has wintered in the area for several seasons.

SANTA BARBARA MUSEUM OF NATURAL HISTORY: After you have toured the interesting exhibits, wander around the Museum grounds, often good for wintering oak woodland species. The Museum can be reached on foot by crossing Mission Canyon Rd. west of Rocky Nook Park and walking a short distance on Puesta del Sol. By car, you will have to go a block further north on Mission Canyon Rd., and turn left on Las Encinas Rd. (Puesta del Sol is one way.) Follow the signs.

SANTA BARBARA BOTANIC GARDEN: Return to Mission Canyon Rd.

and go north to its intersection with Foothill Rd. Turn right (east) on Foothill and shortly bear left to continue again on Mission Canyon Rd., which leads up the canyon to the Botanic Garden. An early morning walk, especially around the central meadow, can produce many chaparral species including California Thrasher, Wrentit, Rufous-sided and Brown Towhees, and the oaks harbor the typical woodland avifauna, including Nuttall's Woodpecker and Hutton's Vireo.

Santa Barbara area: Winter birding for landbirds can be good at several city parks and on residential streets (respect private property) in the Santa Barbara area. For waterbirds, try the Bird Refuge and the Harbor.

THE RIVIERA: The Riviera section of Santa Barbara, on the hillsides overlooking the city, lures wintering birds to its sunny slopes, while they feed on ornamental shrubs and flowering trees. Two spots on Mission Ridge Rd. have been productive for Western Tanager, Scott's Oriole (rare), Northern Oriole and Costa's Hummingbird, along with the typical oak woodland and chaparral species.

To reach Mission Ridge Rd., retrace your route back to Rocky Nook Park on Mission Canyon Rd. Heading back to the Mission (south), take an immediate left (east) off Mission Canyon onto Mountain Dr. Follow Mountain Dr. one block, and make the hairpin turn to your right onto Mission Ridge Rd. Keep on Mission Ridge, past the entrance to Marymount School on your left and park where Ridge Ln. intersects on your right. Bird the area along Mission Ridge and walk the length of Ridge Ln.

To reach Franceschi Park, continue another mile along Mission Ridge to Franceschi Rd. Turn left (north) on Franceschi Rd. to the Park entrance. Anywhere along Mission Ridge Rd. between Ridge Ln. and Franceschi Park can be good winter birding, but traffic is sometimes a problem, so start early.

THE MESA: The Mesa is the round-topped hill rising to the west of the waterfront. La Mesa Park (or Lighthouse Park as it's sometimes called) on the Mesa has stands of blooming eucalyptus which attract birds to this coastal park.

It can be reached easily from the Harbor area, by following Cabrillo Blvd. west along the shore, until it becomes Shoreline Dr. Keep on Shoreline Dr. about 1.5 mi. until it makes a right angle north, becoming Meigs Rd. La Mesa Park is to your left (west). En route, you may wish to stop at Shoreline Park, a grassy area on the bluff from which you can gaze out to sea. Pelagic species are sometimes spotted offshore.

HOPE RANCH: Hope Ranch is a beautiful sector of the city with lovely homes. Laguna Blanca Lake in the middle of La Cumbre Country Club Golf Course (private property) has held its share of good shorebirds and wintering waterfowl, depending upon water levels. Use a scope from the road.

Certain areas in Hope Ranch have been good for wintering montane species such as Mountain Chickadees, Pygmy Nuthatches and Red Crossbills, because of the pines lining the streets.

To reach Hope Ranch, exit U.S. 101 south on La Cumbre Rd. Keep on La Cumbre Rd. until you see the gates of Hope Ranch straight ahead, where the road becomes Las Palmas Dr. This is the main street in Hope Ranch, and winds along beside Laguna Blanca. Any of the residential streets off Las Palmas can be good birding. One of the better spots is on Estrella Dr., reached by proceeding through the Ranch on Las Palmas which becomes Roble Dr. which becomes Marina Drive. After about 4 mi., at the intersection of Marina Dr. and Estrella (to your left, north), park the car on Las Palmas and bird Estrella and Creciente Dr. to your right (south). The stands of pines here have had wintering Hermit Warblers, and may contain other warblers, plus montane species in invasion years.

ANDREE CLARK BIRD REFUGE: This little lake is good in winter for waterfowl and gulls. You can walk right up to the gulls and study Western, California, Ring-billed, and Bonaparte's Gulls, as well as Glaucous-winged, Mew, and Heermann's. Thayer's Gull is fairly regular (usually in first winter plumage) and Herring Gull is occasional. Glaucous and Franklin's Gulls have been seen.

In fall, the vegetation to the north between the lake and the railroad tracks has held some good Eastern vagrants such as Eastern Kingbird, Tropical Kingbird and Swamp Sparrow. The islands in the middle of the refuge are good perches for Double-crested Cormorant, Great Blue Heron, and Black-crowned Night-Heron. Wood Ducks can be seen here, as well as Eared Grebes, Western and Clark's Grebes, and wintering ducks.

The Bird Refuge is scheduled for major improvements in 1989, which should make it even more attractive to birders.

To reach the Bird Refuge, exit U.S. 101 at Hot Springs Rd., crossing back under the freeway on Cabrillo Blvd. towards the ocean (south). Take the first right turn, Los Patos Way, and you'll see the lake at once. Park beside the lake.

SANTA BARBARA HARBOR: Protected from the ocean by a breakwater and sandspit, the harbor is good for wintering waterbirds such as loons, grebes and diving ducks, as well as gulls, terns and shorebirds. Look for Western and Clark's Grebes, Common, Red-throated and possibly Pacific Loons, Surf and White-winged Scoters. A walk out to the end of the breakwater, particularly at low tide so the sandspit promontory at the end is exposed, can produce Snowy Plover, Whimbrel, Marbled Godwit, Black and Ruddy Turnstones, and sometimes Wandering Tattler. Elegant Terns are common July-October and Royal Terns present November-March. Scan offshore for seabirds. Parasitic Jaegers are possible in fall and spring.

To reach the harbor area, get on Cabrillo Blvd. from the Bird Refuge by turning to your right (west). Proceed along the waterfront for about 3 mi. to the intersection of State St. and Cabrillo Blvd., where you will see Stearns Wharf (which is sometimes good birding). Continue west on Cabrillo Blvd. to the harbor. Make a left turn into the harbor parking lot. Follow the sidewalk past the Naval Reserve Training Center out to the breakwater.

For another vantage point, retrace your steps and walk over to the east side of the harbor parking lot, where the sportfishing marina extends out into the harbor. Double-crested Cormorants and Brown Pelicans enjoy sunning themselves on the buoys here.

Montecito area: Montecito, a lovely suburb southeast of the city of Santa Barbara proper, can be good winter birding. Several trails lead up into the chaparral foothills from here, which are attractive for birding in late winter and early spring.

MANNING PARK: Manning Park, on both sides of San Ysidro Rd., is good birding on weekday mornings or in early morning hours on weekends. Lower Manning Park has nice sycamores along the creek, and, if the creek has water, is attractive to wintering tanagers, warblers and finches. Black-throated Gray Warblers are occasionally seen here in winter, and Townsend's Warblers are common.

To reach Manning Park, exit U.S. 101 north at San Ysidro Rd. After .5 mi. you will see a sign on your left indicating the park. This is Upper Manning Park. Both it and Lower Manning Park (reached by crosswalk across San Ysidro, or, by car, turn east at Santa Rosa Ln.) can be good winter birding.

SAN YSIDRO TRAIL: This trail follows San Ysidro Creek up into the chaparral. Look for many of the typical chaparral species, and, in wet years when the creek is flowing well, a pair of American Dippers has nested about 1.5 mi. up the canyon. Canyon Wrens are often found around the bridge or near the buildings of the San Ysidro Ranch. Northern Pygmy-Owls live in the canyon, at a spot about a half-mile up the trail, but they are difficult to find. In late winter and early spring, wildflowers line the trail.

To reach San Ysidro Trail, return to the intersection of East Valley Rd. and San Ysidro Rd. Take a right (east) on East Valley Rd., and continue 1 mi. to Park Ln. Turn left (north) at Park Ln. and keep to your left at the next 2 forks in the road. The road dead-ends into the San Ysidro Ranch stables, and a bridge crossing the creek. Park beside the road and hike the trail beginning on the east side of the creek. To reach the dipper spot, follow the trail about 1.5 mi. above the bridge. About halfway there, the trail forks and crosses the creek, but you should stay to your right and proceed until the trail begins to make steep switchbacks. Scan the rocks in the creek for dipper sign.

Other foothill trails to explore are those in Cold Springs Canyon (in Montecito) and Rattlesnake Canyon (in Santa Barbara). Refer to *Day Hikes of the Santa Barbara Foothills* by Ray Ford. Start early in the day.

Goleta area: The coastal plain reaches its widest point north of Santa Barbara in the Goleta area. Numerous good birding destinations listed below fluctuate in activity depending upon the season and water levels.

ATASCADERO CREEK: This weedy creek on the Goleta coastal plain is best in fall (August—October), when Bobolink, Lazuli and Indigo Buntings, Blue Grosbeak, and several species of sparrows join the Savannah and

Lincoln's Sparrows that feed on the grasses in the middle of the creekbed. It can also be good for wintering sparrows, and other species in the willows along the creek. The best viewing is from the dirt walkway bordering the bike path, looking down on the birds from the bank rather than flushing them by walking in the creekbed.

To reach Atascadero Creek, exit U.S. 101 at Turnpike Rd. and go south on Turnpike, crossing Hollister Ave., to where Turnpike dead-ends into a bike path. Park here and walk to your right (west) downstream along the bike path beside Atascadero Creek.

SAN JOSE CREEK: This riparian creekside habitat is good in some years for wintering birds, as well as migrant landbirds in spring and fall.

To reach San Jose Creek, exit U.S. 101 at Patterson Ave. and go north, crossing Cathedral Oaks Rd. Shortly afterwards, you'll come to a bridge (on Patterson). Park here and walk across the street to the spot where a dirt footpath leads down to the creek. You'll be walking along the east side of San Jose Creek. Follow the path until it comes out upon a patch of lawn, and then dips down into the creek again, at which point you may wish to retrace your steps back to the car. Birding the west side of the creek, will lead you back to the bridge also.

WINCHESTER CANYON: A nice creek in a secluded canyon surrounded by agricultural fields has attracted quite a number of good wintering birds. The creek meanders along the edge of a little tract of houses, where blooming ornamental trees attract migrants in late winter and early spring. Look for Red-breasted Sapsucker and Red-naped Sapsucker, Nuttall's Woodpecker and other woodpeckers in the walnut trees that stand as remnants of an old orchard here. Frequently, overwintering warblers— Wilson's, Black-throated Gray—may be found in the willows by the creek.

To reach Winchester Canyon, exit U.S. 101 north at Winchester Canyon Rd. Proceed along Winchester Canyon Rd. toward the mountains, bearing left down a hill and turning right into the housing tract. Once in the tract, make an immediate left turn on Rio Vista Dr. and drive west until the road turns. Stop directly opposite a little green park. Bird the park (via a bridge across the creek), and up and down the creek.

GOLETA BEACH PARK: This is a good spot for loons, grebes, diving ducks and gulls that winter on the lagoon to the north of the parking lot. Look for Western and Clark's Grebes, a variety of ducks, and all the common gulls, including Bonaparte's, Heermann's, Mew, Ring-billed, California, Western, and Glaucous-winged. In spring, Great Blue Herons nest in the eucalyptus trees on the bluff directly across the lagoon, and overhead in the trees around the parking area. Look for Tri-colored Blackbirds amongst the flock of Brewer's Blackbirds that hangs around the snack shop and the restaurant.

To reach Goleta Beach, exit U.S. 101 south at California 217 (toward UCSB) and be sure to exit Ward Memorial Blvd. at Sandspit Rd. From Sandspit Rd., make a left, following the signs to Goleta Beach. After entering the park, turn into the lefthand parking area. A walk out the fishing pier may be good for loons, grebes, and scoters in late winter/early spring.

UCSB LAGOON/GOLETA POINT: The University of California, Santa Barbara, has two good locations. The campus lagoon is sometimes good for wintering waterfowl (especially Blue-winged Teal), shorebirds, gulls and terns. Goleta Point (also known as "Campus Point") is next to the lagoon and is great in spring for watching the northward seabird migration. From this lookout atop the bluffs, you can follow the huge flocks of loons (Pacific most abundant), brant and scoters as they fly up the coast close to shore. The best time for viewing is late March to mid-May; afternoon hours are most productive, when the onshore breeze helps to bring the birds within closer range. Watch for migrating Surfbirds, turnstones and tattlers on the rocks below the bluff in spring.

To reach UCSB Lagoon/Goleta Point, exit U.S. 101 at California 217 and follow it to the entrance kiosk to the campus (fee). Ask here for directions and a map to the Marine Laboratory, near where you can park. From the parking lot, walk west to overlook the lagoon. (Note: The Marine Science Institute has offices nearby. Pick up a permit for Devereux if you wish.) To reach the Point, keep walking west along the campus beach and proceed on a trail up a hill to the bluffs that look out over the ocean. Bring a scope if possible.

DEVEREUX SLOUGH: This slough is one of Santa Barbara birders' favorite spots, excellent (depending on water level) in fall and winter for shorebirds, waterfowl and even vagrant landbirds. Devereux Slough is part of Coal Oil Point Reserve, owned and administered by the Marine Science Institute at UCSB. Walking out into the marsh is prohibited. Most birds can be readily seen from the road.

In fall and winter, Great and Snowy Egrets, Black-crowned Night-Heron, Green-winged, Blue-winged and Cinnamon Teal, Northern Pintail, American Wigeon, Canvasback, Redhead, and Greater and Lesser Scaup are some of the waterbirds represented. Snowy Plover (usually out on the beach to the west), Semipalmated and Black-bellied Plovers, and many species of sandpiper, including Western and Least Sandpipers, Greater and Lesser (fall) Yellowlegs, dowitchers, and Dunlin are present. In fall, Lesser Golden-Plover, Pectoral, Baird's and Solitary Sandpiper are possibilities.

The Ocean Meadows Golf Course, which borders the slough to the north, has attracted one or two Tropical Kingbirds every winter, along with the handful of Cassin's Kingbirds that winter, and breed, here. The kingbirds are visible from the slough side, perching on the isolated pines on the course. While walking the length of the road that skirts the slough, bird the pines and eucalyptus for all kinds of migrants in spring and fall.

To reach Devereux Slough, exit U.S. 101 at Storke Rd./Glen Annie Rd. off-ramp. Proceed south on Storke Rd., crossing Hollister Ave. When Storke Rd. angles sharply to the left, becoming El Colegio Rd., you'll turn to your right at the entrance of the road to Devereux Slough.

Parking regulations on this west portion of UCSB are STRICTLY ENFORCED. You must have a day permit (small fee on weekdays only) in order to park at designated locations, weekdays and weekends. For further information and a permit write to Shirley Clark, Marine Science Institute,

UCSB, Santa Barbara, CA. 93106, phone (805) 961-4127. Open weekdays 8:00 a.m. to 5:00 p.m.

Permits are also available from Parking Services, UCSB, Santa Barbara, CA. 93106, phone (805) 961-2346, open weekdays 7:30 a.m. to 4:00 p.m.

Should you arrive on a weekend with no prior permit, parking spaces on nearby surface streets in Isla Vista are sometimes available, from which you can walk into the area surrounding Devereux Slough. Try looking for a space on Camino Corto, which turns off El Colegio to your right (south). You can also try parking on any of the streets bordering the extreme west edge of Isla Vista, and walk west along the bluffs to approach the southwest end of the slough.

LAKE LOS CARNEROS at STOW HOUSE: The specimen trees planted around this historic house attract numerous landbird species and the adjacent lake holds a variety of wintering ducks. A walk through the grounds and around the lake should prove fruitful for winter birding.

To reach Lake Los Carneros, exit U.S. 101 north at Los Carneros Rd. After a short distance, watch for the fire station on your right, in front of which a road leads to Stow House and a parking lot. Park here and walk southeast to the house and lake.

Santa Ynez Valley area: This tour starts at the base of San Marcos Pass Rd. (California 154), which can be reached by exiting U.S. 101 north at State St. (Follow the signs to Cachuma Lake.)

EAST CAMINO CIELO: San Marcos Pass Rd. winds up over the Santa Ynez Mountains. Pure stands of hard chaparral cover the hills all the way. After approximately 6 mi., East Camino Cielo Rd. turns off to the right (east) at the top of the pass. East Camino Cielo follows the crest of the mountains 9.4 mi. to La Cumbre Peak. In winter, check the pines at La Cumbre Peak for Townsend's Solitaire. Common Ravens soar overhead. By mid-April, you might see Costa's Hummingbird, Ash-throated Flycatcher, Blue-gray Gnatcatcher, Lazuli Bunting, Rufous-crowned Sparrow, and Black-chinned Sparrow, as well as Mountain Quail, Canyon Wren and Rock Wren. On the way, admire the wonderful views of the Channel Islands and the Pacific on one side of you, and the backcountry of the San Rafael Mountains on the other.

LAKE CACHUMA: From November-March, Lake Cachuma is frequented by hundreds of wintering ducks and grebes. Hooded and Common Mergansers, and Common Goldeneye are the attraction here. Numbers of Ospreys and Bald Eagles winter on the lake, and a Golden Eagle or two are usually around.

Inside the county park entrance, bird the picnic and camping areas for a nice assortment of oak woodland birds such as Acorn and Nuttall's Woodpecker, White-breasted Nuthatch, Plain Titmouse, Western Bluebird, Lark Sparrow, White-crowned and Golden-crowned Sparrows, Dark-eyed Junco and American and Lesser Goldfinches.

To reach Lake Cachuma, drive 9.7 mi. from the top of San Marcos Pass and turn off California 154 at the sign on your right to Cachuma County Park (fee). Once inside the entrance, explore around the lake's edge. Try driving to the right (east) to the campsites marked "Overflow Area" and beyond. Park here and walk down to the lake on any of the sandspits that lead down to the water's edge. Bring a scope if possible.

If you wish to rent a boat, large or small, follow the signs to the boat dock. This is a fun outing on a winter day and the only way to examine all the waterfowl on the lake plus see the eagles up close. The phone at Cachuma Boat Rentals is (805) 688-4040.

After leaving Cachuma County Park, continue on California 154 west for 2.4 mi to the Bradbury Dam Vista Point (turn right, north). This is another spot overlooking the lake; grebes and ducks rest on the water just behind the dam. A scope is necessary because the birds are far away.

HAPPY CANYON RD.: This section of the Santa Ynez Valley can be good in winter for spotting Ferruginous Hawk, Lewis' Woodpecker and, at any time of the year, Yellow-billed Magpie. The bird life is typical of oak woodland/savanna, augmented in winter by an influx of raptors. Watch for a Golden Eagle soaring overhead.

To reach Happy Canyon Rd. from Bradbury Dam, drive 2.1 mi. on California 154 to Armour Ranch Rd., where you make a right (north) turn. After 2.4 mi. Armour Ranch Rd. intersects Happy Canyon Rd., where you make a right turn (east). Anywhere along Happy Canyon Rd., pull over and watch the dead oak snags for a Lewis' Woodpecker flycatching from the top. Magpies abound.

Should you wish to visit Figueroa Mountain, continue up Happy Canyon Rd. where it winds to Cachuma Saddle (8.3 mi.) and then turn left (west) 6.6 mi. to the summit of Figueroa. This road is partial dirt and can be rough after rains.

Although Figueroa can be interesting in winter, the best time to visit is April and early May, when wildflowers blanket the mountainsides and Western migrants are moving through. Year-round residents on Figueroa are Mountain Quail, Steller's Jay, Mountain Chickadee and Pygmy Nuthatch. In spring, Olive-sided Flycatchers, Black-throated Gray Warblers and Western Tanagers arrive, among others.

At the summit of Figueroa Mountain, there are two good birding spots: one is Figueroa Campground on the side of the mountain, and the other is Pino Alto Campground, reached by a 2 mi. dirt road (impassable after heavy rains) to the top.

To return to the Santa Ynez Valley, continue west on Figueroa Mountain Road for 12 mi. to regain California 154. It is a lovely scenic loop.

NOJOQUI FALLS COUNTY PARK: This small park is a prime sample of oak woodland habitat in a shady north canyon of the Santa Ynez Valley. By mid-April, the area resounds with the calls of resident Acorn and Nuttall's Woodpeckers, Yellow-billed Magpies, Plain Titmice, and Western Bluebirds, along with the newly arrived Black-chinned Hummingbirds, Western Flycatchers, Purple Martins (rare elsewhere in the county), Violet-green Swallows, and Black-headed Grosbeaks.

There are two ways to reach Nojoqui Falls. The first is to approach via U.S.

101, at a sharp right turn off 101, (it comes 2.3 mi. north of the turn-off to Lompoc), but the sign to Nojoqui is small. The second approach is to come from the Santa Ynez Valley. Turn west off California 154 at California 246 (Santa Barbara Ave.) and head into the little Danish village of Solvang (nice for picnic supplies). In downtown Solvang, the first major street to your left (south) is Alisal Rd. Take Alisal Rd. 6.5 mi. to Nojoqui (pronounced NAW-ho-wee) Falls. The entrance is on your left.

SANTA BARBARA:
Birding a famous winter hot spot
Checklist of Common Birds by Habitat

CHAPARRAL
Red-tailed Hawk
California Quail
Mountain Quail (rare)
Greater Roadrunner (uncommon)
Anna's Hummingbird
Costa's Hummingbird (summer)
Ash-throated Flycatcher (summer)
Scrub Jay
Common Raven
Plain Titmouse
Bushtit
Ruby-crowned Kinglet
Canyon Wren
Bewick's Wren
Blue-gray Gnatcatcher
Hermit Thrush
American Robin
Wrentit
California Thrasher
Cedar Waxwing
Phainopepla (summer)
Orange-crowned Warbler
Yellow-rumped Warbler
Lazuli Bunting (summer)
Rufous-sided Towhee
Brown Towhee
Rufous-crowned Sparrow
Black-chinned Sparrow (summer)
Sage Sparrow (summer)
Fox Sparrow
Golden-crowned Sparrow
White-Crowned Sparrow
House Finch

**OAK WOODLAND AND
OAK WOODLAND/SAVANNA**
Turkey Vulture
Black-shouldered Kite
Red-shouldered Hawk
Red-tailed Hawk

Golden Eagle (uncommon)
American Kestrel
Band-tailed Pigeon
Mourning Dove
Western Screech-Owl
Great Horned Owl
Northern Pygmy-Owl
Anna's Hummingbird
Acorn Woodpecker
Red-breasted Sapsucker
Nuttall's Woodpecker
Downy Woodpecker
Hairy Woodpecker
Northern Flicker
Scrub Jay
Yellow-billed Magpie (local)
Plain Titmouse
Bushtit
White-breasted Nuthatch
House Wren
Ruby-crowned Kinglet
Western Bluebird
Loggerhead Shrike
Hutton's Vireo
Orange-crowned Warbler
Yellow-rumped Warbler
Townsend's Warbler
Rufous-sided Towhee
Brown Towhee
Lark Sparrow
Savannah Sparrow
Song Sparrow
Dark-eyed Junco
Western Meadowlark
Purple Finch
House Finch
Lesser Goldfinch

COASTAL CREEKS
Cooper's Hawk
Red-shouldered Hawk

Anna's Hummingbird
Downy Woodpecker
Northern Flicker
Black Phoebe
Scrub Jay
Plain Titmouse
Bushtit
White-breasted Nuthatch
Bewick's Wren
House Wren
Hermit Thrush
American Robin
Orange-crowned Warbler
Yellow-rumped Warbler
Townsend's Warbler
Common Yellowthroat
Brown Towhee
Song Sparrow
Lincoln's Sparrow
White-crowned Sparrow
House Finch
American Goldfinch
Lesser Goldfinch

FRESHWATER LAKES
Common Loon
Pied-billed Grebe
Horned Grebe
Eared Grebe
Western Grebe
Clark's Grebe
Double-crested Cormorant
American Bittern (rare)
Great Blue Heron
Black-crowned Night-Heron
Wood Duck
Green-winged Teal
Mallard
Northern Pintail
Gadwall
American Wigeon
Canvasback
Redhead
Ring-necked Duck
Greater Scaup (uncommon)
Lesser Scaup
Common Goldeneye
Bufflehead
Hooded Merganser (rare, local)
Common Merganser

Ruddy Duck
Turkey Vulture
Osprey
Bald Eagle (local)
Virginia Rail
Sora
American Coot
Spotted Sandpiper
Bonaparte's Gull
Heermann's Gull
Mew Gull
Ring-billed Gull
California Gull
Herring Gull (uncommon)
Thayer's Gull (uncommon)
Western Gull
Glaucous-winged Gull

HARBORS, SLOUGHS AND BEACHES
Red-throated Loon
Pacific Loon
Common Loon
Pied-billed Grebe
Horned Grebe
Eared Grebe
Western Grebe
Clark's Grebe
Brown Pelican
Double-crested Cormorant
Brandt's Cormorant
Pelagic Cormorant
Great Blue Heron
Great Egret
Snowy Egret
Green-backed Heron
Black-crowned Night-heron
Green-winged Teal
Mallard
Northern Pintail
Blue-winged Teal
Cinnamon Teal
Northern Shoveler
Gadwall
Canvasback
Redhead
Greater Scaup (uncommon)
Lesser Scaup
Surf Scoter
White-winged Scoter (uncommon)

Bufflehead
Red-breasted Merganser
Ruddy Duck
Black-shouldered Kite
Northern Harrier
Merlin (uncommon)
Peregrine Falcon (rare)
Black-bellied Plover
Snowy Plover
Semipalmated Plover
Killdeer
Greater Yellowlegs
Willet
Whimbrel
Marbled Godwit
Black Turnstone
Sanderling

Western Sandpiper
Least Sandpiper
Dunlin
Long-billed Dowitcher
Bonaparte's Gull
Heermann's Gull
Mew Gull
Ring-billed Gull
California Gull
Herring Gull (uncommon)
Thayer's Gull
Western Gull
Glaucous-winged Gull
Royal Tern
Forster's Tern
Belted Kingfisher

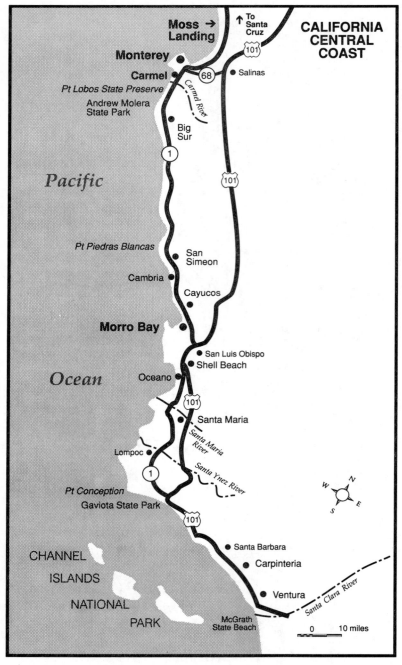

Moss → Landing

↑ To Santa Cruz

CALIFORNIA CENTRAL COAST

Monterey

101

68 • Salinas

Carmel

Pt Lobos State Preserve

Andrew Molera State Park

Big Sur

Carmel River

1

101

Pacific

Pt Piedras Blancas

San Simeon

Cambria •

Cayucos

Morro Bay

• San Luis Obispo

• Shell Beach

Oceano •

Ocean

101

Santa Maria

Santa Maria River

Lompoc •

Santa Ynez River

1

Pt Conception

Gaviota State Park

101

• Santa Barbara

Carpinteria

Santa Clara River

CHANNEL

ISLANDS

NATIONAL

• Ventura

PARK

McGrath State Beach

0   10 miles

N
W   E
S

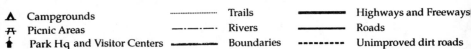

▲ Campgrounds   ⋯⋯⋯ Trails   ▬▬▬ Highways and Freeways

⛫ Picnic Areas   —·—·— Rivers   ▬▬▬ Roads

⛺ Park Hq and Visitor Centers ▬▬▬ Boundaries   - - - - - Unimproved dirt roads

8

FROM MORRO BAY TO MONTEREY:

Chasing fall migrants along the Pacific Coast

Even before the foggy mornings of summer give way to the clear, calm days of autumn on California's coast, birders don their wading boots and shoulder their scopes in eager anticipation of the shorebird migration. By mid-July, shorebird aficionados begin to haunt the estuaries and salt marshes, where extensive tidal mudflats invite multitudinous flocks of sandpipers and plovers to pause for food and shelter on their annual southern journey. With flashing wings and plaintive calls, the shorebirds alight briefly—perhaps only an hour, perhaps a few days—to partake of the feasts available in these bountiful wetlands.

And as the shorebirds flee their tundra breeding grounds, frequently navigating unbelievable distances from one end of the continent to another, birders are on the alert for the hotlines to start ringing. The Siberian rarity, the off-course Eastern migrant, the accidental occurrence—in short, the stuff of which birding history is made—burns up the phone lines, the news spreading instantly from one end of the state to the other. The chase is on, and hard core enthusiasts think nothing of driving hundreds of miles to add a record bird to their life or state lists!

237

The excitement is not confined to shorebirds alone. In recent years, field ornithologists have begun to realize the role of the isolated clumps of vegetation on coastal promontories as magnets for small landbirds in fall migration. Termed "migrant" or "vagrant traps," these birding locations—often simply a grove of pines at a beach campground or a willow-lined creek near the coast—truly earn their reputations as birding hot spots, attracting numerous species of flycatchers, vireos, warblers, tanagers and sparrows, some of which may be rarities.

This bird trip starts at one of the well-known shorebird localities in Southern California, the Santa Clara River estuary about fifty miles north of Los Angeles. From there, the route goes north, stopping at river mouths and landbird hot spots in Santa Barbara and San Luis Obispo Counties.

At Morro Bay, the large, shallow bay bordered by salt marsh gives ample opportunity to view transient and wintering shorebirds, as well as pelicans, herons and waterfowl.

Proceeding north on California's famous Highway 1, other good spots promise further birding breaks, perhaps to be sandwiched between sightseeing along this beautiful drive, or before or after a tour of Hearst Castle.

Finally, on the Monterey Peninsula and north to the Moss Landing area, birders will recognize sites often included on the Rare Bird Alert of the region. From birding at the mouth of the Carmel River, to a possible pelagic trip on Monterey Bay, to exploring the salt marsh at Elkhorn Slough, this finale to a journey up the California coast has the potential for delivering not only rarities, but an exceedingly high species total of birds.

"The restlessness of shorebirds, their kinship with the distance and swift seasons, the wistful signal of their voices down the long coastlines of the world make them . . . the most affecting of wild creatures. I think of them as birds of wind, as 'wind birds'." Peter Matthiessen in his poetic book *The Wind Birds* has captured the feeling shorebirds evoke in those of us who wait for their return every fall.

As the sea breeze wafts the salty air in from the beach, and the tide slips slowly from the pools and channels of the estuary, the sun sets over the teeming forms of hundreds of shorebirds feeding. Watching them snatching and probing in the mud, their subtle shades of chestnut and white and gray turning to gold with the evening light, one marvels at the innate forces guiding these birds of passage. Perhaps birders' affection for shorebirds is part of a shared wanderlust, a tacit understanding of the wind birds' free spirit and their far travels.

Early ornithological history of Monterey was shaped by the settlement of the first Californians there, which later became the political headquarters of Alta California under the Spanish, Mexican and American flags.

Monterey was one of the few adequate harbors on the West Coast, a port of call for many of the first explorers. In the 18th and early 19th centuries, European expeditions made their voyages of discovery around the world and often a naturalist was on board to collect and record new plants and animals of scientific interest. In 1792, when Captain George Vancouver and his British ship stopped in Monterey on his way north to Puget Sound, the naturalist Archibald Menzies collected a number of birds, among them the specimens on which were based the descriptions of the California Condor and the California Quail.

Thomas Nuttall, the English botanist and ornithologist who lived in the United States from 1808 until 1842, made a voyage to California visiting Monterey harbor in 1836, when he came ashore from March to May to study the natural history of the area. Besides being a curator of the botanical gardens at Harvard University, Nuttall contributed to scientific history a two-volume manual on the ornithology of the United States and Canada. He is commemorated in the scientific names of the Common Poorwill *(Phalaenoptilus nuttallii)*, the Nuttall's Woodpecker *(Picoides nuttallii)*, the Yellow-billed Magpie *(Pica nuttallii)*, the Olive-sided Flycatcher *(Nuttalornis borealis)* and the California coastal subspecies of the White-crowned Sparrow *(Zonotrichia leucophrys nuttallii)*.

In 1842, William Gambel described three more new species first collected in the Monterey area: the Plain Titmouse, the Wrentit, and the California Thrasher. William Hutton, another American scientist living in Monterey in 1847, was honored by John Cassin, then curator of the Philadelphia Academy of

Sciences, after Hutton's discovery of the little gray-green vireo that bears his name, the Hutton's Vireo.

Monterey's prominence as a settlement in early California is easy to understand when you review a map of the coastline. Few large embayments and estuaries stand out, along a rugged shoreline that stretches 1100 miles, comprising two-thirds of the length of the United States' western coast. South of San Francisco Bay, which is California's largest bay and salt marsh (what's left of it), you will notice the tiny harbor of Moss Landing, where rambling Elkhorn Slough meets the sea in Monterey County. Southward, Monterey Bay is the only deep water inlet along the central California coast.

From Monterey to Morro Bay, the coast ranges hug the coastal plain tightly, offering no breaks in the spectacular cliffs that tumble into the Pacific. At Morro Bay, a sandspit shields a shallow lagoon that reaches inland, creating a wide salt marsh with mudflats. Then, from Morro Bay to Southern California, only small estuaries and river mouths breach the outer beaches.

A bird's eye view of this section of the California coast instantly shows the importance of the coastal wetlands—the fastest disappearing of all the state's natural habitats—for migrating waterbirds. Many have nested on the Arctic tundra to the north, or far inland, and their major southerly migration route brings them along California's coast. Some are autumn transients, pausing only briefly on their way south. Others are winter visitors arriving in the autumn and remaining until the following spring. Whatever their destination, hungry grebes, cormorants, herons, waterfowl, shorebirds, gulls and terns converge upon the estuaries and marshes en route. And as the wetlands dwindle, the few remaining ones receive concentrations of more and more birds.

Ornithologists believe many landbirds, too, follow the southeastward direction of California's coast, particularly during fall migration. Although considerable numbers of Western migrants trace routes south along the major mountain ranges and inland deserts, many birds—perhaps the majority of species—may head along the coast, stopping to rest and refuel at coastal creeks and willow clumps.

The California state bird list is second only to Texas in its great number of species, and this diversity is due in part to California's position on the West Coast. In fall, when the waterbird and landbird migration is in full swing, the variety of birds passing through guarantees an exciting bird venture.

Climate and Habitats of California's Central Coast

The Pacific Ocean acts as an air conditioner in the summer and a heater in the winter, producing comfortable year-round temperatures on the coastal strip. The early morning fog and low clouds so prevalent in summertime are the result of a high pressure system, known as the Pacific High. In late spring, the Pacific High moves north from the subtropics. Winds circulate around the system in a clockwise direction, hitting the coast from the Northwest. The warm, interior low-pressure air sucks the ocean air inland, and as the air crosses the cool California Current offshore, it loses its ability to hold moisture. The moisture condenses, forming fog and low clouds during the night and early morning.

These coastal fogs are an important source of moisture in arid California. One location near San Francisco Bay measured nearly ten inches annually in fog drip, accumulated when eucalyptus and pine groves intercepted the moist air, which collected and fell in a rain-like deposit of moisture on the surrounding ground.

The winds circulating around the Pacific High also bring cooler ocean temperatures to the coast. From March to August, the prevailing northerly winds and the Coriolis effect of the earth's rotation cause the southerly flowing waters of the California Current to move away from the coast. They are replaced by cooler, more saline waters upwelling from deeper regions. The upwelling may make swimming a bit chilly, but birds and fishermen love it. As the layers of water rise, they bring up nutrients from the depths of the ocean, which attract schools of fish, and many species of seabirds.

In September and October, when the northwesterly winds subside and before the winter storms come, a period of clear, warm weather is a harbinger of California's autumn. With cool nights and warm days, the blue Pacific sparkles, the summer fogs dissipate, and fall is in the air.

On the immediate coast the fogs never stay away for more than a few days, and birders like it that way. Foggy, overcast weather during migration tends to bring the birds down and keep them there. On clear nights, when most small landbirds migrate, guiding landmarks are clearly visible. Heavy fog, on the other hand, obscures the coastline and the stars, disorienting the birds and forcing them to land wherever they find themselves, often at coastal migrant traps. Although not as true for shorebirds—the larger of which may migrate by day—still, there's nothing like a good high fog to make the migrants stay and send birders out in hopes of finding them.

Sandy Beach: Whether climbing the dunes at the mouth of the Santa Maria River or walking on the white strand of Carmel Beach, you notice that the area of sandy beach exists as a narrow transition zone between the ocean waters and the bluffs. If you walk up beyond the high tide mark, small beach plants appear. They are succulent perennials, with thick, fleshy leaves, which help store what water the plant can absorb. They grow in small mounds as a protection against the salt-laden sea winds and shifting sandy substrate. Many have tiny white hairs that give a soft gray look to their foliage.

Watch for the little pink blossoms of sea rocket, purple-flowered sand verbena, sea fig, and beach pea. In southern coastal counties, the delicate yellow flowers of beach primrose can be found, along with beach strawberry and an abundance of introduced ice plant.

The more stabilized backdunes host a number of low shrubs including mock heather, coastal bush lupine and coyote brush.

The open beach lacks the abundance of birds found on its two borders: the vast ocean on one side and the shallow mud-flats on the other.

Only two species of birds, the Least Tern and the Snowy Plover, nest on the sandy beaches. The Least Tern, now on the federal- and state-endangered lists in California, and the Snowy Plover seek the upper part of the beach, where they deposit their well-camouflaged eggs in little depressions in the dry sand. Unfortunately, this is the portion of the beach coveted by sunbathers and surfers too, greatly diminishing the chance of successful breeding by the plovers and terns.

The Snowy Plover breeds from Baja to southern Washington and seems to withstand human disturbance a little better than the Least Tern. The West's smallest plover, the pale, fawn-colored Snowy Plover, can be descried on your beach walks, as it nestles perfectly hidden in the dry sand. By contrast, the Least Tern breeds only on beaches south of Monterey, and is much less approachable. Its nesting habits are highly colonial, and, should one member of the group be disturbed by a human intruder, the others will fly up, leaving their nests unguarded and deserting their young for long periods of time.

By early September, the Least Terns depart the sandy beaches, and a new group of birds is already in residence. These are the large shorebirds that visit the wet sand to forage for sand crabs, marine worms and various crustaceans living at the water's edge. Black-bellied Plovers, Willets, Whimbrels and Marbled Godwits pause to plunge their long bills into the sandy burrows uncovered by the waves. With stately gait and obvious skill, they hunt for the sea creatures hidden just beneath the moist sand.

Probably more than any other shorebird, the Sanderling sparks the attention of the casual observer. Anyone who is even distantly aware of birds, has walked by a flock of Sanderlings on the shore and marked their behavior. The preeminent sandpiper of the open beaches, this tiny, white automaton runs up and back in rhythmic reflection of the breaking waves. When the waves subside, the Sanderling makes a series of little holes in the damp sand, probing for beach fleas and little crabs. At rest, Sanderlings gather in tight flocks, huddled together on the upper beach in what look like delicate aggregations of gray and white stones.

So familiar have birders become with this common fall and winter inhabitant of Pacific shores, we forget its circumpolar range. The Sanderling nests in the Arctic of both hemispheres, and migrates through all continents as far as the southern tip of Africa and South America, and even Australia. Globetrotting birders can take comfort in knowing there are few beaches of the world where they will not see the universal Sanderling.

Other birds gathering on the sandy outer beaches are Brown Pelicans and a mixed assortment of gulls and terns, resting and preening as they face into the wind. When the tide ebbs, they will return to feed and bathe in the shallow pools of the estuaries and lagoons.

Representative birding sites:

Ventura/Santa Barbara Counties Area: outer beaches at Santa Clara River, Santa Ynez River and Santa Maria River estuaries.
Morro Bay area: Morro Bay sandspit.
Monterey Bay area: beach at Carmel River mouth.

Tidal Mudflat and Salt Marsh: The two major types of wetland along the California coast—the tidal mudflat and the salt marsh—exist in such proximity, and their bird life is so interchangeable, they will be discussed as one habitat.

The salt marsh can be separated into two regions: a lower one where very little vegetation except cordgrass thrives, and an upper one where pickleweed and saltgrass take over. The lower one is characterized by monotonous, bare mudflats, at least to the untutored eye. These flats bridge the gap between the open water of the bay or lagoon and the higher marsh. Twice daily, the mudflats are submerged in tidal water, conditions difficult for most plants to withstand.

Cordgrass has adapted to prolonged inundation by salt water. It and saltgrass (which lives at higher levels in the marsh) excrete excess salt by means of special glands. At close range, a film of salt can be seen in little white patches on the plant. Cordgrass also has hollow passageways in its leaves and roots so air can circulate throughout the plant even when it is underwater.

Above the cordgrass, in the vicinity of the average high tide level, the pickleweed grows in branching stems appearing as a gray-brown mat of vegetation. If you hold a piece of pickleweed in your hand, you can examine the plant, which looks like a string of tiny pickles put together stem by stem. The pickleweed also gets its name from its use as a pickling agent. Like cordgrass, pickleweed is a halophyte, a plant which has the ability to concentrate soil salts in their cell fluids and so maintain the important chemical balance necessary for osmosis, the movement of water through the plant's cells.

The roots of the pickleweed support the dikes and banks of the salt marsh, holding the drainage channels open. In addition, pickleweed provides safe resting and roosting spots at high tide for rails, herons, ducks, and shorebirds. The endangered Clapper Rail, which breeds in a few remaining salt marshes in California, uses the pickleweed tangles to support its nest.

The salt marsh habitat merges with freshwater habitats where streams or rivers meet the coast, such as at the mouths of the Santa Clara, Santa Ynez and Santa Maria Rivers. In these estuaries, the marsh vegetation is much poorer, because tidal access is often blocked by a sand barrier or silt build-up at the river mouth and freshwater weeds take over. Like all marshy areas, the salinity of the water decreases during the winter and spring, when rain run-off dilutes the brackish water. The presence of freshwater allows cattails, tules and sedges to grow along the river channels, side by side with the saltbushes and salt-tolerant grasses.

Perhaps the lack of variety in the vegetation accounts for the few species of birds actually nesting in the salt marsh: the Clapper Rail, the rare Black Rail, the dark Belding's race of the Savannah Sparrow, and a race of the Song Sparrow. Yet the salt marsh and nearby mudflats are one of the richest environments for birds.

The birds inhabiting these wetlands, then, are for the most part outsiders, fall migrants and winter visitors attracted by the vast biological productivity of the mudflats. The mud is a giant larder, thrown open twice a day, when the ebb tide reveals the wealth of food available to the waiting birds.

The secret lies in the nutrients trapped in the mud itself, released by the incoming flushing of seawater mixing with freshwater. The resulting turbulence stirs up the plankton and algae, which are fed upon by many filter feeding creatures like mussels, clams, and cockles. Elna Bakker, in *An Island Called California*, says there are also deposit feeders, those which "ingest the rich oozy mud, and extract from it what would be an unsavory mess to human consumers." The California horn snail, the most abundant snail in the high tide zone of mud-flats, is a deposit feeder. Both the deposit feeders and the filter feeders help maintain the health of the wetlands, while providing sustenance for hordes of birds.

Birdwatching on the open mudflats offers a unique window on the feeding and flocking behavior of shorebirds, and many studies have been conducted on the activities of this group of birds.

Scanning a group of feeding shorebirds, the first thing that strikes you is the differences in bill and leg length among them. The variety of bill sizes and shapes foster an array of food items, while leg length dictates different feeding locations within the marsh or mudflats. Ornithologists speculate that feeding on different prey in different locations on the tidal mudflats may lessen the competition for food sources in what at first glance appears to be a fairly uniform habitat.

Members of the Plover family with short, stubby bills pick at the surface of the wet sand. Species such as the Black-bellied Plover, Lesser Golden-Plover, Snowy and Semipalmated Plovers, as well as the ubiquitous Killdeer, snatch their prey. In characteristic Plover style, they run a bit, pause, then run further and snatch. As well as visual location of prey, it is thought they may be "palming" the sand with their dainty feet, sensing prey as they run. The Plovers usually remain apart from the sandpipers feeding at the water's edge, avoiding other bird species which might disturb their potential food.

The Recurvirostridae—the striking American Avocet and its relative the Black-necked Stilt—are in a family by themselves named for the recurved bill of the avocet. Both the stilt and the avocet are long-legged waders, skim-feeders that use a side-to-side sweeping motion to capture swimming aquatic insects from the deeper puddles. The bill of the female avocet has a more pronounced curve than that of the male, which may further differentiate the feeding habits of this species on mudflats—the female sieving prey from the surface of the water and the male plunging his bill slightly beneath.

Any attempt at generalization about the bills of the Sandpiper family seems hopeless—their diversity of size and shape is extraordinary. Even the littlest sandpipers, known as "peeps" in America and "stints" in Europe, show variable bill length and thickness. The tiniest American sandpiper, the Least Sandpiper, feeds more like the plovers, preferring the higher mudflats, grassy margins and other spots where they can snatch rather than probe with their needle-like short bills.

The Western Sandpiper, another peep, prefers to feed at the margins of shallow pools, where the water is not too deep for its short legs, but where its tapered bill can probe in wet mud. The Dunlin, a somewhat larger sandpiper with a longer, drooping bill, is found wading further out still.

Medium-sized sandpipers such as the Red Knot and the Long-billed and Short-billed Dowitchers feed more successfully in deeper water than the peeps. In devouring polychete worms and other invertebrates, these chunky sandpipers move their heads up and down in a continuous probing motion, often described as a sewing machine movement.

Greater Yellowlegs walk briskly through shallow water, changing direction frequently, which evidently surprises small fish. Sometimes, like the avocet, the yellowlegs will form a line with other yellowlegs to drive little fish into the shallows.

The largest waders in the Sandpiper family, the Willets, Whimbrels, Long-billed Curlews, and Marbled Godwits, can plumb the deeper puddles as well as the mudflats, accommodating their very long legs and long bills suitable for probing. The Willet seems to be the generalist in the group, subsisting on numerous kinds of prey. Willets can be found in a wide array of marine habitats, from rocky shore to sandy beach.

The Marbled Godwit, with its long, very slightly upturned bill, and the Long-billed Curlew, with its tremendously long, decurved bill, are able to detect the burrows of tiny crabs and shrimps. Tiny sensory organs in the tips of these shorebirds' bills alert them to crustaceans hiding well below the muddy surface.

Black-bellied Plovers, Lesser Golden-Plovers, Killdeers and Long-billed Curlews are often found inland, feeding in wet, grassy agricultural fields, where they find insects and other prey.

Shorebirds' flocking behavior is as crucial a mechanism for

survival as their feeding patterns. In an open environment with few places to hide, flocking together in groups of varying size helps protect from hunting raptors.

Who has not watched in awe as the dark, swift form of a Peregrine Falcon stoops at an escaping, swirling flock of peep and dowitchers? In closed ranks, the shorebirds bank and dive to elude the marauding falcon. They have a good chance of doing so, if the birds stay in unison. But should one falter or become disoriented, it will present a likely target for the Peregrine.

Shorebirds benefit by flocking together, not only on the wing, but while engaged in feeding. The more birds in the flock, the more watchful eyes available to alert the group to an approaching predator. *The Birder's Handbook* by Paul R. Ehrlich, et al., cites an interesting study on the size of shorebird flocks. In this experiment, the most effective flocks were made up of from four to fifteen birds. Smaller flocks were able to flee a hawk, but they fed poorly, always nervous and jittery. Larger flocks were more watchful, except when they got in territorial squabbles over the food, which distracted them from vigilance and often allowed the raptor to approach unnoticed.

Representative birding sites:

Ventura/Santa Barbara Counties area: Santa Clara River, Santa Ynez River, and Santa Maria River estuaries.

Morro Bay area: Morro Bay State Park, viewpoints at Baywood Park and Los Osos.

Monterey Bay area: Carmel River mouth.

Moss Landing area: Salinas State Wildlife Area, Jetty Road, Moss Landing Wildlife Area, Elkhorn Slough National Estuarine Reserve.

Rocky Shoreline: The rocky shoreline habitat from Morro Bay north on the coast to and including the Monterey Peninsula lures a number of bird species: Double-crested, Brandt's and Pelagic Cormorants join American Black Oystercatchers, Wandering Tattlers, Ruddy and Black Turnstones, and Surfbirds to forage and rest on the rocky coast. Visible from shore, grebes, loons and scoters dive in nearby bays. Brown Pelicans and an assortment of gulls—including Bonaparte's, Heermann's, Mew, Ring-billed, California, Western and Glaucous-winged—roost on the coastal outcroppings and feed in the nearshore waters. A complete habitat description of the West Coast's rocky shore can be found in Chapter Four.

Representative birding sites:
Shell Beach area: Shell Beach Road.
Morro Bay area: Morro Rock, Montana de Oro State Park.
California's Highway 1: San Simeon State Beach to Pt. Piedras Blancas, Andrew Molera State Beach at the mouth of the Big Sur River, Point Lobos State Reserve.
Monterey Bay area: Monterey Peninsula at all locations.

Coastal Migrant Trap: With the realization that isolated clumps of vegetation growing on or very near the coast may attract large numbers of landbirds in migration, birders routinely check a handful of birding hot spots along California's central coast, particularly in fall.

Two types of growth characterize migrant traps: native riparian trees and shrubs lining freshwater streams where they meet the ocean, and planted non-native trees around ranch houses or beach campgrounds near the coast. The first, the streamside vegetation, lures birds to bathe and feed in the protection of dense willows, cottonwoods, sycamores or alders. Here, the migrant passerines (perching birds) merge with resident chickadee and bushtit flocks to seek food as a respite from their long journey south. Birding at the mouth of the Carmel River or at Carpinteria Creek typifies this type of migrant trap.

Monterey pine, eucalyptus, oak, willow and Monterey cypress—sometimes growing naturally but more often planted—comprise the second kind of migrant trap. For example, although Monterey pine and Monterey cypress grow naturally only in certain areas of the Monterey Peninsula and south to Cambria, both are widely planted as well in windrows and around buildings up and down the California coast. Their significance for small birds appears to be their high visibility on coastal bluffs, where the weary migrants drop in for resting and feeding after flying long distances. These isolated plant islands concentrate the birds, acting as magnets to birds returning from over the ocean, perhaps after having overshot land in nocturnal migration.

This type of migrant trap occurs at Oceano Campground, Montana de Oro State Park and Morro Bay State Park, as well as at Gaviota State Park. At Gaviota, where rows of tamarisk trees planted in the campground lure migrants, the aggregations of little green leafhoppers infesting the trees on certain years assure birders of interesting migrants to watch. (On the years of no infestation, Gaviota attracts many fewer birds.)

In the last two decades, the discovery that vagrant or off-course birds regularly visit these vegetation clumps has revolutionized the way we think about fall landbird migration. One theory—that many of the vagrants have malfunctioning internal compasses—may explain why they stray from their normal migration route or become easily lost.

Another theory postulates the vagrant's internal compass may be distorted like a mirror-image navigational chart, with the bird ending up on the opposite coast from that which it should follow to Central America. For example, a warbler breeding in the woods of Minnesota might fly southwest to the Southern California coast, rather than flying to the East Coast, and then south crossing the Gulf of Mexico to Central America.

Regular Western migrant species can also become disoriented while migrating at night, a process furthered by marine overcast conditions blocking out the stars many birds use to navigate. The birds may have drifted out over the ocean, and, at dawn, beat their way back again to shore, and safety.

Migrants and vagrants face certain death if they continue a route out over the Pacific. Hopefully, many will be able to correct their course, flying due south again once they hit the coast. Before that happens, the Rare Bird Alerts will be humming, and local birders will drop everything and dash to see the bird. A sense of urgency is inherent in chasing vagrants; at any minute the rare bird could be on its way, leaving frustrated but resigned birders behind.

Migrant traps keep local birders busy every fall combing coastal creeks and cypress clumps. An example of an incredible year was the fall of 1979, when one hot spot drew a total of 86 species of migrants during a three month period, with 27 species of warblers noted, 13 of which were considered rare fall vagrants. However, be warned that certain locations can be very good one year, and lackluster the next. Call the Rare Bird Alerts for the latest information.

Representative birding sites:

Ventura/Santa Barbara Counties area: Carpinteria Creek, Gaviota State Park.

Shell Beach area: Oceano Campground.

Morro Bay area: Morro Bay State Park (campground), Los Osos, Montana de Oro State Park (campground).

California Highway 1: Cambria (mouth of Santa Rosa Creek), Andrew Molera State Beach at the Big Sur River mouth.

Monterey Bay area: Carmel River mouth, Monterey Peninsula (Esplanade Park, Crespi Pond).

Watching Shorebirds

The most important tip on unravelling the mysteries of shorebird identification is the simplest: you've got to get close to the birds. This may involve tramping around in the wonderful, black gooey mud that lies beneath all healthy estuaries—preferably in wading boots—or it may mean acquiring a spotting scope, and probably both. In other words, get your feet wet!

Shorebirds often cooperate with birders. If you walk slowly and approach quietly, shorebirds are astonishingly tame, especially the juveniles in fall. Intent upon grabbing as many morsels of prey as they can during the ebb tide feeding period, all manner of shorebirds can be observed at close range.

The daunting task of sorting out the subtleties of shorebird plumages suddenly gets much easier once you can examine the species in their natural habitat. Comparing body size, bill length, and plumage characteristics from one species of shorebird to another helps enormously, and you cannot achieve this scrutiny from a great distance.

Once you walk out into the estuary, and see the myriad shorebird sizes and shapes spread out, a somewhat methodical approach may help organize the familiar species by size. Starting with the larger, more obvious ones first—the Long-billed Curlew, the Marbled Godwit, the Whimbrel, and the Willet in order of descending size—you can also easily separate the American Avocet with its black and white plumage and the Black-necked Stilt, with long, pink legs. The Greater Yellowlegs comes next in size, and soon you find you have already reached the medium-sized shorebirds: most of the plovers, the two kinds of dowitchers, the Lesser Yellowlegs, and the Red Knots.

But it is the peeps, the tiniest shorebirds in the genus *Calidris,* that birders fret over the most. Due to their small size, and the complexity of their plumage molts, the peeps prove the ultimate challenge in shorebird differentiation. The Western Sandpiper and the Least Sandpiper have given generations of shorebird-watchers a lot of headaches. However, the Dunlin, the largest of the peeps, is fairly straightforward in identification. In winter plumage, it is a shorebird with a gray bib and a longish bill, drooping at the tip.

Part of the problem lies in the ability to distinguish generally the stage of molt the bird has achieved, a necessity in the correct identification of peeps. For example, most shorebirds have three plumages: breeding (confusingly called "alternate") plumage, winter (called "basic") plumage, and juvenile plumage. Birders on the West Coast, looking at a group of Western Sandpipers in August, might find a bird in each of these three plumages. Some adult birds will still be in left-over breeding plumage, although it will be dull and worn; some adults will already have acquired their winter plumage; and some juveniles will be present, in fresh, brand new plumage.

Learning these differences is not as complicated as it sounds, and an awareness of dates makes them more understandable. In southbound migration, adult birds begin appearing in mid-July, most of them in worn breeding plumage after the rigors of Arctic nesting. By the end of August, many adults have passed through, but some may stay to winter, already assuming their drab winter plumage. From early August through mid-October, the lovely juvenile birds migrate through, the little peeps outstanding in their crisply edged feathers of white, gold and buff, complete with snow-white underparts and lots of rufous on the head and scapulars. Juvenile species of all shorebirds are the most likely to go astray in migration, accounting for many unusual records.

Thus, shorebird feathering can be as distinct from one season to the next as the different species are from one another. Understandably, not everybody will have a penchant for mastering the molts of the shorebirds, but it is a prerequisite for spotting many of the rarities, and birders who do so deserve accolades.

Back to Western vs. Least Sandpipers: there are certain classic ways of telling the two apart, above and beyond molt. The Western is a larger sandpiper, with a tapered bill, whiter underparts, and lacks a definite breast band. It is grayer above than the much browner-toned Least Sandpiper. The Least Sandpiper, having a less elegant air than the Western, appears more hunkered-down and shorter-legged. It is browner in all plumages than the Western, has a slender bill of even thickness, and a brownish breastband. The leg color of the Least is light, either greenish or pale yellow, but this can be obscured by mud. The Western has black legs.

From the minute you arrive at the mudflats, the shorebird calls become part of your birding experience, too. The clarion warning of the Greater Yellowlegs' cry signals danger. The drawn-out mournful whistle of the Black-bellied Plover *chu . . . chu—wheet?* —the second note lower than the first and the last note the high query—carries over the estuary to others of its kind.

Shunning the elaborate songs of the perching birds, shorebirds communicate with each other above the noise of the wind and waves with loud, piercing cries. In the open spaces of beach and mudflat, the trills and chirps employed by woodland birds to advertise their whereabouts would go unnoticed. The loud calls of the shorebirds serve them well on their lengthy journeys from here to South America, binding the flocks together and signaling departure and arrival. Birders are more apt to master shorebird plumage differences first, rather than shorebird calls. Perhaps because of their high visibility, we do not depend on shorebird calls to detect their presence the way we do with woodland birds, which conceal themselves in dense foliage.

With the wild cries of the shorebirds lingering in the air around you, another fall morning of birding comes to a close. Each visit to the tidal mudflats brings greater familiarity with the nuances of shorebird plumages, greater confidence in the arena of shorebird calls, and a feeling of immense wonder at the complexity of the lives of these long-winged migrants.

The Red-necked Phalarope: A Birding Close-Up

The Red-necked Phalarope (formerly called Northern Phalarope) and the Wilson's Phalarope visit the West Coast in fall migration, their special whirligig method of feeding making them look like little tops spinning on the surface of the water. In the deeper pools of estuarine mudflats and in shallow lagoons, these little shorebirds pirouette round and round on the surface of the water, their bills dabbing at the mosquito larvae dislodged by the swimming movements of their lobed feet. Their singular feeding habits and dainty mien, easily recognizable to even the casual birder, proclaim the phalaropes' presence among a gathering of other shorebirds.

Seeing the petite Red-necked Phalarope along the California coast, few people are aware of the oceanic nature of these shorebirds. Except for a three-month breeding period, Red-necked Phalaropes spend most of their lives roaming the seas of the Southern Hemisphere. To this end, they have dense breast and belly feathers and a layer of down which traps warm air, protecting the birds from the cold ocean waters on which they feed and sleep in huge floating flocks.

If you have ever been on a pelagic trip and found the boat to be suddenly surrounded by one of these enormous aggregations of phalaropes—all spinning and dabbing in individual circles—it is an unforgettable experience.

But it is the phalaropes' behavior while on land that has aroused the curiosity of naturalists for years. The three species of phalarope (the Red and the Red-necked, which breed in the Arctic and the Wilson's, which breeds in interior North America) all belong to the less than one percent of bird species in which the males are entirely responsible for incubation and brood rearing. This leaves the females free to be polygamous, or polyandrous, as it's termed when one female is mated to more than one male.

The phalaropes embody the ultimate reversal of the sex roles: the females are more brightly plumaged and they conduct the entire courtship cycle from start to finish, pausing only to lay the eggs.

Many observers have written accounts of the unusual mating antics of the Red-necked Phalarope. Herbert Brandt in Arthur Cleveland Bent's *Life Histories of North American Shorebirds* describes the following scene, as two females vie for the attention of a male phalarope:

"It is very interesting to watch a struggle between two female phalaropes over a solitary male. They fight by the hour, not after the manner of the males, which rush at each other and boldly lock in a mortal combat, but rather these females fight by flipping their wings and pecking at each other instead of laying hold with determination. This can be likened only to a feminine hair-pulling episode."

The phalaropes, although representing an extreme of sex role reversal, are not the only shorebird species to endow the males with considerable parental responsibilities. In a number of sandpipers, the females are larger than the males, and the males assist with the incubation of the eggs. These adaptations probably arose because many shorebirds do not establish strong territories on the tundra where they nest, the young are precocial and do not require extended care, and female shorebirds have a fixed clutch size.

In the case of the Red-necked Phalarope, therefore, the female's best chance for producing more offspring is to start a new nest with a new male, leaving the first one in the care of the original mate.

In most species of migratory birds, the males arrive first from the south, intent upon grabbing a lucrative territory with which to lure the female. In the case of the phalaropes, however, there are equal numbers of males and females and neither establishes a territory. Therefore, it is to the females' advantage to arrive first, acquire a mate early on, and lay eggs. Late arriving females may lose out, unable to obtain any mates at all.

An amusing account written in 1914 by Misses Best and Havilland of a female phalarope appropriating an exhausted male upon arrival is also found in Bent:

". . . we found a male and female in the long herbage at the water side. Perhaps we ought to reverse the usual order and say female and male, for the traditional dominance of the masculine sex is entirely unknown in this species. Certainly this little cock bird was a most henpecked little fowl. Possibly he had been captured immediately on his arrival from the sea. At any rate, he was apparently tired out, and whenever the hen stopped, as she frequently did, to preen herself or feed, he sat down where he was, and tucking his bill under his feathers, went to sleep. Before he had dozed for more than a minute, however, the female would peck him awake, and, calling querulously, force him to follow her while she led the way through the marsh. Now and then she flew at him and chased him about, as if losing patience."

Female Red-necked Phalaropes in breeding plumage are bound to win the attention of the males—their gorgeous red necks, blue-gray heads, and buff-streaked sides are only dully reflected in the male's cryptic coloring, helping him hide on the nest. In fall on the California coast, most female Red-necked Phalaropes pass through first in late July; from August through October the males and particularly the juveniles appear. Both the males and females may retain a vestige of their breeding dress early in the season, but soon fade into winter plumage.

The Red-necked Phalarope is easily told from the Wilson's Phalarope in winter plumage. The white-striped pattern on the Red-necked's back is very different from the smooth gray back of the Wilson's. The Red-necked's bill is a little thicker, not as long and needle-like as that of the Wilson's. Look for the Red-necked Phalarope in freshwater ponds and on tidal mudflats along California's central coast.

NOTES FROM A BIRDER'S DIARY
Santa Maria, California

● September 16, 1984, 10:00 P.M. The phone rings and a voice on the other end of the line, one of the local expert birders, says excitedly:

"There's a Little Curlew in Santa Maria!"

A what? I try to picture the bird in my mind, but draw a blank.

"Joan, the Little Curlew is a first North American record! You've got to try for it in the morning."

I hang up the phone and start frantically leafing through my North American field guides. I cannot even find an illustration of the Little Curlew, but resolve immediately to drive the 75 miles to Santa Maria the next day.

Wondering if the bird will migrate before dawn, I spend a sleepless night. Anyway, previous commitments make it impossible for me to leave for Santa Maria before late morning tomorrow, which adds to my frustration. Will the rarest bird ever to hit Santa Barbara County wait for my arrival?

● September 17, 1984, 11:00 A.M.: A heat wave sends the temperature soaring into the 90's as the day unfolds. Two birding companions have eagerly agreed to make the drive north with me, and we have just checked by phone with one of the birders who has been at the Little Curlew site in Santa Maria. The bird has not been seen since last night, despite a mob of birders combing the area. My friends and I are pessimistic, but finally we're on our way, the air-conditioned car shielding us from the unbearably hot temperature outside.

● 12:30 P.M.: We drive up to the appointed field at the corner of Black and Betteravia Roads on the outskirts of Santa Maria. Our worst fears are confirmed when we see the horde of birders staring aimlessly into the lush, green pasture. A motley selection of cars parked by the roadside marks the spot, and conversation is desultory, centered around the fact that the bird has probably migrated overnight.

A hot, overcast sky arcs over the grassy agricultural fields—some dry and some wet—and the humidity and temperature must both be approaching 100. Irrigation by sprinklers has attracted numerous shorebirds to the pastures, and we can see Black-bellied Plovers, Greater Yellowlegs, Whimbrels, Long-billed Curlews and a couple of Lesser Golden-Plovers, none of which seem of interest to the experts who are scanning the original field where the precious Little Curlew was last glimpsed at sundown the night before.

● 1:30 P.M.: After standing idly in the hot sun for awhile, my friends and I decide to drive over and explore another spot. Despite one of the hotshot birders assuring us that every shorebird in every field has been checked since 5:30 A.M., we depart on our own.

I pull up near a promising-looking field wet enough to support shorebirds and we get out, hauling the scopes. We must look an odd sight as we tramp along the shoulder of this rural road. Huge produce trucks rumble by, nearly knocking us over.

If the trucks don't get us, the heat will. I raise my binoculars once more to scan the shorebird specks in yet another wet field. By this time, we are half a mile from the car, and I am muttering about returning to the original field to check on what the experts might have found.

All at once, one of the many farmers who have been speeding by pulls over to the side of the road. He leans out his window.

"Whatcha looking for?" he asks.

"Birds," we say patiently, trying to explain we are looking for a rare shorebird called a Little Curlew.

"Curlews," he says, "heck, I've got tons of curlews on my property. Wanna have a look?"

We glance at each other, then shrug our shoulders. What have we got to lose?

We hop into the back of his dusty pick-up, scopes and all, and hitch a ride to our car. Then, we follow the rancher a couple of miles to his property. Opening the gate, he proudly ushers us onto the dirt track running through the middle of his green pasture. I feel a twinge of hope as I notice that, indeed, there are lots of Whimbrels walking around.

"See . . . there are the curlews," the rancher gestures expansively at the flock of Whimbrels.

We don't pause to correct him, but hurriedly set up the scope and scan the birds.

Suddenly, something small flushes from the main flock. It is half the size of the other Whimbrels and its delicate bill has only a slight decurvature.

THAT'S IT!

Nervously fumbling through my field guide, I turn to the sandpiper page. The bird before us resembles a miniature Whimbrel, somewhat like the picture of the Eskimo Curlew in the *National Geographic* guide. Not twenty yards away this long-necked little shorebird from Siberia is marching around in the grass, and we three are the only birders who know its whereabouts!

I still can't believe we have found the Little Curlew, but there's no time to waste. We must alert the others.

The friendly rancher has long since disappeared, so we jump in the car and hurtle down the road. As we drive up, we see that the restless group of birders are still gazing dejectedly into the wrong pasture.

Birders are not generally known for their quick coordination or fast running ability, but I've never seen so many excel at both when we shouted the news. Instantaneously, the long line of cars formed behind us, as we led them elatedly towards the most serendipitous Little Curlew ever to visit the North American continent!

*   *   *

The Little Curlew ended up staying for an unusually long time, nearly a month, and people came from as far away as New Jersey to see this vagrant that breeds in Siberia and chose to migrate to Santa Maria rather than to Australia. Mr. Mahoney, the generous rancher, became famous as the guy who helped over 300 birders from 18 different states get a look at a Little Curlew. Eventually, he even moved his cattle into a neighboring pasture to accommodate the birders.

Like all good birding yarns, this story has appeared in at least three versions, notably by Brad Schram in *Birding,* by Karen

Bridgers in *Birdwatcher's Digest,* and by Paul Lehman, who found the bird originally, in *American Birds.*

And ... typical of birding records which never stand for long, another Little Curlew was glimpsed very briefly in September of 1988, close to the same field where the first one visited, but definitely not as cooperative.

TRAVELERS' TIPS

Before You Visit: To guide you, two excellent maps, one of San Luis Obispo County and one of Monterey County, published by Compass Maps, Inc., P. O. Box 4369, Modesto, CA. 95352, (209) 529-5017, are available. They may be obtained, among other places, from the Morro Bay Chamber of Commerce, 895 Napa St., Suite A-1, Morro Bay, CA. 93442 (805) 772-4467, the San Luis Obispo Visitor's and Conference Bureau, 1041 Chorro St., Suite E, San Luis Obispo, CA. 93401, (805) 541-8000, or the Monterey Peninsula Chamber of Commerce, P. O. Box 1770, Monterey, CA. 93942, (408) 649-1770.

Santa Barbara and Ventura County are available on Compass Maps, too. For further information about Ventura County, write the Visitors and Convention Bureau, 785 S. Seaward Ave., Ventura, CA. 93001. For Santa Barbara information, write the Chamber of Commerce, Visitor Information, 1 Santa Barbara St., Santa Barbara, CA. 93101, phone (805) 965-3021.

When you visit Morro Bay, stop at the Morro Bay Museum of Natural History in Morro Bay State Park on State Park Rd. (805) 772-2694, to learn more about the ecology of the bay and obtain a checklist of the birds of San Luis Obispo County.

In the Monterey area, two natural history institutions well worth a stop are the Pacific Grove Museum of Natural History and the Monterey Bay Aquarium. The Museum of Natural History is at the corner of Forest and Central Aves. in Pacific Grove, phone (408) 372-4212. Specimens of the wildlife of Monterey County, including over 400 mounted birds, are on display.

The Monterey Bay Aquarium at 886 Cannery Row in Monterey has gained worldwide attention since its opening. Dramatic, innovative exhibits of a variety of live marine creatures makes the aquarium an absolute must on a Monterey visit. The well-stocked book store offers a large selection of everything from bird books to checklists. For a chance to fully enjoy the walk-in shorebird aviary, with birds so close you can nearly touch them, try to get an early or late admission time, especially on the weekends. Tickets for the Aquarium must be purchased in advance, available from all the usual ticket outlets. Phone (408) 649-6466 for further information on the Aquarium.

For information on state park campsite reservations up and down the coast, available up to eight weeks in advance, write Reservations, Department of Parks and Recreation, Box 942896, Sacramento, CA. 94296-0420, or call 800-446-7275 in California, (619) 452-1950 out of state.

Several organizations operate short excursions for watching gray whales and other mammals out of Monterey Harbor, but birders wishing to participate in a pelagic trip should schedule a reservation ahead of time with one who specializes in bird finding: Shearwater Journeys. Organized by Debra Shearwater, these trips leave almost every weekend from mid-August to mid-October, and less frequently at other times of the year. Most trips are around $45 and some overnight excursions run $120. For information and schedules write or phone Shearwater Journeys, P. O. Box 1445, Soquel, CA. 95073, (408) 688-1990.

For information on Channel Islands National Park, reached by boat from Channel Islands Harbor in Ventura, write the Visitor Center at 1901 Spinnaker Dr., Ventura, CA. 93001 (805) 644-8262. Island Packers is the concessionaire designated to transport visitors to Channel Islands National Park. They can also provide information on charter boat trips for birders. Located at 1867 Spinnaker Dr., Island Packers can be reached by writing P O. Box 993, Ventura, CA. 93002, phone (805) 642-1393.

The Rare Bird Alert phone numbers are: Morro Bay (805) 528-7182 and Monterey (408) 375-9122 or 375-2577. Santa Barbara's Rare Bird Alert often has information about the Santa Clara, Santa Ynez and Santa Maria river estuaries, (805) 964-8240.

When To Visit: This tour emphasizes hot spots for viewing the fall shorebird and landbird migration occurring between

August and mid-October along California's central coast. The river mouths and tidal estuaries are particularly exciting for viewing migrant shorebirds at this season and the recognized vagrant traps of vegetation on the coast often yield many a rare warbler, vireo or flycatcher.

Indeed, California's mild winters make this trip productive well into the late fall and winter. Though most of the fall migrants have passed through by late October, ducks, geese and gulls are still arriving from the north to winter on the coast. Then, when the greater portion of wintering waterfowl have settled in joining the many wintering shorebirds, the large salt marshes such as Morro Bay and Elkhorn Slough remain prime birding spots throughout the winter.

In late summer and fall, the species to be seen on a pelagic trip out of Monterey Bay include storm-petrels, shearwaters, jaegers, alcids and gulls in great numbers, with the possibility of Black-footed Albatross, Flesh-footed Shearwater, Buller's Shearwater, and other rarities. In winter, you might see Laysan Albatross, Northern Fulmar, Short-tailed Shearwater, Fork-tailed Storm-Petrel and Black-legged Kittiwake, plus several species of alcids.

Despite California's reputation for mild fall and winter temperatures, birding in the coastal fog belt calls for light, water-repellent outerwear as protection against morning drizzle and chilly onshore breezes. If you plan to wade in to look at shorebirds, pack a pair of rubber boots or old tennis shoes.

Length of Visit: Excursions up the California coast tend to take longer than planned, so leave yourself time to enjoy the scenery and the full spectrum of good birding locations. If you take the entire trip, expect to spend four days, especially if you drive from Morro Bay to Monterey via California's Highway 1. (Taking U.S. 101, the parallel inland route, saves time but is much less appealing for birds.)

This bird trip can easily be split into two parts, the more southerly destinations such as the Santa Clara River Estuary and Morro Bay in one and the Monterey area in another. Morro Bay beckons as a weekend sojourn in late fall and winter. Charming Carmel and Monterey provide enough good birding—with a side trip up to Moss Landing—for a long weekend or longer in late August and September.

THE BIRDING SITES

Ventura/Santa Barbara Counties area: The Santa Clara River estuary near McGrath State Beach just south of Ventura, and the Santa Ynez and Santa Maria River estuaries north of Santa Barbara provide excellent shorebird viewing in late summer and fall.

SANTA CLARA RIVER ESTUARY: When the water level is down, the extensive mudflat habitat here attracts innumerable shorebirds. (Be sure to scan the estuary from the bridge above to ascertain whether the area is flooded, in which case most shorebirds will be absent.) One of the finest places for fall shorebirds in southern California, the Santa Clara River mouth supports the following species when conditions are suitable: Black-bellied, Snowy and Semipalmated Plovers, Black-necked Stilt, American Avocet, Greater and Lesser Yellowlegs, Whimbrel, Marbled Godwit, Ruddy and Black Turnstones, Western and Least Sandpipers, Dunlin, and Long-billed and Short-billed Dowitchers. Black Skimmers are possible in summer, as are Pectoral, Baird's and Solitary Sandpipers and Red Knots in early fall. Many rarities have been recorded. Towards the outer beach, on the north sandspit enclosing the estuary, Least Terns and Snowy Plovers nest.

To reach the Santa Clara River estuary, from the north exit U.S. 101 west at Seaward Ave.; turn left (south) onto Harbor Blvd. and proceed 3 mi. to the north end of the bridge spanning the estuary. (from the south, exit Victoria Ave. west to Olivas Park Dr.; turn right (west) on Olivas Park Dr., which shortly brings you to Channel Islands Blvd. just north of the river mouth). Once at the bridge, park at a pull-out on your right and follow a trail beginning to your right (west) leading directly down under the bridge, across a channel (usually negotiable in wading boots), and out to the mudflats which lie between the bridge and the open beach. McGrath State Beach (fee), just south of the bridge, is another place to park and gain access to the estuary. You can't bird this spot without getting your feet wet, so bring boots.

Channel Islands National Park Headquarters, located in the Ventura marina at the western terminus of Spinnaker Dr. (just north of the Santa Clara estuary bridge) has interesting exhibits about the Channel Islands. Most Channel Islands charter boat cruises, run by Island Packers, leave from this marina—a good way to see some common pelagic species.

Note: You can reach the north sandspit, which encloses the river estuary, by parking on Spinnaker Drive just where it makes a right angle turn to the north, and walking south along the beach (no boots needed).

CARPINTERIA CREEK: Approximately 18 mi. northwest of the Santa Clara River estuary on U.S. 101, this slender ribbon of riparian growth bordering a coastal creekbed can be phenomenal for migrants in fall. The place has recently been responsible for more landbird rarities than any other Santa

Barbara County location. Between late August and mid-October, the cotton-woods, sycamores and willows are filled with regular Western migrants such as Western Wood-Pewee, Western Flycatcher, Swainson's Thrush, Solitary (uncommon) and Warbling Vireos, Orange-crowned, Nashville, Yellow, Black-throated Gray, MacGillivray's, and Wilson's Warblers, Western Tanager, Black-headed Grosbeak, and Hooded and Northern (Bullock's) Orioles. Carpinteria Creek can also be good birding in winter.

To reach Carpinteria Creek, in the town of Carpinteria just south of Santa Barbara, exit U.S. 101 south at Casitas Pass Rd. and go one block to Carpinteria Ave. Turn right (west) on Carpinteria Ave., then make an immediate left on Palm Ave. Follow Palm Ave. 2 blocks and turn left (east) on Sixth St., which ends at a dirt parking lot by the creek. During weekdays, a nursery school uses the lot, so park your car further back on Sixth St.

Rubber boots are needed to adequately bird Carpinteria Creek. The best method is to get into the creekbed and walk upstream (to your left), the most productive stretch being from the parking lot to a bike bridge that crosses the creek in about 200 yards.

GAVIOTA STATE PARK: Approximately 34 mi. northwest of Santa Barbara, this vagrant trap can be very good or very boring, depending upon the time of year and the numbers of leafhoppers on the tamarisk trees. Fall is always best, and the list of migrants and vagrants can be impressive in a good year.

To reach Gaviota State Park, turn west off U. S. 101, making a lefthand turn (cross the highway here with care) onto an entrance road leading to the kiosk. Parking is a problem, unless you wish to pay the small fee.

SANTA YNEZ RIVER ESTUARY: This estuary can produce interesting gulls, terns and shorebirds in season. To reach the mouth of the Santa Ynez River, exit U.S. 101 west (2.5 mi. north of Gaviota State Park) on California 1 and proceed 18 mi. to Lompoc. Turn left (west) at Ocean Ave. (California 246) and go 9.5 mi. to the turn off to Ocean Beach County Park. Turn right and go 1 mi. to the little park at the river mouth.

SANTA MARIA RIVER ESTUARY: The Santa Maria area has several good spots for shorebirds, but by far the most reliable is the estuary at the river mouth, water level permitting. Several agricultural fields near the intersection of Black and Betteravia Roads just west of the town of Santa Maria have produced shorebird rarities, notably Little Curlews. Because there is no way of knowing from one year to the next which of these grassy fields will be irrigated enough to attract shorebirds, and all of them are on private property, consult local birders for exact information. Scanning from the road can produce Lesser Golden-Plovers (*fulva* race), Black-bellied Plovers, Marbled Godwits, Willets and Long-billed Curlews. By November, the Mountain Plovers may have arrived. Look for wintering raptors such as Ferruginous Hawk, Prairie Falcon and Merlin, plus Burrowing Owl.

At the Santa Maria River mouth, all the representative shorebirds are present in numbers in fall, plus gulls and terns. Snowy Plovers and Least Terns nest in the vicinity. A Peregrine Falcon is a possibility, especially in fall and winter. By scanning offshore, good numbers of Sooty Shearwaters (summer), and Black-vented Shearwaters (late fall, winter) may be espied.

To reach the Santa Maria River mouth and adjacent agricultural fields, exit U.S. 101 west at Betteravia Rd. in Santa Maria and proceed west 4.2 mi. to Black Rd. The potential shorebird pastures are in the vicinity of this intersection. To visit the river mouth, turn right (north) on Black Rd. for 2.4 mi. to Main St., then left (west) on Main St. and head out to the ocean 7.7 mi. The county park at the river mouth is open from 8 a.m. to dusk, and large 4-wheel drive vehicles are prohibited to protect the dunes. (The willows near the entrance station can be good for migrants, mornings being best; Chestnut-backed Chickadees here are at the southern limit of their range.) At the river mouth, wear rubber boots to get as close to the birds as possible.

Shell Beach area: Sixteen miles north of Santa Maria at Oceano and Shell Beach, two very different locations provide good birding. The first, Oceano, is a well-known migrant trap for landbirds, and the second, an overlook near Shell Beach, can produce interesting waterbirds offshore.

OCEANO CAMPGROUND: Birding the willows and pines around the lagoon that winds through the campground can yield numerous landbirds, including vagrant eastern warblers in fall migration from mid-August to mid-October. Although many rarities have been discovered here, it's also good for regular Western migrants.

To reach Oceano from the Santa Maria River mouth, retrace your route on Main St. back to its intersection with California 1 (2.9 mi.) and follow California 1 north 10.6 mi. to the town of Oceano. Here, California 1 (Cienega St.) turns west; follow it and turn right (north) on Front St., which then becomes Pacific Blvd. Watch for Pier Ave. to the left (west) which leads you to Oceano Campground (part of Pismo State Beach). Before crossing the bridge to the campground entrance, take the first right turn (Norswing Dr.) and proceed north 3 blocks to Coolidge Dr., which turns back to your right. Park here and bird the east side of the pond along the nature trail immediately to your left among the willows; walk up, cross the bridge, and bird the west side of the creek to the corrals, and the campground itself.

SHELL BEACH ROAD: This coastal overlook spot, marked by a small city park with a gazebo (Margo Dodd Park), provides opportunities to view Pigeon Guillemots, American Black Oystercatchers and (sometimes) Rhinoceros Auklets, which nest on nearby rocky cliffs. Scanning offshore in summer may turn up Sooty Shearwaters and in fall and winter Black-vented Shearwaters. A Peregrine Falcon pair formerly nested in the area, to the delight of birders who could spy the bird on the rocks as they drove by on U.S. 101!

To reach this stretch of coastline, exit U. S. 101 west on Mattie Rd. in Pismo Beach from the south (from the north, use Price St. exit west) and turn right (north) onto the frontage road, which becomes Shell Beach Rd. Look for some tennis courts on the cliffs to your left, which are a good spot for scanning offshore. Then continue on Shell Beach Rd. to Cliff Ave., where a left turn will take you two blocks toward the ocean and the little park with the gazebo.

Morro Bay area: From a plethora of migrating shorebirds, to huge flocks of wintering ducks, to several locations attractive to landbird migrants, the entire Morro Bay area has a lot to offer birders. The town has been designated a bird sanctuary, and you'll understand why when you explore here, particularly in fall and winter.

To reach the Morro Bay area (about 12 mi. north of Shell Beach), exit U.S. 101 and go west on Los Osos Valley Rd. south of San Luis Obispo, or take California 1 (North Santa Rosa St.) west in San Luis Obispo.

MORRO ROCK: This monolithic rock can be seen for miles around, situated across from the stacks of the power plant at the entrance to Morro Harbor. Morro Rock and the adjacent harbor waters make interesting birding. The rock is used for roosting by numerous gulls, and Double-crested, Brandt's and Pelagic Cormorants. Its most famous denizens, the Peregrine Falcons which nest here, can be seen fairly regularly by scanning the rock surfaces above you. Rock Wrens bounce around the base of the giant boulders.

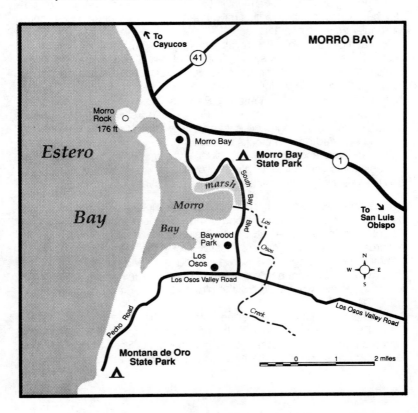

In the harbor waters, look for wintering loons and scoters, as well as American White Pelicans and Brant.

To reach the base of Morro Rock, take Harbor St. west off California 1, and proceed to Embarcadero, which runs along the waterfront. Turn right (north) on Embarcadero to its end at Morro Rock.

To take the Clam Taxi or Sand Spit Shuttle, for service between the end of the sandspit and the town of Morro Bay, go to the marina at the end of Pacific St. and Embarcadero. On the weekends the taxi (fee) runs hourly; weekday service is sporadic. Information: (805) 772-8085. Once on the sandspit, you can walk to its southerly end (4 mi.) or just enjoy the dune vegetation and the shorebirds feeding on the bay side. Snowy Plovers nest here.

MORRO BAY STATE PARK: The pines and eucalyptus trees in Morro Bay State Park Campground lure Chestnut-backed Chickadees and other interesting landbirds at all seasons, plus migrant warblers—occasionally rare ones—in fall. In spring, Great Blue Herons noisily occupy a rookery at the northwest edge of the park in the trees beside the bay.

The Museum of Natural History is worth a visit, possessing an excellent viewpoint over the bay. Southeast of the museum the State Park Marina marks the start of a trail leading out to the edge of the bay (see directions below), good for watching roosting shorebirds at high tide. From this trail, you can scan the salt marsh for American Avocets, Greater Yellowlegs, Willets, Whimbrels, Long-billed Curlews, Marbled Godwits, Least Sandpipers, Dunlins, and Short-billed and Long-billed Dowitchers. American White Pelicans, Great Blue Herons, Green-backed Herons and Great and Snowy Egrets can be seen.

To reach Morro Bay State Park from Morro Rock, take Embarcadero to Harbor St., turn left (east) on Harbor and right (south) on Main St., which becomes State Park Rd., winding along the edge of the bay. Shortly after the turn-off for the Museum of Natural History on your right, turn right into the marina and go all the way to its southeast end. Park here and follow a trail that skirts the end of the marina and leads straight out to the edge of the marsh.

The entrance to the state park campground and the picnic area are a short distance further east of the marina on State Park Rd.

BAYWOOD PARK: This small community at the southeast end of Morro Bay sports several locations where coastal access allows a good view of the tidal mudflats.

The Turri Road ponds, at the intersection of South Bay Blvd. and Turri Rd. (just north of Baywood Park), have good shorebirds and ducks depending upon water level.

The Audubon Overlook at the end of 4th St. in Baywood Park, reached by taking Santa Ysabel Ave. right (west) off South Bay Blvd. and turning right (north) on 3rd St. and doubling back to 4th St., is good for shorebird viewing at mid-tide.

At the western terminus of Santa Ysabel Ave., where it meets Pasadena Dr., another overlook allows views out into the bay, where American White Pelicans, Brown Pelicans and numerous ducks feed.

The little Baywood Park Pier, reached by retracing your route on Santa Ysabel Ave. and turning right (south) on 2nd St., is found between 2nd and 3rd St. on the edge of the tidal flats.

LOS OSOS: Another small resort community on the south side of Morro Bay, Los Osos has additional bay access points which lead to good birding.

One of the best locations is reached by taking Pine Ave. right (north) off Los Osos Valley Rd. After Pine Ave. dead-ends into Bay St., go right one block to Broderson Ave. and park. Follow the end of Broderson Ave. as it becomes a dirt path and leads to the edge of a lovely shallow bay. When the tide is low, the exposed mudflats attract shorebirds. In winter, a large flock of American Wigeon congregate here, and an occasional Eurasian Wigeon can be found among them.

MONTANA DE ORO STATE PARK: This lovely park combines two habitats attractive to birds: the rocky coastline of Spooner's Cove and the bluffs to the south, plus the willows and pines of the campground. The former are home to such rocky shorebird species as Pigeon Guillemots and American Black Oystercatchers, which nest there, while the latter shelter numerous fly-catchers, vireos, warblers and tanagers in migration—some of which may be rarities.

To visit Montana de Oro, continue south on Los Osos Valley Rd. from Los Osos, bearing left at Pecho Road. After approximately 5.5 mi., the road ends at the state park headquarters and campground. If you wish to hike the bluffs and watch for waterbirds, park at the last parking lot to the south, beyond Spooner's Cove. To bird the campground, park near the headquarters and walk down to the extensive willows by the creek and the pines around the campsites.

California's Highway 1: This scenic, winding drive, wedged between the bluffs and the Coast Range on California 1, from Morro Bay north to Monterey, has several good birding spots. Among the best are:

CAYUCOS: Walk out the pier at the foot of Cayucos Dr. in Cayucos (5.7 mi. north of Morro Bay on Highway 1) and scan for seabirds in fall and winter. In late summer Marbled Murrelets have been seen.

CAMBRIA: The Monterey pines in this pretty seaside village are the southernmost location for nesting Pygmy Nuthatches along the coast. Good landbirding for migrants occurs at the mouth of Santa Rosa Creek, reached by exiting Windsor Blvd. west from Highway 1 (14.2 mi north of Cayucos) and proceeding toward Shamel County Park. Between the park and the Windsor Blvd. bridge, bird the willows, walking along the creekbed. (Good for Chestnut-backed Chickadees, too.)

SAN SIMEON STATE BEACH to PT. PIEDRAS BLANCAS: A variety of birds inhabiting the rocky shoreline are visible along the coast here, in a stretch beginning a mile north of Cambria and extending north for about 15 mi. Look for oystercatchers, turnstones, Brown Pelicans and all three species of cormorants, plus loons and scoters offshore. Easiest access to the bluffs is at San Simeon State Beach and William Randolph Hearst Memorial State Beach.

ANDREW MOLERA STATE BEACH at the MOUTH OF THE BIG SUR RIVER: Approximately 65 mi. north of San Simeon State Beach, this is one of the best spots on Highway 1. Since it's only 27 mi. south of Carmel, you can bird the Big Sur River mouth on a trip from the north even if you don't attempt the full drive down the coast to Morro Bay. Breeding landbirds in the willows near the river mouth include Chestnut-backed Chickadee, Swainson's Thrush, and Wilson's Warbler. In fall migration, many migrants turn up here. Out in the bay, scoters, grebes and loons can be seen, and Harlequin Ducks have occurred several times.

To bird Andrew Molera State Beach, you can either park at the main lot and walk along the trails on both sides (north is best) of the river out to the river mouth, or park at a pullout .5 mi. north of the main entrance on the west side of California 1. From here you walk down a trail leading to the river mouth.

POINT LOBOS STATE RESERVE: Approximately 2 mi. south of Carmel on Highway 1, this beautiful park (fee) has a network of roads and trails leading to viewpoints over the ocean. Brown Pelicans formerly nested this far north, and they roost here on the spectacular bird rocks. Scan for three kinds of cormorants. Wandering Tattlers, Black Turnstones and other rocky shorebirds prowl the beaches at low tide.

Monterey Bay area: This beautiful peninsula comprised of the towns of Carmel, Pacific Grove and Monterey provides excellent birding locations, the highlights of which are covered below. For a more detailed discussion, consult *Monterey Birds* by Don Roberson.

CARMEL RIVER MOUTH: Approximately 2 mi. north of Pt. Lobos Reserve, and a mile south of the town of Carmel, Highway 1 crosses the Carmel River. The region around the mouth of the Carmel River is a famous bird finding area. The willows from the highway bridge west to the lagoon attract all sorts of landbirds in migration, including vagrants which often tag along with the chickadee and Bushtit flocks in fall. The lagoon and surrounding marsh, where the river meets the beach, lures herons, egrets, shorebirds and gulls. Two ways to reach this hot spot are:

(1) Immediately after the bridge over the Carmel River, take Rio Rd. right (east) and turn right again into the nearest shopping center. By locating the movie theater and parking near it, you can climb down into the creekbed (which is dry in late summer and fall) and walk west, downstream, birding the willows until you come to the lagoon. Shorebirds, such as Baird's and Pectoral Sandpipers in season, may be spied from this approach, too.

(2) Take Rio Rd. left (west) to the Carmel Mission, turn left on Lasuen Ave. Proceed on Lasuen, bear left onto I5th Ave., and follow it to its intersection with Carmelo St. Turn left (south) on Carmelo St. and continue to a parking lot

at Carmel River State Beach. From the parking lot, you can see the small marsh, alive with a variety of waterbirds, or you can walk out to the open beach and bird along the rocky coast to the south. In fall of 1988, a rare Terek Sandpiper was discovered here!

MONTEREY PENINSULA: The Monterey Peninsula can be reached from Carmel to the south via Highway 1, or by exiting U.S. 101 west on California 68 and thence to Highway 1.

This mini-tour will take you to a few of the most outstanding bird spots in Monterey and Pacific Grove. To begin the tour, exit Munras Ave. west off Highway 1 in Monterey (3.2 mi. north of the Rio Rd. intersection in Carmel). Follow Munras as it becomes Abrego St., and then Washington St. Turn right off Washington St. onto Franklin, go two blocks to Figueroa St., and turn left. At the base of Figueroa St., a large metered parking lot marks the Municipal Wharf/Fisherman's Wharf area of the waterfront. You can see Fisherman's Wharf, where most of the pelagic trips depart, to the west across the marina. At the end of the Municipal Wharf, scope the harbor waters for seabirds. Especially in winter, gulls of all kinds perch on the wharf buildings.

Leaving the Municipal Wharf area, turn right on Del Monte Blvd. and follow Lighthouse Ave. through the tunnel. Emerging from the tunnel, pull-outs on your right afford access to a walking path that follows the coast around the entire Peninsula to the west. For birding the rocky shoreline, or simply enjoying a brisk walk, this walkway accompanies our route out to Pt. Pinos.

Continuing west, take a right turn on Foam Ave. and a right again on Cannery Row. The Coast Guard Wharf here, and a road on which you can walk to the end of the jetty, has good potential for seabird watching.

Continue right (west) on Cannery Row or go straight up the hill and turn right on Wave St.—either way will lead you past the Monterey Bay Aquarium at the corner of Cannery Row and David Ave.

Wave St. now becomes Ocean View Blvd., which follows the peninsula in a beautiful drive along the coast at Pacific Grove, with opportunities to stop and bird the rocky shoreline as you go. The walking tour path on the ocean side of the street parallels Ocean View Blvd., providing excellent birding all the way for waterbirds. At Lover's Point, there are good views out over the bay.

Esplanade Park (.5 mi. further west from Lover's Point) is a two block long park containing pines and cypresses, good for Eastern vagrants in fall. The park is often mentioned on the Rare Bird Alert.

Crespi Pond (.3 mi. further west) is a small freshwater pond (sometimes dry in late summer) to your left (south) on the Pacific Grove Golf Course. When the pond has water, many rarities have been found here in fall and winter, including unusual gulls and waterfowl. The cypress trees around the pond have been good for eastern warblers in fall. Be sure not to bother the golfers in any way; early morning is best.

Pt. Pinos, the rocky point practically across the street from Crespi Pond, is another great place from which to watch for waterbirds. Look for gulls and shorebirds on the beach at low tide.

At the Point, the road turns sharply left (south) ending our tour. (A pond inside the cyclone fence on the ocean side of the road just a little further is worth a check.) More good birding spots can be found off Sunset Dr. at Asilomar State Beach.

To return to Highway 1, follow Sunset Drive and turn right (south) on California 68 (the W. R. Holman Highway), which will connect with Highway 1 north of Carmel. To drive back through Pacific Grove, take Forest Ave. left (north) and visit the Pacific Grove Natural History Museum at the corner of Forest and Central Ave. Lighthouse Ave., just south of the Museum, will route you back toward Monterey and Del Monte Blvd., which joins Highway 1 east of Monterey harbor.

Moss Landing area: Moss Landing, 15 mi. north of Monterey on Highway 1, is a little fishing village and harbor that has given its name to one of the most famous areas in California for sighting shorebirds, gulls and other waterbirds. En route to Moss Landing, stop and bird the Salinas river mouth.

SALINAS RIVER STATE WILDLIFE AREA: This interesting birding spot consists of good shorebird-watching in the river channel and raptor-watching in the open fields nearby. Northern Harriers and Black-shouldered Kites breed here, and Short-eared Owls can occasionally be found (fall, winter). A walk out to the beach produces huge flocks of pelicans, terns and gulls. Snowy Plovers nest on the sand dunes.

To reach the Salinas River Wildlife Area, go 10 mi. north of Monterey on Highway 1, and exit west at Del Monte Blvd. (the only Del Monte Blvd. exit between Marina and Castroville). The paved road ends shortly after crossing over the freeway, and at the start of the dirt road (may be impassable after heavy rains) a sign says "Salinas River Wildlife Area 1/2 Mile". At the end of the road, park in the lot and take the trail to the right (north) which leads across a field to the south bank of the Salinas River. From there, a path follows the river bank out to the ocean, with views of shorebirds feeding in the channel on the sand bars and little islands.

MOSS LANDING AND JETTY ROAD: Good birding here is along Jetty Rd., which follows the northern part of the Moss Landing Harbor and ends at the rock jetty on the outer beach. At low and mid-tide, the exposed mudflats north and south of Jetty Rd. prove good feeding and roosting grounds for numerous shorebirds; many rarities have been found over the years.

To reach Jetty Rd., follow Highway 1 north from the Salinas River Wildlife Area for about 2 mi. to the intersection with California 156. Bear left here, following the sign to Santa Cruz/Watsonville, on Highway 1. In about 3 mi. the highway crosses Elkhorn Slough—with the big power plant to your right—and after another mile, a sign indicates Jetty Rd. to the left (west). Immediately after turning onto Jetty Rd., park your car and bird the stretch between the highway and the entrance to Moss Landing State Beach (fee).

In addition, check the Moss Landing Harbor area and the power plant outfall area in winter for loons, grebes, scoters and gulls and maybe a Harlequin Duck.

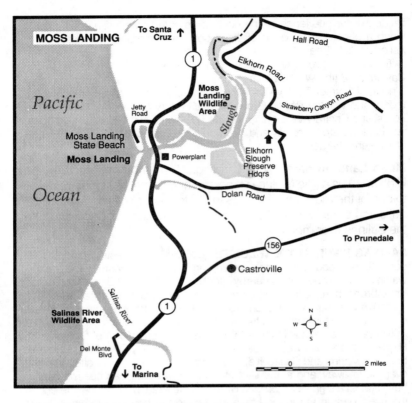

MOSS LANDING WILDLIFE AREA: On the east side of Highway 1, just a mile north of Jetty Rd., the California Department of Fish and Game recently purchased part of a complex of former salt ponds, which often draws shorebirds and waterfowl in fall and winter. Snowy Plovers, Caspian Terns and Forster's Terns have nested here. Access is obtained at an entrance road off Highway 1. Watch for a big eucalyptus tree which marks the turn-off on your right (east). For information, call (408) 649-2870.

ELKHORN SLOUGH NATIONAL ESTUARINE RESERVE: Huge Elkhorn Slough meanders inland from Moss Landing Harbor, embracing a prime segment of estuarine marsh. This large Reserve has miles of hiking trails through oak woodland adjacent to the slough and several boardwalks (the South Marsh Loop Trail is good) lead through the marshy areas. Watch for typical oak woodland species plus raptors (Black-shouldered Kites breed here; Peregrine Falcons are sometimes present near the slough). Be sure to obtain a map and a checklist of birds when you stop at the interpretive center on the Reserve. A publication entitled "Natural Resources of Elkhorn Slough and Central Monterey Bay Area: Access to Parks, Reserves & Wildlife Refuges & Boating Facilities" is useful as an explanation of the wildlife facilities in the area. For further information contact the Reserve at 1700

Elkhorn Rd., Watsonville, CA. 95076. Phone: (408) 728-2822, 728-0560. Open 9–5:00 Wednesday through Sunday (possible fee by publication date).

To reach Elkhorn Slough from the Jetty Rd. area, go south once again on Highway 1 and turn left (east) on Dolan Rd. (at the powerplant).

After going 4.8 mi. on Dolan Rd., turn left (north) on Elkhorn Rd. and go 5.7 mi. to the Elkhorn Slough Reserve entrance on your left.

FROM MORRO BAY TO MONTEREY:
Chasing fall migrants along the Pacific Coast
Checklist of Common Birds by Habitat

SANDY BEACH (INCLUDES NEARSHORE WATERS)
Red-throated Loon
Pacific Loon
Common Loon
Horned Grebe
Western Grebe
Clark's Grebe (uncommon north of Morro Bay)
American White Pelican
Brown Pelican
Surf Scoter
White-winged Scoter
Black-bellied Plover
Snowy Plover
Willet
Whimbrel
Marbled Godwit
Sanderling
Parasitic Jaeger
Heermann's Gull
Bonaparte's Gull
Mew Gull
Ring-billed Gull
California Gull
Western Gull
Glaucous-winged Gull
Caspian Tern
Elegant Tern
Forster's Tern
Least Tern (summer, local)

TIDAL MUDFLAT AND SALT MARSH
American Bittern (rare)
Great Blue Heron
Great Egret
Snowy Egret
Green-backed Heron
Black-crowned Night-Heron
Merlin

Peregrine Falcon
Clapper Rail (rare)
Virginia Rail
Sora
Black-bellied Plover
Lesser Golden-Plover (uncommon, local)
Snowy Plover
Semipalmated Plover
Killdeer
Black-necked Stilt
American Avocet
Greater Yellowlegs
Lesser Yellowlegs
Solitary Sandpiper (rare)
Willet
Spotted Sandpiper
Whimbrel
Long-billed Curlew
Marbled Godwit
Red Knot
Western Sandpiper
Least Sandpiper
Baird's Sandpiper (uncommon)
Pectoral Sandpiper (uncommon)
Dunlin
Short-billed Dowitcher
Long-billed Dowitcher
Common Snipe
Wilson's Phalarope
Red-necked Phalarope

ROCKY SHORELINE
Double-crested Cormorant
Brandt's Cormorant
Pelagic Cormorant
American Black Oystercatcher
Willet
Wandering Tattler
Spotted Sandpiper
Ruddy Turnstone

Black Turnstone
Surfbird
Common Murre
Pigeon Guillemot
Rhinoceros Auklet (rare)

COASTAL MIGRANT TRAP
A sampling might include:
Olive-sided Flycatcher
    (uncommon)
Western Wood-Pewee
Western Flycatcher
Western Kingbird
Cassin's Kingbird (uncommon)
Chestnut-backed Chickadee
Bushtit
Winter Wren
Ruby-crowned Kinglet
Swainson's Thrush
Hermit Thrush
Solitary Vireo
Warbling Vireo
Orange-crowned Warbler
Nashville Warbler
Yellow Warbler
Yellow-rumped Warbler
Black-throated Gray Warbler
Townsend's Warbler
Hermit Warbler (uncommon)
Black-and-white Warbler
    (uncommon)
MacGillivray's Warbler
Common Yellowthroat
Wilson's Warbler
Western Tanager
Black-headed Grosbeak
Lazuli Bunting
Chipping Sparrow
Savannah Sparrow
Northern Oriole (Bullock's)

Suggested Reading

General

ABA Checklist. 3d ed. American Birding Association, 1986.

The Audubon Society Nature Guides. New York: Alfred A. Knopf, 1985.
McConnaughey, Bayard H. and Evelyn. *Pacific Coast.*
McMahon, James. *Deserts.*
Whitney, Stephen. *Western Forests.*

Bent, Arthur Cleveland. *Life Histories of North American Birds.* New York: Dover Publications, 1964.
Shorebirds, Part I
Cuckoos, Goatsuckers, Hummingbirds and Their Allies
Jays, Crows, and Titmice, Part I
Thrushes, Kinglets and Their Allies
Nuthatches, Wrens, Thrashers and Their Allies

Matthiessen, Peter. *The Wind Birds.* New York: The Viking Press, 1973.

Pearson, T. Gilbert, ed. *Portraits and Habits of Our Birds.* 2 vol. New York: Doubleday Page & Co., 1921.

Peterson, Roger Tory, and Fisher, James. *Wild America.* Boston: Houghton Mifflin Co., 1963.

Pettingill, Olin Sewall, Jr. *A Guide to Bird Finding West of the Mississippi.* 2d ed. New York: Oxford University Press, 1981.

Pettingill, Olin Sewall, Jr., ed. *The Bird Watcher's America.* New York: McGraw-Hill, 1974.

Reilly, Edgar M., Jr. *The Audubon Illustrated Handbook of American Birds.* New York: McGraw-Hill, 1968.

Terres, John K. *The Audubon Encyclopedia of North American Birds.* New York: Alfred A. Knopf, 1980.

Welty, Joel Carl. *The Life of Birds.* 2d ed. Philadelphia: W. B. Saunders Co., 1982.

Zimmer, Kevin J. *The Western Bird Watcher.* New Jersey: Prentice-Hall, 1985.

Field Guides

Ehrlich, Paul R.; Dobkin, David S.; and Wheye, Darryl. *The Birder's Handbook*. New York: Simon & Schuster, 1988.

Farrand, John, Jr., ed. *The Audubon Society Master Guide to Birding*. 3 vols. New York: Alfred A. Knopf, 1983.

Field Guide to the Birds of North America. 2d ed. Washington D. C.: The National Geographic Society, 1987.

Peterson, Roger Tory. *A Field Guide to Western Birds*. Boston: Houghton Mifflin, 1961.

ARIZONA

Bowers, Janice Emily. *100 Roadside Wildflowers of Southwest Woodlands*. Tucson: Southwest Parks and Monuments Association, 1987.

Brandt, Herbert. *Arizona and Its Bird Life*. Bird Research Foundation of Cleveland, 1951.

Davis, William A. and Russell, Stephen M. *Checklist of Birds of Southeastern Arizona*. Tucson: Tucson Audubon Society, 1984.

_ *Birds in Southeastern Arizona*. 2nd ed. Tucson: Tucson Audubon Society, 1984.

Elmore, Francis H. *Shrubs and Trees of the Southwest Uplands*. Tucson: Southwest Parks and Monuments Association, 1976.

Lane, James A. *A Birder's Guide to Southeastern Arizona*. Denver: L & P Press, 1988.

Lowe, Charles H. *Vertebrates of Arizona*. Tucson: University of Arizona Press, 1964.

McMoran, Charles W. *Trail Guide and Map of Huachuca Mountains*. Sierra Vista: 1976.

Monson, Gale, and Phillips, Allan R. *Annotated Checklist of the Birds of Arizona*. 2nd ed. Tucson: The University of Arizona Press, 1981.

Phillips, Allan; Marshall, Joe; and Monson, Gale. *Birds of Arizona*. Tucson: University of Arizona Press, 1964.

CALIFORNIA: GENERAL

Bakker, Elna S. *An Island Called California*. 2d ed. Berkeley: University of California Press, 1984.

Dawson, William Leon. *The Birds of California*. 3 vols. San Diego: South Moulton Company, 1923.

Hoffmann, Ralph. *Birds of the Pacific States*. Boston: Houghton Mifflin, 1927.

Small, Arnold. *The Birds of California*. New York: Macmillan Publishing Co., Inc., 1974.

MOJAVE DESERT

Bird Checklist Joshua Tree National Monument. Twentynine Palms: Joshua Tree Natural History Association, 1982.

Checklist of the Birds of the Big Morongo Canyon Area. Big Morongo Canyon Preserve.

Cowles, Raymond B. *Desert Journal.* Berkeley: University of California Press, 1977.

Miller, A. H., and Stebbins, R. C. *The Lives of Desert Animals in Joshua Tree National Monument.* Berkeley: University of California Press, 1964.

Munz, Philip A. *California Desert Wildflowers.* Berkeley: University of California Press, 1962.

Siebecker, Alice. *Key to the Cacti of Joshua Tree National Monument..* Joshua Tree Natural History Association.

Ward, Grace B. and Onas M. *Colorful Desert Wildflowers of California and Arizona.* Palm Desert: Living Desert Association, 1978.

SIERRA NEVADA

Arno, Stephen F. *Discovering Sierra Trees.* Yosemite Natural History Association, 1973.

Beedy, Edward C., and Granholm, Stephen L. *Discovering Sierra Birds.* Yosemite Natural History Association, 1985.

Gaines, David. *Birds of Yosemite and the East Slope.* Lee Vining: Artemisia Press, 1988.

Hart, Terry, and Gaines, David. *Field Checklist of the Birds of the Mono Basin.* Lee Vining: Mono Lake Committee, 1983.

Hood, Mary and Bill. *Yosemite Wildflowers and Their Stories.* Yosemite: Flying Spur Press, 1969.

Horn, Elizabeth. *Wildflowers 3. The Sierra Nevada.* Beaverton: The Touchstone Press, 1976.

McCaskie, Guy; De Benedictis, Paul; Erickson, Richard; and Morlan, Joe. *Birds of Northern California, An Annotated Field List.* 2d ed. Berkeley: Golden Gate Audubon Society, 1979.

Muir, John. *The Yosemite.* New York: The Century Co., 1912.

Munz, Philip A. *California Mountain Wildflowers.* Berkeley, University of California Press, 1963.

Ryser, Fred A. *Birds of the Great Basin.* Reno: University of Nevada Press, 1985.

Smith, Genny Schumacher, ed. *Mammoth Lakes Sierra.* 4th ed. Palo Alto: Genny Smith Books, 1976.

Storer, Tracy I., and Usinger, Robert L. *Sierra Nevada Natural History.* Berkeley: University of California Press, 1963.

Weeden, Norman F. *A Sierra Nevada Flora.* Berkeley: Wilderness Press, 1981.

SANTA BARBARA

Belzer, Thomas J. *Roadside Plants of Southern California* Missoula: Mountain Press Publishing Co., 1984.

Bevier, Louis. *Field List of the Birds of Santa Barbara County.* Santa Barbara Audubon Society, 1982.

___ *Wildlife in the Santa Barbara Botanic Garden.* Santa Barbara Botanic Garden Checklist.

Ford, Ray. *Day Hikes of the Santa Barbara Foothills.* Santa Barbara: Kimberly Press, 1984.

Smith, Clifton F. *A Flora of the Santa Barbara Region, California.* Santa Barbara: Santa Barbara Museum of Natural History, 1976.

Smith, Dick. *Condor Journal.* Santa Barbara: Capra Press and Santa Barbara Museum of Natural History, 1978.

Webster, Richard; Lehman, Paul; and Bevier, Louis. *The Birds of Santa Barbara and Ventura Counties.* Santa Barbara: Santa Barbara Museum of Natural History, 1980.

MONTEREY

Davis, John, and Baldridge, Alan. *The Bird Year.* Pacific Grove: The Boxwood Press, 1987.

Edell, Tom; Marantz, Curtis; McDonald, John; Persons, Phil; Schram, Brad; and Smith, Gregory P. *The Birds of San Luis Obispo County, California.* Morro Bay: Morro Coast Audubon Society, Inc., 1985.

Gilliam, Harold. *Weather of the San Francisco Bay Region.* Berkeley: University of California Press, 1962.

Munz, Philip A. *Shore Wildflowers of California, Oregon and Washington.* Berkeley: University of California Press, 1964.

Richmond, Jean. *Birding Northern California.* Walnut Creek: Mt. Diablo Audubon Society, 1985.

Roberson, Don. *Monterey Birds.* Monterey: Monterey Peninsula Audubon Society, 1985.

COLORADO

Beidleman, Richard G. *Checklist of Birds of Rocky Mountain National Park and Arapaho National Recreation Area.*

Dannen, Kent and Donna. *Rocky Mountain Wildflowers.* Estes Park: Tundra Publications, 1981.

___ *Short Hikes in Rocky Mountain National Park.* Estes Park: Tundra Publications, 1986.

Folzenlogen, Robert. *Birding Guide to the Denver-Boulder Region.* Boulder: Pruett Publishing, 1986.

Lane, James A., and Holt, Harold R. *A Birder's Guide to Colorado.* Denver: L & P Press, 1987.

Johnsgard, Paul A. *Birds of the Rocky Mountains.* Boulder: Colorado Associated University Press, 1986.

Mutel, Cornelia Fleischer, and Emerick, John C. *From Grassland to Glacier.* Boulder: Johnson Books, 1984.

Nelson, Ruth Ashton. *Handbook of Rocky Mountain Plants.* Estes Park: Skyland Publishers, 1979.

Perry, John and Jane Greverus. *The Sierra Club Guide to the Natural Areas of Colorado and Utah.* San Francisco: Sierra Club Books, 1985.

Ryder, Ronald A. *Field Checklist, Birds of the Pawnee National Grassland.*

Zwinger, Ann H., and Willard, Beatrice E. *Land Above the Trees. A Guide to American Alpine Tundra.* New York: Harper & Row, 1972.

WASHINGTON

Atkinson, Scott, and Sharpe, Fred. *Wild Plants of the San Juan Islands.* Seattle: The Mountaineers, 1985.

Clark, Lewis J. *Wildflowers of Field and Slope in the Pacific Northwest.* Seattle: University of Washington Press, 1984.

Gabrielson, Ira N., and Jewett, Stanley G. *Birds of the Pacific Northwest* New York: Dover Publications, 1970.

Lewis, Mark G. *San Juan Islands Seasonal Status of Birds and Wildlife Checklist.* Friday Harbor: San Juan Islands Audubon Society, 1985.

Lewis, Mark G., and Sharpe, Fred A. *Birding in the San Juan Islands.* Seattle: The Mountaineers, 1987.

Mueller, Marge. *The San Juan Islands Afoot and Afloat.* Seattle: The Mountaineers, 1983.

Nehls, Harry B. *Familiar Birds of the Northwest.* Portland: Portland Audubon Society, 1981.

Wahl, Terence R., and Paulson, Dennis R. *A Guide to Bird Finding in Washington.* Bellingham: 1986.

Yocum, Charles, and Dasmann, Ray. *Pacific Coastal Wildlife Region.* Happy Camp: Naturegraph Publishers, 1965.